Crusaders, Scoundrels, Journalists

Crusaders, Scoundrels, Journalists

The Newseum's
Most Intriguing Newspeople

Edited by Eric Newton

Foreword by Tim Russert, host of *Meet the Press*

Copyright © 1999 by The Freedom Forum Newseum, Inc.

All rights reserved under International and Pan-American Copyright Conventions. Published in the United States by Times Books, a division of Random House, Inc., New York, and simultaneously in Canada by Random House of Canada Limited, Toronto.

Library of Congress Cataloging-in-Publication data is available.

ISBN 0-8129-3080-0

Random House website address: www.atrandom.com

Manufactured in Singapore on acid-free paper

9 8 7 6 5 4 3 2

First Edition

Design by Patrice L. Casey

"News is history

in its first and best form,

its vivid and fascinating form."

Mark Twain

"So let us today drudge on

about our inescapably impossible task of providing

every week a first rough draft of a history

that will never be completed about a world

we can never really understand."

Phillip Graham

"To the reporter:

... In the beginning he chiselled in living rock

the news of the first dawns of promise.

In the great ending, he will write 'thirty' —

his own mystic symbol of conclusion —

and the strange history of man will be complete."

Franklin Delano Roosevelt

Contents

Foreword

by Tim Russert

Join the Debate

NEWS. WE SEE IT, HEAR IT AND READ IT EVERY day. It swirls around us like the air we breathe. But we go about our daily lives understanding very little about how and why news is the way it is. As Americans, we agree we need news to run our lives, to govern ourselves. But we don't agree on much else about it. If a snow storm shuts down the city of Buffalo, I'd like to know — but then, that's my hometown. You might use the same story to line your birdcage.

Just what is news? A scholar would say news is a report of something new — fresh data, a current event, a revealing analysis, a bright idea. But a report about *what*, exactly? What makes news is often in the eye of the beholder. Like the Cannery Row in John Steinbeck's novel, news can be many things: "a poem, a stink, a grating noise, a quality of light, a tone, a habit, a nostalgia, a dream ... gathered and scattered."

The most important news of all is often news we don't *want* to know, but *need* to know. With my colleagues at NBC, I spend a great deal of time trying to be sure *Meet the Press* gets at this very news. We hold politicians' feet to the fire because we think the world is better off knowing the truth in all its ugly beauty. This may not make us popular with politicians, but it has worked for 50 years with you, the audience.

You'd think working in news would be easy. But news has the soul of a candle flame, flickering, ephemeral. Even the best of us have gone with stories too soon, have gotten things wrong. I can only hope, for example, that eventually everyone forgets that I was the one who told the world President

Clinton would probably name his new dog Luke, not Buddy.

My tenure as an adviser and a trustee of the Newseum, the nation's news museum, has helped me appreciate this all the more. In the Early News Gallery there, I have learned that even in ancient Egypt, in a culture where scribes were as important as scholars or priests, the almighty Pharaoh had to assign four scribes to write about an important trial, hoping the truth would somehow emerge from their varying reports.

We can't precisely define news and don't know the best of it until we see it. By its very nature, news is imperfect. Is it surprising then that Americans today — or people of any nation — are wary of news and newspeople? That the public sometimes sees journalists as people with agendas, the ethical equals not of priests and teachers but of politicians and lawyers? I'm not surprised. Some journalists deserve it, especially the ones who have traded in healthy skepticism for rabid cynicism.

Every generation should debate the quality of its news. Yet these debates take us to the brink. The same Americans who tell pollsters they respect newspeople also agree "there are times when the press should not be allowed to publish or broadcast certain things." Censorship remains in horrifyingly good standing. Have the newsmongers ruined it for everyone? Will the First Amendment be amended into extinction? Will news be stripped of controversy? I doubt it. During the past 200 years, the free expression guaranteed by our First Amendment has grown. It may ebb, but it won't evaporate. We won't let it.

If any group needs to take a stroll through its own history, it's journalists. In news, the most important thing, always, is the *next* story — the future, not the past. Some journalists pine for the quality and independence of the good old days. But lost to nostalgia are the facts: professional codes of ethics are a relatively recent trend. A generation ago, a college degree was a newsroom handicap, not an asset. Almost a century ago, journalists predicted disaster from moral decay, government control and the new electronic medium — radio. But the disaster never arrived.

Take an honest look back, and you'll see there is more accurate, fair, responsible news today than ever before. Of course, inaccuracy, bias and sensationalism also are growing. But that's the digital age: There's more news and information available to you, the consumer, than ever before. There's more good and more bad, more to choose from, more to know.

That wide array of voices — loud, crazy and

otherwise — is healthy for us. Different people see things differently. If everyone is at the table, everything can get *onto* the table. That was Milton's idea: "who ever knew Truth put to the worse in a free and open encounter?" The free exchange of ideas has served Western civilization well.

So join the debate. Read your history, do your homework, ask questions, prod. Or in the words of one of my own journalistic heroes, *Meet the Press* founder Larry Spivak: "Learn everything about your guests' positions on the issues — and take the other side!"

Introduction

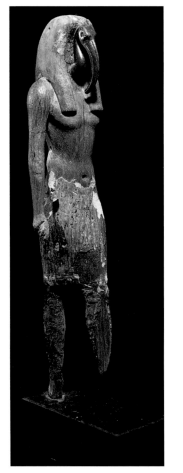

Above: Thoth, the Egyptian god of scribes, comes in two forms: as a scholarly Ibis-headed creature (here in the c. 500 B.C. statue) or as a dog-faced baboon.

Crusaders and Scoundrels

Even though we never like it, and even though we wish they didn't write it, and even though we disapprove, there isn't any doubt that we could not do the job at all in a free society without a very, very active press.

— John F. Kennedy, 1962

The press is the enemy.

— Richard Nixon, 1969

AROUND CAMPFIRES, OUR EARLIEST ANCESTORS trade stories. At ancient crossroads, they spread the word. News, ancient and universal, fills a basic human need — the need to know. Spoken, written and printed, news helps turn clans into civilizations.

News, we need.

It's the people who bring it to us we have problems with.

In Africa, the singing storytellers — the griots — are denied the right of burial because their corpses might pollute the land. In Sumer, a king can negotiate by killing another king's messenger. "No one," Socrates explains, "likes the bringer of bad news." In Rome, Cicero condemns "tittle-tattle" reports about gladiators (he wants serious news from the Senate). In London, printers who stray from royal truth are tortured.

America attacks its printers not with the rack or machete but with words. Before Thomas Jefferson is president, he declares "our liberty depends on the freedom of the press, and that cannot be limited without being lost." But after becoming president, he says "the man who never looks into a newspaper is better informed than he who reads them."

The love-hate relationship with the press is endemic.

On the one hand, our presidents see journalists as free-press heroes, "martyrs," as James Garfield calls them, "in the long fierce struggle for freedom of opinion." Dwight Eisenhower will fight, even die, "for the freedom of newspapers that call me ... a good deal less than ... a gentleman." Bill Clinton says "America is stronger and freer because of them." But presidents also call newspeople every epithet imaginable, including "assassins" (John Quincy Adams), "infamous" (Ulysses S. Grant), "unscrupulous" (Teddy Roosevelt), "disagreeable" (Harry S Truman) and "vicious" (Jimmy Carter). When he thinks his microphone is off, Ronald Reagan lets slip his view of Washington's elite press corps: "sons of bitches."

Given that generalized disdain, why would anyone go into the business? What exactly is a newsperson — and why are they telling us all these things we don't want to hear?

This book strives to shed some light on these questions by bringing a bit of history to current debates about news and newspeople. Perhaps, if we better understand who our newspeople have been, why they have been loved *and* hated, reviled *and* needed — crusaders *and* scoundrels — we can better understand news and newspeople today.

Anybody can be a journalist — and usually is.
— Walter Lippmann

The people in this book represent the many faces and voices of news. They are strikingly diverse, but one way or another shaped how the news was reported in their day.

Any student of journalism could find a role model (or anti-role model) among them. They are men and women, people of all creeds and color, young, old, gay, straight, walking and in wheelchairs. They come from big-city dailies and small-town weeklies. They are rich, they are poor. They lean right, they lean left. They are owners, editors, reporters, broadcasters, photographers, artists. They're crusaders like Ida B. Wells and sleuths like Ida Tarbell; lovable sorts like Ernie Pyle and detestable cynics like Ambrose Bierce; broadcasters like Edward R. Murrow and Global Villagers like Bill Gates.

In the broadest sense, anyone who helps spread news is a newsperson. In fact, the word *newes* (1382) enters the language hundreds of years before the word *journalist* (1718). Yet, within journalism, the word *journalist* is debated passionately. Do commentators or talk show hosts qualify? No, say hard news reporters. Yes, say the talk show hosts. Phil Donahue protests "long, hand-wringing discussions" about who is a journalist. "We should remember," he says, "that the guy who ran into the bar at Chernobyl and said, 'Holy cow, this thing blew,' is a journalist."

So this work contains a deliberately motley crew. We profile journalists and other types of newspeople. Who is who? That's up to you. Our point is that their gathering illustrates the vast, rich domain that is the news business. Just ask newspeople why they do what they do, and hear the array of voices: Is it "to inform people so they can help themselves" (Sarah McClendon) or to "be where the action is" (Clarence Page)? To "live a kind of floating existence between heaven and earth" (Morley Safer) or "to come as close as possible to the heart of the world" (Henry R. Luce)? "For love, not money" (Howard K. Smith); to "sell abuse" (Ambrose Bierce); "to get to the truth ... our Holy Grail" (Helen Thomas); because "every day is fresh, every

'The greatest news-people are simply fine people ... the worst, simply lousy people.'

day is something new" (Mike Wallace); or simply because "it's fun" (Sam Donaldson)?

Ask Associated Press correspondent Terry Anderson, hostage of Muslim fundamentalists from 1985 to 1991: "Why? Why is such force mustered against reporters? Because what journalists do is important. An active press often plays a key role in bringing freedom to a society."

The news is hardly perfect, and neither are newspeople. Horace Greeley, father of the modern editorial page, calls for slaves to be freed, but ignores the slaughter of Native Americans. But many newspeople do share admirable qualities. They tend to be curious and to think critically. They can be quick, with facile, active (sometimes overactive) minds. Many consider what they do a public trust. The greatest newspeople often are simply fine people — smart, compassionate, brave. In the same way, the worst newspeople often are simply lousy people. They possess the flip-side qualities — a kind of thick-headed, cold-hearted cowardice. Witness Walter Duranty, who ignored millions dying in a Soviet famine to protect his access to top officials, and thus his renown as the world's top foreign correspondent.

This book is full of both types, as well as some who are blended so thoroughly it's hard to tell where the bad one ends and the good one begins. *Crusaders, Scoundrels, Journalists* is by no means a hall of fame. It is, rather, a reflection of what news and newspeople have been and can be.

Compare front pages of 500-year-old European news books with the front pages of today. Weather, sports, crime, business, politics, human interest — page one then, page one now. Human nature hasn't changed much in half a millennium.

Nor have the larger issues of news changed all that much. Chain ownership? Ben Franklin tried it. Censorship? Ernie Pyle suffered it. Sensationalism? Benjamin Harris, the first publisher in British North America, hoped to thrive on it.

What is the importance of such a history today? Today, America is entering a digital age. We demand our news when and how we want it. We can drown in it or pluck what we need from the deluge of data. Uplinked citizens of the new millennium, we can download into our homes in one day what a shoe-leather journalist of the 1970s couldn't have carted home from city hall in a year.

The digital revolution has the potential to make all of us into newspeople of sorts. And what kind will we be? Newsmongers, peering into our computers for salacious gossip? Sleuths, digging through government data to aid a community cause? Crusaders for truth, justice, the greater good — nitpicking naysayers?

The questions we face are the same as they have been since news began — the battle between oppression and freedom, between those who would control news, and those who would free it; between those who would use news for private gain, and those who would use it for public good.

These are fresh, timeless tales, told in the active voice of the Newseum's News History Gallery. There on the wall is a text panel that says it all: "The story of news is the story of our need to know and our need to tell, of many voices struggling to be heard."

— **Joe Urschel**
Executive Director, Newseum

Crusaders, Scoundrels, Journalists

Newsmongers

BOSTON, 1690 —

B ENJAMIN HARRIS LAUNCHES THE FIRST NEWSPAPER in British North America with a really sexy story on page three and a promise to print monthly, "or if any Glut of Occurrences happen, oftener."

But *Publick Occurrences* appears only once. The page three story, that King Louis XIV of France is having sex with the prince's wife, scandalizes Boston's Puritan clergy. Proclaim authorities: "Great inconvenience may arise by the liberty of printing." Their rule: No printing without a license.

Still, the flood of sensation comes. Followed by reporters on his honeymoon, President Grover Cleveland calls it "ghoulish glee." For 500 years, from ballads and early newspapers to tabloid TV, we've heard all about it: sex, scandal, bloody battles, bizarre blizzards, slasher murders, witches, freaks, dragons and aliens. If news is important, good; if it's strange, even better. Such is the beat of the newsmonger, the peddler of tales, the one who doesn't let the facts ruin a good story.

At *The New York Times*, Walter Duranty's portrait hangs on a long wall of Pulitzer Prize winners. Moscow correspondent Duranty wins in 1932 for his stories on

Joseph Stalin's rise to power. But while the *Times* lionizes Stalin, nine million people are dying. Convinced the dictator will transform Russia, Duranty ignores a great famine sweeping the Ukraine. "Having bet his reputation on Stalin, he strove to preserve it by ignoring or excusing Stalin's crimes," the *Times* says in a 1990 editorial. "He saw what he wanted to see." On the Pulitzer Prize wall, Duranty's portrait carries a footnote: "Other writers in the *Times* and elsewhere have discredited this coverage."

At least Duranty didn't have to give back his Pulitzer. That dishonor belongs to Janet Cooke, in 1980 an up-and-coming *Washington Post* reporter who writes a heart-wrenching account of Jimmy, an 8-year-old heroin addict. The boy (as are most of the story's main sources) is unidentified. "At some point," Cooke says, "it dawned on me that I could simply make it all up." She does, taking readers on a riveting, fictional ride through *Jimmy's World*, "a world of hard drugs, fast money and the good life he believes both can bring."

Says Bob Woodward, famed Watergate reporter and one of the *Post*'s duped editors: "I should have tried to save the kid and then do the story. If I had worried about the kid, I would have learned that the story was a fraud."

— Courtesy Steve Lomazow/Ben Lourie photo

Cooke wins the 1981 Pulitzer Prize for feature writing. But the fraud is exposed, and she loses her job. Such is the state of newsmongering at the nation's largest newspapers. A hundred years earlier, in a century before professional codes of ethics, she might have been a hero. In 1835, Benjamin Day's New York *Sun* — America's first successful "penny paper," appealing to the masses — prints a series about long-legged man-bat creatures living on the moon. Circulation jumps to a world-record 19,000, or so the *Sun* claims. When a reporter in a bar admits the spoof, the *Sun* doesn't apologize, but takes credit for "diverting the public mind, for a while, from that bitter apple of discord, the abolition of slavery."

Edgar Allan Poe calls the hoax "the greatest hit in the way of sensation ... ever made by any similar fiction either in America or Europe." Poe himself is in the midst of hoaxing the world about a mythical balloon flight.

This is, of course, in the days before facts take on a more scientific importance, when newspapers still are a purposeful blend of news and entertainment, the important and interesting — even if the interesting is gossip, stunts, rumors or front-page poetry. As John Holt's *New-*

Inset: R. F. Outcault creates America's first popular cartoon character, the Yellow Kid, in 1895. When New York publishers fight over it, and two immigrant Kids appear in two different newspapers, sensationalism gets a new name, 'Yellow Journalism.'

York Journal puts it: "Our service you can't express, the good we do you hardly guess; There's not a want of human kind, but we a remedy can find."

Wilbur Storey, owner of the *Chicago Times*, tells his Civil War reporter: "Telegraph fully all news ... and when there is no news send rumours." Another Storey vision becomes a time-honored journalistic motto: "Print the news and raise hell."

Another part of the time-honored newsmongering tradition: If you don't like the news, go out and make some of your own. Writing for Joseph Pulitzer's New York *World*, "stunt girl" Nellie Bly feigns insanity to expose conditions inside an asylum on Blackwell's Island, and circles the globe in 72 days to upstage Jules Verne's *Around the World in Eighty Days*. Her sensational success inspires newspapers in the United States and Europe to imitate Pulitzer's "New Journalism" by introducing aggressive, intelligent news mixed with illustrations, crusades, high-quality editorials, colorful Sunday sections and shameless self-promotion.

In the 1920s, newsmongering acquires another dimension. Ben Hecht helps immortalize the fast, loose, hard-drinking reporters who will cheat and steal for a scoop in the 1928 play, *The Front Page*. The play's influence extends to hundreds of novels and movies, in which wise-cracking, hat-wearing reporters swear the scoop is still the biggest thrill of all. Hecht's hero, Hildy Johnson, calls them "lousy daffy buttinskis, swelling around with holes in their pants, borrowing nickels from office boys." Amplifies Hecht, in *Nothing Sacred:* "Newspapermen ... The hand of God reaching down into the mire couldn't elevate one of them to the depths of degradation."

Early celebrity journalist Walter Winchell would've taken powerful exception to that. The columnist sets his sights beyond The Story to The People — collecting his fans, that is, and paving the way for such populists-to-come as Geraldo and Oprah. The kingmaker's format in the tabloid New York *Evening Graphic* and later the *New York Mirror* — brief items separated by ellipses — is a three-dot hit. Writes Winchell's editor at the *Mirror*, Arthur Brisbane: "You have neither ethics, scruples, decency or conscience." Replies Winchell: "Let others have those things ... I've got the readers."

A generation later, TV talk show host Geraldo Rivera — crusader-turned-showman — calls objectivity "a word that was made up by some journalism professor." In 1986, Rivera has the viewers when he opens Al Capone's vault on live TV in the most-watched syndicated special to date. But the crypt is empty. And so, Geraldo learns, for every newsmonger, there lurks in the world of news a

'Telegraph fully all news ... and when there is no news send rumours.'

— WILBUR STOREY

serious critic. "I have every ratings record there is on documentaries," he complains, and "nothing but scathing reviews." In 1998, he tries to return to his hard-news roots, giving up his talk show altogether.

No chance that will happen with Hunter S. Thompson. At *Rolling Stone* magazine in the 1960s and 1970s, the writer names his style "gonzo journalism." It's a premeditated blend of truth, fiction, alcohol and drugs that takes Thompson on trips with Hell's Angels, through fear and loathing in Las Vegas and into a restroom with Richard Nixon. For fun, he shoots his typewriter. The God of Gonzo speaks: "Absolute truth is a very rare and dangerous commodity in the context of professional journalism."

The folks at *The Bee* of New London, Connecticut, in 1800, would agree:

"Here various news we tell, of love and strife,
Of peace and war, health, sickness, death and life,
... Of prodigies, and portents seen in air,
Of fires, and plagues, and stars with blazing hair,
... Of old mismanagements, taxations new,
All neither wholly false, nor wholly true."

Benjamin Harris

c. 1660–1720

Scandal-loving journalist Benjamin Harris flees England for a new life as a Boston bookseller. In 1690, he starts the first newspaper in British North America, *Publick Occurrences,* to appear monthly, "or oftener." Officials, upset by a French sex scandal and other reports, kill the paper after one edition, calling it a "great inconvenience." In time, the sensationalist heads back to England, where printing is somewhat less Puritanical. No portrait of Harris survives.

A statement of intent from the only issue of Publick Occurrences, *Sept. 25, 1690:*

'Considerable things'

It is designed that the Countrey shall be furnished once a month (or if any Glut of Occurrences happen, oftener) with an Account of such considerable things as have arrived unto our Notice. In order here unto, the Publisher will take what pains he can to obtain a Faithful Relation of all such things; and will particularly make himself beholden to such Persons in Boston whom he knows to have been for their own use the diligent Observers of such matters.

James Thomson Callender

1758–1803

Thomas Jefferson kept a slave mistress, seduced a friend's wife — even paid a debt with bad money. So writes Richmond *Recorder* co-owner James Thomson Callender, whose scandal-mongering has already landed him in jail for sedition. Once financially supported by Jefferson, Callender punishes the president with "entertaining facts" meant to humiliate. The partisan editor defends his work: "Until the people are well-informed, there cannot be a correct and firm government." No portrait of Callender survives.

THE PRESIDENT AGAIN.

IT is well known that the man, *whom it delighteth the people to honor*, keeps, and for many years past has kept, as his concubine, one of his own slaves. Her name is SALLY. The name of her eldest son is TOM. His features are said to bear a striking although sable resemblance to those of the president himself. The boy is ten or twelve years of age. His mother went to France in the same vessel with Mr. Jefferson and his two daughters. The delicacy of this arrangement must strike every person of common sensibility. What a sublime pattern for an American ambassador to place before the eyes of two young ladies !

If the reader does not feel himself *disposed to pause* we beg leave to proceed. Some years ago, this story had once or twice been hinted at in *Rind's Federalist*. At that time, we believed the surmise to be an absolute calumny. One reason for thinking so was this. A vast body of people wished to debar Mr. Jefferson from the presidency. *The establishment of this* SINGLE FACT would have rendered his election impossible. We reasoned thus; that if the allegation had been true, it was sure to have been ascertained and advertised by his enemies in every corner of the continent. The suppression of so decisive an enquiry serves to shew that the common sense of the federal party was overruled by divine providence. It was the predestination of the supreme being that they should be turned out; that they should be expelled from office by the *popula-*

In September 1802, James Thomson Callender writes in the Richmond Recorder *about Thomas Jefferson and his slave, Sally Hemings:*

'Her name is Sally'

It is well known that the man, whom it delighteth the people to honor, keeps and for many years has kept, as his concubine, one of his slaves. Her name is SALLY. … By this wench Sally, our president has had several children. There is not an individual in the neighbourhood of Charlottesville who does not believe the story, and not a few who know it.

Benjamin Day

1810–1889

Young printer Benjamin Day wakes up journalism in 1833 with his spunky New York *Sun,* "the first penny paper in America, and, as far as I have known, the first in the world." He hires newsboys to sell the *Sun* on the streets. Lively local news, one of the first police beats and a hoax about moon creatures drive sales to more than 19,000 daily, a world record. In a financial panic, Day sells the newspaper in 1837. Later, he says selling was the silliest thing he ever did.

MUSEUM OF THE CITY OF NEW YORK

A statement from the first issue of the Sun, *Sept. 3, 1833:*

Affordable news for all

The object of this paper is to lay before the public, at a price within the means of every one, ALL THE NEWS OF THE DAY, and at the same time afford an advantageous medium for advertising. The sheet will be enlarged as soon as the increase in advertisements requires it, the price remaining the same.

Dan De Quille

1829–1898

Miner-turned-writer Dan De Quille is a master hoaxer. With friend and fellow reporter Mark Twain, he pens wild, sometimes fabricated frontier stories in Nevada for the Virginia City *Territorial Enterprise.* His most famous: A man thrives in the desert wearing a sponge suit with a push-button cooler, but when a valve sticks, he freezes to death. De Quille stays with the paper for more than 30 years.

SPECIAL COLLECTIONS, UNIVERSITY OF NEVADA–RENO

In 1874, Dan De Quille describes in the Territorial Enterprise *how "solar armor" killed a man:*

'Dead and frozen stiff'

The armor consisted of a long, close-fitting jacket made of common sponge, and a cap or hood of the same material. … He was dead and frozen stiff. His beard was covered with frost, and — though the noonday sun poured down its fiercest rays — an icicle over a foot in length hung from his nose.

Wilbur F. Storey

1819–1884

In 1861, Wilbur F. Storey buys *The Chicago Times* for $13,000. He gets his money's worth. One hanging carries the headline: "JERKED TO JESUS." Storey gives bad reviews to plays that don't buy ads and good ones if he gets an invite. When the *Times* describes members of a burlesque troupe as "beefy specimens of the barmaid class," one of the women tackles and horsewhips Storey. At one point, he faces 24 libel suits. "Print the news," he says, "and raise hell." A century later, the *San Francisco Bay Guardian* picks up the credo as its motto.

CHICAGO HISTORICAL SOCIETY

During the Civil War, Wilbur F. Storey attacks Abraham Lincoln and ignores government censorship. In 1864, Gen. Ambrose E. Burnside orders The Chicago Times *seized and suspended for sedition. The president rescinds the order after three days. Storey sums up his attitude in his instructions to a correspondent in the field:*

'Send rumors'

Telegraph fully all news ... and when there is no news send rumors.

Nellie Bly

1864–1922

Elizabeth Cochrane gets a job at the *World* after interviewing New York editors about why they have no female reporters. She becomes Nellie Bly, the most famous of the "stunt girls." In 1889, readers revel as she whisks around the world in just 72 days, "coming home to dear old America with the scalps of the carpers and critics strung on her slender girdle." Cochrane is a newsmonger who wants facts: she pioneers the undercover exposé, feigning insanity to reveal conditions in a notorious asylum. Every story she does for *The World* is so sensational it carries her name in the headline.

In a series beginning Oct. 9, 1887, in the New York World, *Nellie Bly exposes conditions inside the asylum of Blackwell's Island:*

'Produce insanity'

What, excepting torture, would produce insanity quicker than this treatment? Here is a class of women sent to be cured. I would like the expert physicians who are condemning me for my action, which has proven their ability, to take a perfectly sane and healthy woman, shut her up and make her sit from 6 a.m. to 8 p.m. on straight-back benches, do not allow her to talk or move during these hours, give her no reading and let her know nothing of the world or its doings, give her bad food and harsh treatment, and see how long it will take to make her insane. Two months would make her a mental and physical wreck.

Bernarr Macfadden

1868–1955

Bernarr Macfadden enters the New York tabloid wars in 1924 with his *Evening Graphic*. Critics call it the "Porno-Graphic." The tabloid's sensational first-person accounts carry headlines like "I Am Now the Mother of My Sister's Son." The *Graphic* features fictional composite photographs called "composographs." Macfadden defends sensationalism: It is "perfectly proper as long as one adheres to truth." A body-builder and health-food fanatic, he runs for president and prints books featuring nude photos of himself. The *Graphic* folds in 1932.

LIBRARY OF CONGRESS

In 1924, Bernarr Macfadden tells editors at the Evening Graphic *his hopes for the new tabloid:*

'Editorialize the news too'

A paper wholly human, with a serious purpose behind it — which makes it different from all other tabloids. ... We're going to play up physical culture in it. ... That's why I'm starting it. And I want you to editorialize the news too. Don't stop with the bare skeleton of the facts. Point out the moral, the social lesson.

Marcus Garvey

1887–1940

"The Black Moses," Jamaican-born Marcus Garvey, promotes black history and the return of African Americans to Africa in his weekly *Negro World*. The opinion leader's message: Black is beautiful. "Hitch your hopes to the stars," he writes. In 1922, his $10-million emigration scheme goes belly up. Garvey is jailed for fraud. After three years, his sentence is commuted. But then he's deported to Jamaica. Generations later, schools in cities across the United States bear his name.

In a front-page editorial in the June 6, 1925, issue of The Negro World, *Marcus Garvey writes:*

'Create our own martyrs'

The time has come for the Negro to forget and cast behind him his hero worship and adoration of other races, and to start out immediately, to create and emulate heroes of his own. We must canonize our own saints, create our own martyrs, and elevate to positions of fame and honor black men and women who have made their distinct contributions to our racial history. ... Africa has produced countless numbers of men and women, in war and peace, whose lustre and bravery outshine that of any other people. Then why not see good and perfection in ourselves?

Ben Hecht

1894–1964

UPI/CORBIS-BETTMANN

In "A Child of the Century," Ben Hecht writes of a hanging on the eve of World War I:

'Darkness full of little things'

Sweet night in the shadow of death, night of crickets chirping and a clover-smelling breeze, night of heedless youth and bawdy tales, of young breasts glinting over a hanging rope, of a darkness full of little things — starlight and owls and weather reports and a melodeon playing for the salvation of a man, and haphazard human doings eerie and unpolitical and with the sap of life in them — that night is gone. And none like it was ever to be in my time again. For on this August, 1914, night, an innocence was departing the world.

Walter Duranty

1884–1957

New York Times Moscow correspondent Walter Duranty wins a Pulitzer Prize in 1932 by predicting Joseph Stalin's rise to power. The next year, he denies that nine million Ukrainians are dying in a government-inflicted famine. Privately, however, he admits the story is true. His report that "there is no famine" contains the line "you can't make an omelet without breaking eggs." It secures access to Soviet brass and, for a time, his renown as the world's top foreign correspondent. Half a century later, a *Times* writer calls Duranty's Moscow stories "some of the worst reporting to appear in this newspaper."

Walter Duranty dismisses reports of widespread famine in a front-page March 31, 1933, story in The New York Times:

'There is no famine'

The big cities and the army are adequately supplied with food. There is no actual starvation or deaths from starvation, but there is widespread mortality from diseases due to malnutrition. In short, conditions are definitely bad in certain sections — the Ukraine, North Caucasus and Lower Volga. The rest of the country is on short rations but nothing worse. These conditions are bad, but there is no famine.

Walter Winchell

1897–1972

Celebrity-maker Walter Winchell shapes the modern gossip column ... his "three-dot" column is a must-read '20s feature in the New York *Evening Graphic* ... later, the *Daily Mirror* ... he writes, says Ben Hecht, "like a man honking in a traffic jam" ... befriends gangsters, FBI, stars ... says "to become famous ... throw a brick at someone who is famous" ... reigns 40 years as kingmaker ... scrawls "take care of this" on notes he sends to the president ... says "Democracy is where everybody can kick everybody else's ass ... but you can't kick Winchell's."

UPI/CORBIS-BETTMANN

Walter Winchell leaves the Vaudeville News *to join the New York* Evening Graphic *as theater reviewer and Broadway columnist. He spends the bulk of his career holding court at the Stork Club. From a* Graphic *column after he is barred from the Shubert theaters:*

'You get weary'

You get weary being barred from the Shubert theaters. You miss the splendid exercise you got walking out on their shows.

Hunter S. Thompson

1937–

Writer Hunter S. Thompson mixes fact, fantasy and intoxicating substances in a blend of first-person "gonzo journalism." Thompson's popular books and magazine articles cover everything from barroom life with Hell's Angels to restroom interviews with Richard Nixon. Good fiction, he says, is "far more true" than journalism. College professors make Thompson's *Rolling Stone* screeds required reading on college campuses. Cartoonist Garry Trudeau draws him in *Doonesbury* as the hard-drinking, gun-toting Uncle Duke.

THE ASSOCIATED PRESS

In Fear and Loathing in Las Vegas, *Hunter Thompson writes about journalism:*

'Pompous contradiction'

So much for Objective Journalism. Don't bother to look for it here — not under any byline of mine; or anyone else I can think of. With the possible exception of things like box scores, race results and stock market tabulations, there is no such thing as Objective Journalism. The phrase itself is a pompous contradiction in terms.

In Fear and Loathing on the Campaign Trail '72, *he writes about candidates:*

There is no avoiding Hubert Humphrey in Wisconsin this week. The bastard is everywhere: on the tube, on the box, in the streets with his sound trucks ... and now the bastard is even breaking into Easter morning sermons with his gibberish.

Janet Cooke

1954–

The 1981 Pulitzer Prize for feature writing goes to young *Washington Post* reporter Janet Cooke for a profile of Jimmy, an 8-year-old heroin addict. But the story is untrue. So is Cooke's résumé. She resigns. For the first time, the prize is returned. A litany of *Post* editors call the story the biggest mistake of their careers. "What I did was horrible," Cooke tells *GQ* in 1996. But she maintains that her ostracism doesn't "fit the crime."

THE ASSOCIATED PRESS

An excerpt from Janet Cooke's Pulitzer Prize-winning article in The Washington Post, *Sept. 28, 1980, later revealed as a hoax:*

'Jimmy's World'

The needle slides into the boy's soft skin like a straw pushed into the center of a freshly baked cake. Liquid ebbs out of the syringe, replaced by bright red blood. The blood is then reinjected into the child. Jimmy ... climbs into a rocking chair and sits, his head dipping and snapping upright again, in what addicts call "the nod."

Geraldo Rivera

1943–

Before talk TV, Geraldo Rivera is an award-winning investigative reporter. Rivera starts in New York television, exposing the Willowbrook State School for the Mentally Retarded: It "smelled of filth, it smelled of disease, and it smelled of death." He becomes a correspondent for ABC's *20/20*. All this before becoming the 1980s personification of a new brand of broadcasting: tabloid TV. With shows on male strippers and "Kids Who Kill," his talk show, *Geraldo*, is accused of masking entertainment as news. But people watch.

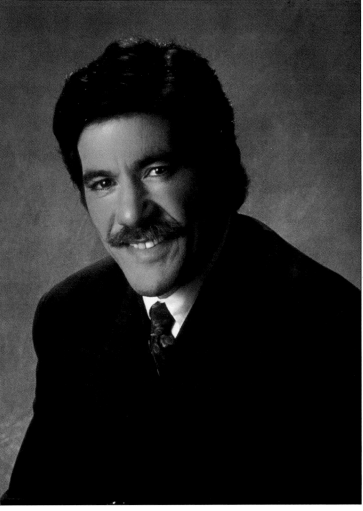

CAPITAL CITIES/ABC, INC.

In his 1991 memoir, Exposing Myself, *Geraldo Rivera talks about the fallout from his exclusive TV opening of Al Capone's vault, which turns out to be empty:*

'Thrill of commercial victory'

I had done better work, but never before such a vast audience. Whatever our winged-monster of a program turned out to be, it crapped on the networks. We absolutely crushed the competition ... The thrill of commercial victory was made even richer against ... negative reviews, and the embarrassment of digging for a vault that turned out to be virtually nonexistent.

Jerry Springer

1944–

Talk show host Jerry Springer rules tabloid TV with brawling guests and themes like "My Boyfriend Is a Girl." The *Jerry Springer Show* is second only to *Oprah* in ratings. In 1997, a longtime Chicago TV anchor quits when Springer — a former mayor and TV anchor — joins her station as a commentator. He quits after two programs. Springer calls his own show a "cultural cartoon." "No one ever gets on our show," he says, "who doesn't desperately want to get on."

COURTESY THE JERRY SPRINGER SHOW

An excerpt from a Jan. 15, 1998, Jerry Springer show, "Teenage Call Girls":

'Stop selling her body'

Eighteen-year-old LaTanya has been working as an escort for the past year, but she told her boyfriend, Craig, that she was a waitress at a club. Today she'll tell him the truth about her job and about her secret affair with her best friend, Tracy. Next, Michelle is 19 years old, but has been working as a prostitute since she was just 12. Her best friend, who is a former prostitute, and her mother make passionate pleas to convince Michelle to stop selling her body and leave the boyfriend they hate!

Matt Drudge

1967–

Internet columnist Matt Drudge scours newspapers and wire services for his 85,000-reader entertainment-and-politics column, the *Drudge Report*. He also relies on anonymous sources, an approach that brings a libel suit from a White House adviser and calls to regulate online gossip. Drudge is unrepentant: "Anyone can report anything. You don't have to work for ABC." When Drudge reports allegations that President Bill Clinton had sex with a White House intern, he finds himself a national celebrity and instant guest on *Meet the Press*.

TODD BIGELOW

On Jan. 18, 1998, the Drudge Report *breaks the story of a presidential sex scandal:*

'Shake official Washington'

At the last minute, at 6 p.m. on Saturday evening, *Newsweek* magazine killed a story that was destined to shake official Washington to its foundation: A White House intern carried on a sexual affair with the President of the United States! *The Drudge Report* has learned that reporter Michael Isikoff developed the story of his career, only to have it spiked by top *Newsweek* suits hours before publication. A young woman, 23, was a frequent visitor to a small study just off the Oval Office, where she claims to have indulged the president's sexual preference. *The Drudge Report* has learned that tapes of intimate phone conversations exist.

Crusaders

NEW YORK, 1734 —

S TRUGGLING PRINTER JOHN PETER ZENGER'S NEW newspaper, *The New-York Weekly Journal*, is a hit. Its editorial secret? Stir up resentment toward a high-handed colonial governor. But Governor William Cosby is not amused. Suddenly, Zenger finds himself in jail, charged with seditious libel, a crime punishable by death. Even so, he dictates articles through a hole in his jail cell door to his wife, who keeps the *Journal* going.

The printer's hopes are faint. His lawyers are disbarred; their replacement, inexperienced. At the last moment, Philadelphia lawyer Andrew Hamilton rides into town on a white horse to defend Zenger. "It is not the cause of a poor printer ... which you are now trying: No!" he tells the jury. "It is the Cause of Liberty ... the liberty both of exposing and opposing arbitrary power ... by speaking and writing — Truth."

With that, the colonial jury rebels against British law. Zenger is free. Hamilton's oratory establishes the notions that truth is a defense against libel, that Americans can criticize political officials — notions that later become law.

The crusaders are newspeople who believe in their hearts their cause is right and just. Zenger's is the pivotal news crusade in early America, the one that makes all the rest possible. Many a crusader after Zenger does jail time: revolutionary Thomas Paine; abolitionist William Lloyd Garrison; radical John Reed; Japanese-American Fred Makino; Mexican freedom-fighter Ricardo Flores Magón; and birth-control champion Margaret Sanger. Others endured threats of jail, boycotts by advertisers, torches thrown through their windows.

They suffer, but seldom in silence. American revolutionary Thomas Paine is chased out of England, nearly guillotined in France, and shunned back in America. He dies a pauper, leaving this: "Those who expect to reap the blessings of freedom must, like men, undergo the fatigue of supporting it."

Should journalists take sides? Or, as Tom Gish puts it: "Should the editor keep his mouth shut and his typewriter quiet? Or should he seek solutions and, through news stories and features and editorials, try to awaken the town and get some movement underway?" For much of the 20th century, Tom and his wife, Pat, of *The Mountain Eagle* in eastern Kentucky, answer their own question with each weekly edition, crusading against political corruption and the ravages of strip mining.

Some journalists call crusaders too political, propagandists, even. Many crusaders happily admit bias — bias, they argue, toward the truth. Socialist John Reed, whose politics force him to flee his country and die in exile, writes: "My sympathies were not neutral. But in telling the story of those great days, I have tried to see events with the eye of a conscientious reporter, interested in setting down the truth." Radio pioneer H. V. Kaltenborn: "No news analyst could be or would be completely neutral or objective. He shows his editorial bias by every act of selection or rejection from the vast mass of news material on his desk." And, a generation later, feminist Gloria Steinem: "I always wanted to be a writer. I got into activism just because it needed to be done."

The obsessive single-mindedness, the rightness of the crusade, applies also to the rightness of the journalistic methods.

Pamphleteer Tom Paine: "I dwell not upon the vapours of imagination. I bring reason to your ears and in language as plain as A, B, C, hold up truth to your eyes."

William Lloyd Garrison, in his antislavery newspaper, *The Liberator:* "Tell a man whose house is on fire to give a moderate alarm; tell him to moderately rescue his wife from the hands of the ravisher; tell the mother to gradually extricate her babe from the fire into which it has fallen — but urge me not to use moderation in a cause like the present. I am in earnest – I will not equivocate – I will not excuse – I will not retreat a single inch – AND I WILL BE HEARD."

— Courtesy Thomas Paine National Historical Association/Alex Jamison photo

Above: Thomas Paine uses this writing kit during his pamphleteering days.

Women's rights crusader Elizabeth Cady Stanton: "It is a settled maxim with me that the existing public sentiment on any subject is wrong."

William Allen White, small-town editor and free-speech crusader: "My idea of one hundred percent Americanism is an American who has intelligent faith enough in his country and his ideals to allow any other American, however stupid and however crooked and however malicious, to say what he pleases."

The crusaders, of course, are not always right. In the 1720s, James Franklin (Ben's older brother) launches an effort in his *New-England Courant* to fight Puritan leaders Increase and Cotton Mather. Looking for a cause, Franklin decides to *fight against* smallpox inoculation. "The Town is become almost a Hell upon Earth, a City full of Lies," writes Cotton in his diary. Fortunately, the Puritan leaders fight back in competing publications, and Boston is inoculated against smallpox after all. When they are right, media crusades advance the great social issues of our time — freedom, justice and equality — not to mention cleaning up crime, corruption, pollution and faulty products. But when they are wrong, crusades bring about lynchings, political bosses, mass exploitation and more.

Whether they want to admit it or not, many news people are at times infected by the crusading spirit. Publisher Joseph Pulitzer's New York *World* would not rest until its readers contribute enough nickels and dimes to provide a base for the Statue of Liberty. Editor Scott Newhall's *San Francisco Chronicle* feels the same way about making sure every citizen has access to a great cup of coffee. Others crusade for fair bank loans, trauma care for the poor, water conservation, live music in clubs — you name it.

Some crusades come calling. Like John Peter Zenger before him, reporter Earl Caldwell wants to keep his sources confidential. In *The New York Times*, Caldwell reveals the Black Panthers have a cache of arms. When authorities demand his notes, he destroys them. "I shredded almost every document I had ... many should have been saved, for history's sake," he says. "But in America today, a reporter cannot save his notes." That's still the case in states without shield laws to protect the use of anonymous sources.

All along, the greatest crusade is still the first, the one that makes the rest possible. The fight to keep our right, as syndicated columnist Nat Hentoff puts it, to be "exuberantly offensive." The U.S. Supreme Court agrees: the government can't restrain news before printing (1931 ruling), public figures are by definition hard to injure (1964),

> 'Allow any other American, however stupid ... to say what he pleases.'
>
> — WILLIAM ALLEN WHITE

and electronic speech enjoys the same protection as other forms (1997). It is the First Amendment, something Zenger never knew, that is the greatest ally of the crusader, who thinks that facts alone can't pin down the truth, that the world will know it only when they hear it, if only someone is free to tell it.

John Zenger

1697–1746

Anna Zenger

c. 1704–1751

In 1734, printer John Peter Zenger begins the odyssey that makes him a free-press hero. When his *New-York Weekly Journal* angers the colonial governor, Zenger is jailed for seditious libel. His wife Anna keeps the *Journal* going. John dictates stories through a hole in his cell door. Lawyer Andrew Hamilton wins the case by arguing that "every freeman" must feel free to be "speaking and writing – truth" even if he criticizes the government. No portrait exists of the couple.

ERIC C. CAREN COLLECTION

John Peter Zenger, to his readers, in the Nov. 25, 1734, New-York Weekly Journal:

'I was Arrested'

To all my Subscribers and Benefactors who take my weekly *Journall*: Gentlemen, Ladies and Others; As you last week were Disappointed of my Journall, I think it incumbent upon me, to publish my Apoligy which is this. On the Lords Day, the Seventeenth of this Instant, I was Arrested, taken and Imprisoned in the common jail of this Citty, by Virtue of a Warrant from the *Governour* ... whereupon I was put under such Restraint that I had not the Liberty of Pen, Ink, or Paper, or to see, or speak with People, till upon my Complaint to the Honourable the Chief Justice. ... I have had since ... the Liberty of Speaking through the Hole of the Door, to my Wife and Servants, by which I doubt not yo'l think me sufficiently Excused for not sending my last weeks *Journall*, and I hope for the future by the Liberty of Speaking to my Servants thro' the Hole of the Door of the Prison, to entertain you with my weekly *Journall* as formerly. And am your obliged ... J. Peter Zenger.

Thomas Paine

1737–1809

Thomas Paine produces *Common Sense,* a pamphlet that sells an astounding 120,000 copies and rallies American colonists to fight for independence. "The sun never shined on a cause of greater worth," Paine writes. "The blood of the slain, the weeping voice of nature cries, 'TIS TIME TO PART." He fights with George Washington's troops and inspires them with his *Crisis* papers, another best seller. After the revolution, Paine's popularity wanes. He dies penniless. "Those who expect to reap the blessings of freedom must," he says, "undergo the fatigue of supporting it."

On Dec. 23, 1776, Thomas Paine begins the best-selling Crisis *papers, which rally George Washington's troops:*

'Tyranny, like hell'

These are the times that try men's souls. The summer soldier and the sunshine patriot will, in this crisis, shrink from the service of his country; but he that stands it NOW deserves the love and thanks of man and woman. Tyranny, like hell, is not easily conquered.

Benjamin Franklin Bache

1769–1798

He's called "Lightning Rod Junior." At 21, Benjamin Franklin Bache founds the *Aurora* in Philadelphia with a press bequeathed by his famous grandfather. Bache is one of the nation's most strident "partisan" editors. When George Washington retires, young Lightning Rod calls for "rejoicing." Revolutionary War veterans beat Bache and ransack his office. This 1798 caricature shows soldiers marching on his head. He dies of yellow fever before his 30th birthday.

NEW-YORK HISTORICAL SOCIETY

Bache covers George Washington's retirement in the Aurora, *Dec. 23, 1796:*

'A nation ... deceived'

If ever a nation was debauched by a man, the American nation has been debauched by Washington. If ever a nation has suffered from the improper influence of a man, the American nation has suffered from the influence of Washington. If ever a nation was deceived by a man, the American nation has been deceived by Washington. Let his conduct then be an example to future ages. Let it serve to be a warning that no man may be an idol.

Jane Grey Swisshelm

1815–1884

Reporting for the *New York Tribune* in 1850, Jane Grey Swisshelm becomes the first woman from a major newspaper to cover Congress. She's paid $5 a week. Later, she starts her own newspaper, *The St. Cloud Visiter,* to campaign in Minnesota for women and against slavery. In 1858, a pro-slavery mob smashes her press. Her reaction? She starts a new newspaper, the *St. Cloud Democrat.* "Dying is not difficult," Swisshelm says. "Yielding is impossible."

Jane Grey Swisshelm writes in the Nov. 25, 1858, St. Cloud Democrat:

'Women and politics'

[We] chose as our subject "Women and Politics" ... as affording the best plea for urging upon woman their duty toward those outraged children of a common God, who are bought, sold and bartered, as the brute which perisheth, by the government which they are obliged to support and compelled to obey.

William Lloyd Garrison

1805–1879

In 1831, William Lloyd Garrison starts *The Liberator*, a Boston weekly with only one goal — to abolish slavery. Garrison braves insults, assaults and mobs. Georgia offers a $5,000 reward for his arrest. Garrison founds the American Anti-Slavery Society and leads it for 22 years. In 1865, slavery is abolished. *The Liberator* closes, its mission complete.

LIBRARY OF CONGRESS

William Lloyd Garrison responds to a clergyman who says abolitionists are not behaving like "Christian gentlemen":

'Not without excitement'

These are your men of "caution" and "prudence" and "judiciousness." Sir, I have learned to hate those words. Whenever we attempt to imitate our Great Exemplar, and press the truth of God in all its plainness upon the conscience, why, we are imprudent; because, forsooth, a great excitement will ensue. Sir, slavery will not be overthrown without excitement — a most tremendous excitement.

Elizabeth Cady Stanton

1815–1902

In 1840, women are barred from the floor of a London anti-slavery convention. Enter Elizabeth Cady Stanton, who is so outraged she begins a lifelong crusade for women's rights. In 1848, women hold their own rights convention at Seneca Falls, N.Y. Cady takes her zeal to a job at an early feminist publication, *The Lily*, and later edits *The Revolution*. She's elected first president of the National Woman Suffrage Association. Cady dies 18 years before American women win the right to vote.

LIBRARY OF CONGRESS

The motto of Elizabeth Cady Stanton's Revolution:

Men, Their Rights and Nothing More;
Women, Their Rights and Nothing Less.

Frederick Douglass

c. 1817–1895

Four years after escaping from slavery, Frederick Douglass is writing for an abolitionist newspaper. In 1847, he starts *The North Star* to crusade against slavery and for women's rights. The Rochester, N.Y., weekly has worldwide influence; Douglass writes powerfully, living proof that his race is the equal of any. He keeps fighting, even after racists burn his house and papers. "Power concedes nothing without a demand," he says. "It never did, and it never will."

NATIONAL PORTRAIT GALLERY, SMITHSONIAN INSTITUTION

Frederick Douglass explains why he lectures and writes:

'Truth must be told'

I still see before me a life of toil and trials ... but, justice must be done, the truth must be told. ... I will not be silent. (Truth also is part of the *The North Star*'s motto: "Right is of no Sex — Truth is of no Color — God is the Father of us all, and we are all Brethren.")

Francisco Ramírez

c. 1838–c. 1890

In 1855, 17-year-old Francisco Ramírez founds *El Clamor Público*, a Spanish-language newspaper in Los Angeles. The pro-Mexico weekly attacks the North American conquerors of California who "treat us worse than slaves." The democracy so celebrated in the United States is really a "lynchocracy." Money problems close the paper after four years. Ramírez moves to Mexico, urging others to do the same.

From El Clamor Público, *September 1856:*

'Lessons in humanity'

The North Americans pretend to give us lessons in humanity and to bring our people the doctrine of salvation so we can govern ourselves, to respect the laws and conserve order. Are these the ones who treat us worse than slaves?

Ida B. Wells

1862–1931

In 1892, local racists lynch three successful black men. Ida B. Wells proclaims the innocence of lynching victims in searing editorials in her *Memphis Free Speech and Headlight*. "The Afro-American race," she says, is "more sinned against than sinning." Ransacking mobs close her paper. In the *New York Age*, Wells continues to crusade against lynchings. Her goal: To "arouse the conscience of the American people" and do her race "a service."

In the spring of 1892, Ida B. Wells denounces the false accusations against black men in a Memphis Free Speech and Headlight *editorial:*

'Thread bare lie'

Nobody in this section of the country believes the old thread bare lie that negro men rape white women. If Southern white men are not careful, they will over-reach themselves and public sentiment will have a reaction; a conclusion will then be reached which will be very damaging to the moral reputation of their women.

Fred Kinzaburo Makino

1877–1953

Fred Kinzaburo Makino, son of an English father and a Japanese mother, founds *Hawaii Hochi* in 1912 to speak for the large ethnic Japanese population on the islands. Makino's newspaper backs workers' rights in a plantation strike and supports Japanese-language schools. In 1927, the U.S. Supreme Court rules the schools are constitutional.

HAWAII HOCHI

An excerpt of a front-page statement in the inaugural issue of Hawaii Hochi, *Dec. 7, 1912:*

'Further the interests of the Japanese'

This paper, to be published daily in the Japanese language, will endeavor to the utmost of its ability, to further the interests of the Japanese residents in the Territory of Hawaii. This paper is not subsidized by the planters, nor, on the other hand, is it the organ of any Japanese society or institution ... it is free.

Margaret Sanger

1879–1966

Margaret Sanger champions birth control in *The Woman Rebel*. The U.S. Post Office confiscates the first issue in 1914. Sanger is arrested on obscenity charges. "Woman is enslaved by the world machine," she says, "by customs, laws and superstitions." Sanger flees to Europe under the name Bertha Watson. She returns and founds the group that becomes Planned Parenthood.

Margaret Sanger writes about female sexuality in the first issue of The Woman Rebel:

'Have an ideal'

Because I believe that woman is enslaved by the world machine, by sex conventions, by motherhood and its present necessary childrearing, by wage-slavery, by middle-class morality, by customs, laws and superstitions ... [all women must] look the whole world in the face with a go-to-hell look in the eyes; to have an ideal; to speak and act in defiance of convention.

Abraham Cahan

1860–1951

In 1897, Russian refugee Abraham Cahan creates the *Jewish Daily Forward,* for 50 years the leading newspaper voice of Jews worldwide. Cahan's recipe: labor union and socialist crusades blended with stories touching readers' everyday lives. The *Forward* becomes America's largest ethnic newspaper. *Nation* editor Oswald Garrison Villard calls it the "most vital" New York daily.

YIVO INSTITUTE FOR JEWISH RESEARCH

Abraham Cahan recalls the founding of the Jewish Daily Forward, *when workers filled collection plates with personal jewelry, pocket watches and chains:*

'Holy inspiration'

If ever there was a paper supported by the holy spirit — upon holy inspiration — it was ours.

Ricardo Flores Magón

c. 1873–1922

A founder of Mexico City's revolutionary newspaper, *Regeneración*, Ricardo Flores Magón is exiled to San Antonio in 1904 and later chased to St. Louis. But he continues crusading for the overthrow of Mexican dictator Porfirio Díaz. "The dreamer," Magón says, "is the designer of tomorrow." In 1911, Díaz is ousted. Magón turns anarchist, is convicted of violating U.S. Espionage Act and dies in Leavenworth prison.

Ricardo Flores Magón writes about the Mexican revolution in a Sept. 3, 1910, editorial in Regeneración:

'Liberation is near'

We come to tell the Mexican people that the day of their liberation is near. Before our eyes is the splendid dawn of a new day; the noise of the liberating tempest ... echoes in our ears; that rumbling is the revolutionary spirit; the entire Nation is a volcano on the verge of spouting forth the fire within its entrails.

John Reed

1887–1920

After visiting Russia in 1917, John Reed writes *Ten Days That Shook the World*, the Bolshevik Revolution classic. Reviewers dub Reed "America's Kipling." But his radical writing in *The Masses* and elsewhere gets him indicted. Reed flees to Russia and dies of typhus. Thirty-three years after he was born to wealth in Portland, Ore., Reed is buried in the Kremlin.

An excerpt from John Reed's 1919 classic, Ten Days That Shook the World:

'Joy swept the city'

It was on 18 November that the snow came. In the morning we woke to window-ledges heaped white, and snowflakes falling so whirling thick that it was impossible to see ten feet ahead. The mud was gone; in a twinkling the gloomy city became white, dazzling. The droshki with their padded coachmen turned into sleighs, bounding along the uneven street at headlong speed, their drivers' beards stiff and frozen. ... In spite of Revolution, all Russia plunged dizzily into the unknown and terrible future, joy swept the city with the coming of the snow. ... The life of the city grew gay, and the very Revolution ran swifter.

William Allen White

1868–1944

For $3,000 in 1895, William Allen White buys the *Emporia Gazette* and embraces small-town America. In an editorial, "What's the Matter With Kansas?" he attacks "shabby, wild-eyed, rattle-brained" reformers. Later, he fights the Ku Klux Klan, runs for governor and wins a Pulitzer Prize for a three-paragraph editorial backing free speech. "If there is freedom," it says, "folly will die of its own poison."

From the Pulitzer Prize–winning editorial William Allen White writes in the Emporia Gazette, *July 27, 1922:*

'Folly will die'

You tell me that law is above freedom of utterance. And I reply that you can have no wise laws nor free enforcement of wise laws unless there is free expression of the wisdom of the people — and, alas, their folly with it. But if there is freedom, folly will die of its own poison, and the wisdom will survive. That is the history of the race.

H. V. Kaltenborn
1878–1965

Brooklyn Daily Eagle editor Hans von Kaltenborn leads newspaper journalists moving into radio. In 1922, he affects a British accent for his new job as commentator. In 1938, he oversees CBS reports from Europe. He pushes radio networks to allow opinion, saying "no news analyst ever developed a large and loyal following" without it. Kaltenborn broadcasts until he's 75.

UPI/CORBIS-BETTMANN

In his 1950 memoir, Fifty Fabulous Years, *H. V. Kaltenborn recalls his early radio days:*

'Sweat pouring off my face'

Any turn of the head away from the carbon mike would make some words inaudible. For a few early broadcasts my head was placed in a frame, similar to that used by the old fashioned photographers to prevent movement. ... Most of my hot-weather broadcasts were delivered in shirt sleeves with sweat pouring off my face.

John H. Sengstacke

1912–1997

Chicago Defender publisher John H. Sengstacke urges President Truman to combat military racism by integrating the armed forces. The next day, Truman does so. Sengstacke turns his influential weekly into the nation's most powerful African-American daily. The black press should be the "voice of the people," he says, "defender of truth and justice."

JOHN SENGSTACKE, LEFT, COURTESY CHICAGO DEFENDER

John Sengstacke calls for a black publishers association in an April 18, 1942, editorial in The Chicago Defender:

'A practical strategy'

The struggle of the Negro masses to attain democratic parity with the whites on those basic principles that give meaning to American citizenship would be advanced ... were the Negro press, which controls a considerable body of public opinion, willing to consolidate its energy, unify its aims, and concentrate on a practical strategy for a sustained frontal attack on the issues ... blocking the progress of the race.

Hazel Brannon Smith

1914–1994

Lexington Advertiser editor/owner Hazel Brannon Smith crusades for racial equality in Mississippi. Town leaders burn crosses on her lawn. For 17 years, they boycott her newspaper. In 1963, police kill a black World War II veteran for no reason. Smith decries it: "I was one white person who stood up for what was right." She is the first woman to win a Pulitzer Prize for editorial writing.

UPI/CORBIS-BETTMANN

Hazel Brannon Smith talks about her 1963 editorial about Alfred Brown, the mental patient and World War II veteran who is shot in the back by a policeman who wanted to arrest him:

'Low-key factual story'

I got it from eyewitnesses and I was sure I had the truth. ... I wrote a very low-key factual story ... and my memory of it is that I also wrote something in my column condemning the action. ... A friend of mine ... called me and said, "Hazel, what are you trying to do, start a riot?" ... And I said, "Hell, no, I'm not trying to start a riot. I'm trying to stop one." ... My philosophy ... is that I don't have the right to withhold the story when the local law officials who are supposed to uphold the law take the law into their own hands and kill somebody ... without provocation. I don't have the right to withhold a story like that from my readers.

Tom Gish

1926–

Pat Gish

1927–

Journalism school sweethearts Tom and Pat Gish buy *The Mountain Eagle* in Whitesburg, Ky. They crusade for coal workers and against local corruption, survive boycotts and inspire laws to limit strip mining. The *Eagle*'s motto: "It Screams!" In 1974, a policeman hires two men to set fire to the weekly. The Gishes publish from their living room. That week, the motto reads: "It Still Screams!"

LOUISVILLE COURIER JOURNAL

Tom Gish editorializes about strip mining in the Oct. 27, 1960, issue of The Mountain Eagle:

'Sprawled helplessly'

A nightmare of gigantic proportions has been haunting me. ... In that almost constant dream I see Eastern Kentucky sprawled helplessly, slowly dying. ... And as she gasps for breath, giant vultures with wings thousands of feet wide and beaks bigger than a mountain swoop down and nibble at the near corpse, swallowing whole mountaintops at a time.

Gloria Steinem

1934–

She's a star of the trendy New York magazine scene who dresses as a Playboy Club bunny to write an exposé. In 1972, Gloria Steinem finds her calling, co-founding *Ms.*, a magazine edited by and for women. Steinem's sharp intellect makes her a leader of the feminist movement. "Feminism isn't responsible for divorce," she says. "Marriage is responsible for divorce."

PEOPLE WEEKLY, © TIME, INC.

In a 1963 first-person article for Show *magazine entitled "A Bunny's Tale," Gloria Steinem writes about undercover life as a Playboy bunny:*

'Beautiful Bunnies'

I went to see the Playboy doctor ("Failure to keep doctor's appointment, twenty demerits"). ... "So you're going to be a Bunny," he said heartily. "Just came back from Miami myself. Beautiful club down there. Beautiful Bunnies." I started to ask him if he had the coast-to-coast franchise, but he interrupted to ask how I liked Bunnyhood.

Nat Hentoff

1925–

In 1957, former radio announcer Nat Hentoff starts a column for the fledging alternative weekly *The Village Voice*. A self-proclaimed atheist and passionate civil libertarian, Hentoff goes on to write an award-winning syndicated column in defense of the Bill of Rights. In 1984, the free expression advocate angers liberal constituents by calling abortion a violation of the rights of the unborn.

UNITED MEDIA

Nat Hentoff writes in his 1992 book, Free Speech for Me — But Not for Thee:

'Strongest drive in human nature'

I said, among other things, that some of my colleagues were mirror images of Phyllis Schlafly and Jerry Falwell, whom they regularly excoriated. A postcard came. It was from Phil Kerby ... [who] advised me to look at my paper's thought police in perspective: "Censorship," he wrote, "is the strongest drive in human nature; sex is a weak second."

CHAPTER 3

Political Animals

> 'I will have a bias … the men and women (of Congress) are … honorable.'
>
> — SUSAN MOLINARI

WASHINGTON, 1822 —

NATHANIEL CARTER OF THE NEW YORK STATESMAN *and Evening Advertiser* arrives with a mission to this arcane city on a swamp: to make government more understandable to the folks back home. Carter, the earliest known full-time Washington correspondent, learns the rules fast. In one of the first dispatches from the nation's new capital, he writes:

"I have to-day learned from a source, which may be depended on …"

A sign of things to come. Unnamed political sources telling the press something juicy, newsworthy, maybe just hard to get anywhere else, in exchange for … what? Anonymity? Why the big hush? For one thing, there's more information down the line, should this tidbit accomplish what I, provider of the information, want it to. Politics — ever a game of mutual back-scratching, "the science," as labor figure Sidney Hillman says, "of how who gets what, when and why."

Just how far should reporters and editors go? Far enough to get the story? Far enough to share cognac and confidences? So far as to get sucked into the maw of the political beast? Politics and the press. The press and politics. Two American institutions that on some days can't live without each other and, on other days, in the vaunted name of objectivity, can't live with each other.

"Government is the only vessel known to leak from the top," says longtime *New York Times* political columnist James "Scotty" Reston. And, of course, it takes two to leak a leak: the political insider and the reporter. "Secrecy is a disease you get when you move into the White House," says United Press International correspondent Helen Thomas, who tries to stay outside as she looks inside. "Nobody wants a name attached to a quote. They want to be called 'a senior government official' to tell you the color of the walls."

Swallowed whole by politics: editorial page legend Horace Greeley, who runs for president in 1872, loses, and dies 27 days later. Other presidential hopefuls over the years: socialist editor Eugene V. Debs, Ohio publishers Warren G. Harding and James Middleton Cox, New York publisher Frank E. Gannett, Illinois editor-publisher Adlai E. Stevenson, and conservative columnist Pat Buchanan. (Only Warren Harding wins and is rocked by the Teapot Dome scandal, the press swarming over it.)

The crossover can work both ways. Famed pro-creationist and Scopes trial attorney William Jennings Bryan is all-politics first, writing columns and founding a newspaper later to promote his political views. At the other end of the century, Congresswoman Susan Molinari (R-N.Y.) leaves her political post for a short-lived Saturday anchor job at CBS-TV. The move (Molinari's, not Bryan's)

causes uproarious debate over whether soldiers of one kind should defect to the enemy camp. But the press and politics have lived intertwined, sometimes indistinguishably so, since the earliest days of the Republic. Our early newspeople, Thomas Paine, Benjamin Franklin, Samuel Adams and their ilk, were the political leaders and thinkers — architects of the American Revolution with their fiery writings, and many among them soldiers of the revolution with their guns or money. The rabidly partisan, post-revolution press finds each party (sometimes, candidate) supporting its own newspaper. President Andrew Jackson gets so tired of being blasted by the opposition press, he establishes a newspaper himself, supplies it with lucrative U.S. printing contracts and then, for good measure, hands out more than 50 plum government jobs to journalists.

By the time of Lincoln ("that compound of cunning, heartlessness and folly"), many in the press have made a clean break from political patronage. The modern phase of press and pol relations no doubt begins with President Grover Cleveland, who hires the first White House press agent after charges he once fathered an illegitimate child. Cleveland's 1886 honeymoon inspires hordes of reporters to sneak, to stalk, and in the president's words, "to dese-

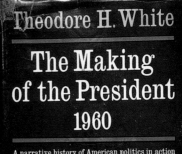

Newseum/Max Reid photo

Above: Theodore White gets behind the scenes to look at how presidents really are elected.

crate every sacred relation of private life."

But that's the press as outsider. What does political insiding look like? For *Times* columnist James Reston, it may look like the day in 1961 when he goes to President John F. Kennedy's Hyannis Port home after Soviet Leader Nikita Krushchev had insulted the president in Berlin. Kennedy wants to let the Soviets know he means business without making the Cold War crisis worse by "making a personal declaration." Says Reston: "It would, however, be 'helpful,' (Kennedy) said mildly, if I wrote in the *Times* on my own authority that this was his clear intention." With the blessings of *Times* editors, that is what he does.

Ben Bradlee, longtime editor of *The Washington Post*, hometown paper of the political center, has been both outsider (when Nixon's White House spies on and sabotages the Democrats) and insider, self-described player in the Kennedy administration by virtue of his long, intimate friendship with the man who becomes president — a president whose sexual indiscretions are not known to Bradlee or reported by the *Post*.

"The experience of having a friend run for President of the United States is unexpected, fascinating, and exciting for anyone," Bradlee says. "For a newspaperman, it is all that, plus confusing: are you a friend, or are you a reporter? You have to redefine 'friend' and redefine 'reporter' over and over again, before reaching any kind of comfort level."

For a time, writes author and syndicated columnist Jules Witcover of the Baltimore *Sun*, presidential candidates and the press are "like fellow passengers on a ship, thrown together for a long voyage on which there is no alternative to peaceful coexistence. There are arguments and disagreements and dissembling and distorting on both sides, to be sure. But the common experience fosters a mutual candor and trust that is indispensible to one who seeks to put down whatever he can learn about what happened, and why." Today "mutual candor" is harder to find.

Lapdogs, watchdogs, or attack dogs? There is Joseph Alsop, along with brother Stewart, whose caste ties to the political elite inform his waging of the Cold War in the pages of the *New York Herald Tribune* and beyond. There is David Broder of *The Washington Post*, who wants "an adversary relationship ... we make them present their best case." There is ABC News correspondent Cokie Roberts, daughter of a powerful Louisiana political family, saying "I don't assume, going in, that they're all a bunch of crooks and scoundrels." Or alternative-press icon I. F. Stone: "Every government is run by liars, and nothing they say should be believed."

A hundred allegiances, but often the reporter's truest

> 'Are you a friend,
>
> or are you a reporter?'
>
> — BEN BRADLEE

is to the story. One minute the press is being accused of liberal bias; the next, "Anonymous" writes a sex-laden best-selling *roman à clef* about Bill Clinton's presidential campaign; turn around again, and papers fill countless columns with an alleged affair between Clinton and a White House intern. The age-old bias is the bias toward scandal, sensation, news. The press on the prowl for a story. Hungry, day after day. Says Dee Dee Myers, former Clinton administration press secretary: "You have to feed the beast."

Anonymous

[Samuel Adams] 1722–1803

Radical patriot Samuel Adams uses the *Boston Gazette* to help spark the American Revolution. Under at least 20 different pen names, Adams fervently attacks the British, joined by his "Caucus Club" — *Gazette* writers, including his cousin John Adams, who goes on to become the second U.S. president. The *Gazette* describes the British as "serpents" and "diabolical Tools of Tyrants" and "Men totally abondoned to Wickedness." It is "curious employment," confirms John, "Cooking up paragraphs, articles, occurrences & working the political engine!"

LIBRARY OF CONGRESS

Samuel Adams writes under the pen name Populus in the March 21, 1768, Boston Gazette:

'A free press'

There is nothing so fretting and vexatious, nothing so justly TERRIBLE to tyrants, and their tools and abettors, as a FREE PRESS.

On Oct. 7, 1771, writing as Candidus: Is it impossible to form an idea of slavery more complete, more miserable, more disgraceful, than that of a people where justice is administer'd, government exercis'd, and a standing army maintain'd at the expense of the people, and yet without the least dependence upon them?

Alexander Hamilton

1755–1804

Alexander Hamilton writes many of *The Federalist* papers, 85 essays urging a strong federal government and a Constitution to protect "your liberty, your dignity and your happiness." Daily journalism is new in America (*Pennsylvania Evening Post,* 1783) when Hamilton enters the field. In 1801, he co-founds the *New-York Evening Post,* the country's oldest continuously published daily. Hamilton opposes and offends Vice President Aaron Burr. In a duel, Burr kills him.

LIBRARY OF CONGRESS

Alexander Hamilton argues that press freedom depends not on the Constitution but on public opinion, in number 84 of The Federalist:

'Impracticable'

What signifies a declaration, that the "liberty of the press shall be inviolably preserved"? What is the liberty of the press? Who can give it any definition which would not leave the utmost latitude for evasion? ... I hold it to be impracticable; and from this I infer, that its security, whatever fine declarations may be inserted in any constitution respecting it, must altogether depend on public opinion, and on the general spirit of the people and of the government. And here, after all, as is intimated upon another occasion, must we seek for the only solid basis of all our rights.

Horace Greeley

1811–1872

At 30, Horace Greeley starts the *New York Tribune,* which soon becomes the most respected newspaper in the nation. Its mission: "to advance the interests of the People, and to promote their Moral, Social and Political well-being." Excluded: "the immoral and degrading Police Reports." An anti-slavery, anti-liquor, anti-corruption crusader, Greeley pioneers the modern editorial page. A disillusioned Republican Party founder, he runs for president as a Democrat. On Nov. 5, 1872, he loses to Ulysses S. Grant. On Nov. 29, he dies.

Here's how Horace Greeley begins his open letter to President Abraham Lincoln, the "Prayer of Twenty Millions," in the Aug. 20, 1862, New York Tribune:

'Deeply pained'

Dear Sir: I do not intrude to tell you — for you must already know — that a great proportion of those who triumphed in your election, and of all who desire an unqualified suppression of the rebellion now desolating our country, are sorely disappointed and deeply pained by the policy you seem to be pursuing with regard to the slaves of rebels.

(The president responds: "If I could save the Union without freeing *any* slaves, I would do it; and if I could save it by freeing *all* the slaves, I would do it; and if I could do it by freeing some and leaving others alone, I would also do that.")

William Jennings Bryan

1860–1925

One of America's grandest political orators, William Jennings Bryan shapes Nebraska Democratic party politics — and American populism — in his editorials for the *Omaha World-Herald.* Named editor-in-chief in 1894, the attorney-fundamentalist promotes creationism, temperance and a switch from the gold standard to silver, all with evangelical zeal. "I must continue to fight the battles of the people," he says. In 1901, the three-time presidential candidate (and one-time congressman and secretary of state) starts his own weekly, *The Commoner,* a vehicle for his common-man views and speeches. The paper lasts 22 years.

William Jennings Bryan delivers one of the most famous pieces of American political oratory — on dropping the gold standard for silver — at the 1896 Democratic National Convention:

'Cross of gold'

Our ancestors, when but three millions in number, had the courage to declare their political independence of every other nation; shall we, their descendants, when we have grown to seventy millions, declare that we are less independent than our forefathers? No, my friends, that will never be the verdict of our people. ... Having behind us the producing masses of this nation ... and the toilers everywhere, we will answer their demand for a gold standard by saying to them: You shall not press down upon the brow of labor this crown of thorns, you shall not crucify mankind upon a cross of gold.

Eugene V. Debs
1855–1926

Critics call union leader Eugene V. Debs a "noted agitator." His supporters call him a hero. Debs, five-time presidential candidate and editor of the socialist newspaper *Appeal to Reason*, calls the press capitalist conspirators trying to hobble the labor movement. "Truth," he says, "is one thing the rotten rulers of this republic cannot stand." In 1920, he receives nearly one million votes for the U.S. presidency.

UPI/CORBIS-BETTMANN

Eugene V. Debs writes on free speech in the Dec. 9, 1911, Appeal to Reason, *at the beginning of a decade in which hundreds of socialist and German publications die, banned from the mails:*

'Strangling the press'

In every struggle, the aim of the ruling power has always been to stifle the voice of discontent by suppressing free speech and strangling the press. On the other hand, the champions of the masses have always fought with valor to keep the clutches of despotism from the throat of the truth ... and through the press to shake off their oppressors.

Willard M. Kiplinger

1891–1967

In 1923, newsletter pioneer Willard M. Kiplinger starts his weekly *Kiplinger Washington Letter.* Subscribers pay $10 a year for mimeographed insights, political and economic, in a chatty, staccato style. Readers "wanted the inner workings," he says, "to know what was going to happen." Newsletters catch on, many of them copying Kiplinger's typographical gymnastics. By the 1990s, there are 5,000.

THE KIPLINGER WASHINGTON EDITORS, INC.

Willard Kiplinger gives clients an economic forecast in the Sept. 29, 1923, inaugural edition of The Kiplinger Washington Letter:

A decline in foreign currency

Rumors of an international <u>German loan</u> are renewed — a loan to revive the mark. Bankers take them seriously in a few cases, but they are foolish. No German loan will come without plenty of advance notice and the paper mark will not come back. Begin to watch for the <u>decline of the franc</u>, too.

Arthur Krock

c. 1886–1974

He's one of the most influential unelected figures in the nation's capital. Arthur Krock, Washington bureau chief of *The New York Times* from 1932 to 1953, writes a column, *In the Nation,* that's widely respected throughout official Washington, granting him special access. "Mr. Krock," as he is called by associates, is one of a handful of journalists to be awarded four Pulitzer Prizes.

GEORGE TAMES/THE NEW YORK TIMES

In his Nov. 28, 1934, Pulitzer Prize–winning article in The New York Times, *Arthur Krock describes Secretary of State Cordell Hull's economic peacemaking skills:*

'Profound student'

No more profound student of history through economics has ever been at the helm of the State Department. ... When he was a young Representative ... he would sit and discuss for hours ... his firm conviction that tariff and trade agreements, the leveling of barriers and the disappearances of quotas formed the surest gateway to peace.

Dorothy Thompson

1893–1961

Before World War II, Dorothy Thompson of the *New York Herald Tribune* writes a column for 170 newspapers, reaching 8 million readers. Her NBC Radio program reaches 5 million. In 1931, she gets kicked out of Germany for calling Adolf Hitler "a man in a trance." *Time* says Thompson is the nation's "most influential woman," next to Eleanor Roosevelt.

UPI/CORBIS-BETTMANN

Dorothy Thompson defends the Jewish murderer of a German official in a Nov. 14, 1939, radio broadcast:

'Chased ... like animals'

Herschel fingered his pistol and thought: "Why doesn't someone do something! Why must we be chased around the earth like animals!" Herschel was wrong. Animals are not chased around the world like this. In every country there are societies for the prevention of cruelty to animals. But there are none for the prevention of cruelty to people.

Joseph Alsop
1910–1989

Stewart Alsop
1914–1974

For a generation, Joseph and Stewart Alsop edify and enrage Washington, D.C. In 1946, they create *Matter of Fact,* a widely syndicated political column. Stewart, who coins such phrases as "hawks and doves," leaves in 1958 for *The Saturday Evening Post.* Older brother Joe (seated) is a hawk who stays on as top political columnist and presidential confidant. "As columnists," they write, "we always regarded ourselves as reporters. We tried ... never to print a column lacking at least one previously unpublished and significant item of factual information."

Joseph and Stewart Alsop passionately oppose both communism abroad and anti-communism demogogy at home. They decry some of the questioning at loyalty hearings in the Aug. 22, 1948, New York Herald Tribune:

None of your 'damn business'

Does it really matter in America whether a man's maternal grandparents came over from Poland, or whether all his ancestors landed decorously on Plymouth Rock? There have been countless instances when, during loyalty hearings, individuals have been asked where their parents and grandparents were born. An entirely American response would be that it was none of the loyalty board's damn business.

James J. Kilpatrick, Jr.

1920–

He's one of the best-known conservative columnists in the post-World War II era. In 1966, James Jackson Kilpatrick, Jr. becomes a full-time pundit after a long career as reporter, editorial writer and editor of *The Richmond News Leader.* There, he leads Virginia's "massive resistance" to school desegregation. His assertion that capitalism will win out over communism proves correct. His column helps some publishers and editors defend themselves against charges that the media has a liberal bias.

THE ASSOCIATED PRESS

In the January 1972 issue of Quill, *James J. Kilpatrick, Jr. decries press alarmism:*

The 'yapping dog'

To the extent that we are good and watchful sentinels, crying alarm when alarm is truly required, we live up to the responsibility of our inheritance. But ... there is little to be said for the dog who barks all night ... having hysterics at shadows. Such a protector in time comes to be known as that goddamned yapping dog.

Theodore H. White

1915–1986

Books can make news. Theodore H. White inspires a new school of political journalism with his acclaimed *The Making of the President, 1960*. White takes an inside look at John F. Kennedy's campaign for the White House, prompting other reporters to describe the human side of political life. White is the first to describe the Kennedy years as "Camelot."

THE ASSOCIATED PRESS

In the Dec. 6, 1963, issue of Life *magazine, Theodore H. White interviews Jacqueline Kennedy after the assassination of President John F. Kennedy:*

'Known as Camelot'

"When Jack quoted something, it was usually classical," she said, "but I'm so ashamed of myself — all I keep thinking of is this line from a musical comedy. ... The lines he loved to hear were: 'Don't let it be forgot, that once there was a spot, for one brief shining moment that was known as Camelot.' "

James "Scotty" Reston

1909–1995

Pipe-smoking James Barrett "Scotty" Reston transforms the Washington bureau of *The New York Times* into a reporting powerhouse. The consummate insider, he decides when to break big stories — and when not to. The future executive editor of the *Times* writes a graceful, influential column. On President John F. Kennedy's assassination: "America wept ... for itself ... for somehow the worst in the nation had prevailed over the best."

James Reston writes about the Pentagon Papers in the June 27, 1971, issue of The New York Times:

'Nation ... seething with distrust'

The fuss over the Pentagon Papers is only a symbol of a much larger problem. ... The nation is seething with distrust, not only of the Government but of the press, and the issue of the Pentagon Papers is merely whether we should get at the facts and try to correct our mistakes or suppress the whole painful story.

William F. Buckley, Jr.

1925–

In 1955, William F. Buckley, Jr. founds the *National Review,* a journal of conservative opinion. His sister Priscilla is the managing editor. Buckley's new journal "stands athwart history, yelling 'Stop' at a time when no one is inclined to do so, or to have much patience with those who do." In 1960, the *Review* has only 32,000 subscribers and a big deficit. By 1990, sales top 180,000. Buckley becomes a one-man media corporation: magazine editor, syndicated columnist, author, and host of TV's *Firing Line.*

UPI/CORBIS-BETTMANN

In the March 19, 1968, National Review, *William F. Buckley, Jr., ponders U.S. involvement in Vietnam:*

'Security of the United States'

Our participation in the Vietnam war is justified only if Vietnam is the contemporary salient of a world enterprise ... that aims ultimately at the security of the United States. If that is what it is, we need to hit back. ... If that is not what Vietnam is all about, then we should get the hell out.

Ben Bradlee

1921–

In 25 years as editor of *The Washington Post,* Benjamin Crowninshield Bradlee's greatest triumph is the Pulitzer Prize–winning coverage of the Watergate scandal — a story that forces President Richard Nixon to resign. Under Bradlee, the *Post* becomes a household name. A young reporter at *Newsweek,* he becomes the archetypical editor, plainspoken, profane, in love with the news business. "Put out the best, most honest newspaper you can today," he says, "and put out a better one the next day."

COURTESY BEN BRADLEE

Ben Bradlee writes in his 1995 memoir,
A Good Life:

'Kerosene journalism'

The press's vision of itself had changed drastically with the Vietnam War and the rise of the counter-culture and with Watergate itself. The best newspapers were still involved in the pursuit of truth with conscience, and newly determined to be interesting, useful, and entertaining in the process. But at the bottom of the barrel, the stain of the tabloids was spreading with the help of television into what could be called "kerosene journalism." In this genre of journalism, reporters pour kerosene on whatever smoke they can find, before they determine what's smoking and why. The flames that result can come from arson, not journalism.

Dan Rather

1931–

In 1981, CBS veteran Dan Rather succeeds Walter Cronkite as the *CBS Evening News* anchor. Rather personifies the press-as-adversary. During a 1974 press conference, President Richard Nixon asks Rather: "Are you running for something?" Rather: "No, sir, Mr. President, are you?" As an anchor, Rather tries on a softer image. But he's still a newsman. In 1998, he's in Cuba covering the pope when the Clinton sex scandal breaks: "You had two choices you get back to Washington... or you ask for asylum in Cuba."

THE ASSOCIATED PRESS

In his 1994 memoir, The Camera Never Blinks Twice, *Dan Rather reflects:*

'Never overconfidence'

My career at CBS has been a puzzlement. I was tagged too intense to be an anchorman, too inclined to get into a confrontation ... too bull-headed. Yet more than a dozen years have passed since I succeeded Walter Cronkite ... during that time, I have been guilty of several misjudgments, but never of overconfidence. I have run scared.

David Broder

1929–

When reporters ask Richard Nixon at the 1968 Republican convention if anyone had predicted Spiro Agnew as his running mate, Nixon answered, "Well, yes. Dave Broder did." While some reporters cover politics every four years, *The Washington Post*'s David Salzer Broder pioneers in the full-time coverage of the process and issues that shape politics, campaigns and presidents. "I admire the professionals ... who view politics not as a holy war between virtue and evil," he says, "but as the glory of the country."

THE WASHINGTON POST

In a Nov. 5, 1972, Pulitzer Prize–winning column in The Washington Post, *David Broder writes:*

'Distrust of government'

But even as he is applauded for using his power, Mr. Nixon is feared and distrusted. ... It would be incorrect, I think, to view this suspicion as a personal problem of this particular president. It has, I'm afraid, become generic — a distrust of government and of government's essence, the exercise of power.

Cokie Roberts

1943–

In 1977, Cokie Roberts joins National Public Radio and soon is known on Capitol Hill as the correspondent who asks real-people questions. Daughter of Louisiana Reps. Hale and Lindy Boggs, Roberts rapidly rises to celebrity status at ABC-TV. Do men and women cover stories differently? Listen to questions asked to federal budget negotiators. "Our male colleagues," Roberts says, "would ask, 'How many MX missiles?' And I'd ask, 'Are mammograms still covered?'"

STEVE FENN/ABC, INC.

Cokie Roberts talks to TV Guide *in a June 19, 1993, interview:*

Gender and politics

Men come up to me on the street and say, "We like your common sense on the Brinkley show." But women say, "We love the way you don't let them interrupt you. ..." I get the feeling that the country is full of women who've never gotten a word in edgewise when men talk about politics.

Sam Donaldson

1934–

Relentless grilling techniques make ABC's Sam Donaldson the "junkyard dog" of White House correspondents. He ruffles presidents, aides and viewers. In 1989, he leaves the White House beat to anchor ABC's *PrimeTime Live*. In his memoir, *Hold On, Mr. President,* Donaldson says of his infamous style: "Questions don't do the damage. Only the answers do." In 1998, he's back covering the White House.

USA TODAY

In Hold On, Mr. President, *Sam Donaldson defends his grilling technique:*

'Nothing to hide'

As to what questions are appropriate and how they should be asked, well, let's put it this way: If you send me to cover a pie-baking contest on Mother's Day, I'm going to ask dear old Mom whether she used artificial sweetener in violation of the rules ... if Mom has nothing to hide, no harm will have been done.

Ted Koppel

1940–

In 1979, Ted Koppel is a little-known State Department correspondent for ABC. He starts a late-night news show to analyze the U.S. hostage crisis in Iran. The show takes issues one at a time, giving Koppel a chance to demonstrate his deft interviewing skills. It snares a mighty TV audience and later becomes *Nightline*. In 1981, Iran releases the U.S. hostages. But *Nightline* goes on. Says Koppel: "When you do something live, if you're great, you're great; if you stink, you stink."

DONNA SVENNEVIK/ ABC, INC.

In the Winter 1994 Media Studies Journal, Ted Koppel talks about television's future:

Shutting off politics

Why should viewers have Peter Jennings, Dan Rather or Tom Brokaw giving them 22 minutes of what "they" think is important? ... Am I worried [interactive TV] is going to allow people to shut themselves out from politics and world and cultural events? ... No, I'm already worried that they've stopped reading newspapers and reading magazines and participating in their communities.

Helen Thomas

1920–

Helen Thomas earns the title "Dean of the White House Press Corps" with energy, talent and class. In 1943, she starts at United Press International as a radio newswriter. Forty years later, she is the first woman to win the National Press Club's Fourth Estate Award. To officially end every presidential press conference, she says: "Thank you, Mr. President."

UPI/CORBIS-BETTMANN

Helen Thomas offers her view of the presidency in her 1975 memoir, Dateline: White House:

'Only honest and wise men'

As for Presidents, my own feeling about what they should be is summed up in John Adams' prayer inscribed on the side of the marble fireplace in the State Dining Room below the brooding portrait of Lincoln: "Blessings on this house. May only honest and wise men live here."

Larry King

1933–

Cable News Network talk show host Larry King offers a welcome oasis away from the grilling political figures get on Sunday-morning TV. Before the November 1992 election, every major candidate visits King, reaching millions of voters in an easy-chair setting. Ross Perot's impressive third-party campaign uses the program as a sounding board, making King a force in presidential politics. The success comes after years of building a national audience for his interview shows on the Mutual radio network. Says King: "I ask the questions people on the street would ask."

THE ASSOCIATED PRESS

Larry King explains his job in a Sept. 15, 1996, interview with Sunshine *magazine:*

'Why?'

I get paid to do what I've been doing since I was 6 years old, which is to ask, 'why?' I was the kind of kid who wanted to know why the bus driver drove the bus. I remember running down the street after Leo Durocher, the Dodgers' manager ... he looked at me and said, "Kid, get off my back."

Pat Buchanan
1938–

Take a *St. Louis Globe-Democrat* reporter and editorial writer. Make him a White House staffer for presidents Nixon, Ford and Reagan. The result? Patrick J. Buchanan, syndicated columnist in 138 newspapers. A spokesman for the conservative wing of the Republican Party, Buchanan launches his own bid for the presidency in 1992 and 1996. "There is a religious war going on in our country for the soul of America," he says. "It is a cultural war." Losing, he returns to writing columns and adds television commentary.

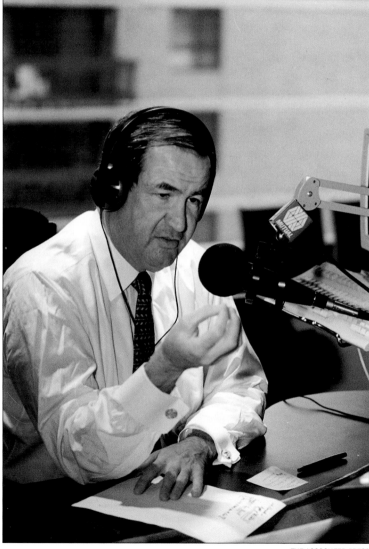

THE ASSOCIATED PRESS

In a Feb. 21, 1995, column, Pat Buchanan declares his candidacy for president:

'Preparing to run for president'

Friends, this is my last column. In it I would like to explain to editors and readers why I'm leaving, giving up a podium I cherish and a vocation I love. Stated simply, I am preparing to run for president. Why? Because America is drifting on a course that, unaltered, will prove fatal to our republic.

Anonymous

[Joe Klein] 1946–

It's the guessing game of 1996: Who is "Anonymous," author of the best-selling political novel *Primary Colors*? Joe Klein, *Newsweek* political reporter and odds-on suspect, denies writing the thinly veiled account of Bill Clinton's 1992 presidential campaign. But a manuscript in his handwriting proves he's the author. "There are times when I've had to lie to protect a source," says Klein when he finally confesses. "I put this in that category." Rich from the book and the movie deal, Klein moves on to write for *The New Yorker.* Klein's friends — not to mention senior managers at *Newsweek* — are piqued at his hiding his identity even from them.

THE ASSOCIATED PRESS

Writing as "Anonymous" in the novel Primary Colors, *Joe Klein mines allegations of Clinton's affairs:*

'Talk of the tabloids'

We hadn't seen the woman, except for pictures, which were sort of hilarious: truck-stop pinups. ... She had breasts, that was clear enough. ... On Thursday the *National Flash* issued a press release and started distributing advance copies: the thing would be smeared across checkout lines all over the country on Monday. On Friday we were the talk of the New York tabloids ... which meant we'd soon become the stuff of Eyewitless News everywhere.

Humorists

VIRGINIA CITY, NEVADA, 1862 —

THE COUNTY CORONER IS WITHHOLDING IMPORTANT information about local deaths. A reporter for the *Territorial Enterprise* decides the coroner needs to be embarrassed.

So Mark Twain pens a satire — "a string of absurdities," he calls it — about a Paleolithic citizen who had been exhumed.

"Every limb and feature of the stone mummy was perfect, not even excepting the left leg, which had evidently been a wooden one during the lifetime of the owner. ...

The body was in a sitting posture, and leaning against a huge mast of croppings; the attitude was pensive, the right thumb rested against the side of the nose; the left thumb partially supported the chin, the forefinger pressing the inner corner of the eye and drawing it partly open; the right eye was closed and the fingers of the right hand spread out."

The story is a hoax, but unfortunately is widely reprinted — as far away as London — as fact. In the end, Twain's stone age man thumbs his nose at the gullibility of the human race.

Humor in the news business is a powerful and dangerous tool. In the hands of its best practitioners, the goal isn't to merely get a laugh, as it might be for an ordinary comic. In news, when a writer turns to wit, it is often to provoke, to outrage, to belittle, to cause such a stir that the reader can no longer bear the obvious absurdity.

The humorist has a valuable tool not licensed to the straight news reporter. The humorist gets to make stuff up. Still, sometimes they don't have to. "God gave me Texas politics to write about," says Molly Ivins. "How can I not be funny?"

P. J. O'Rourke spends the better part of his career TRYING to be funny until an editor points out that the real world is much funnier. "I had an epiphany," he says. "I realized that, for the rest of my life, I'd never lack things to write about. All I had to do was put myself in foolish situations ... and keep my eyes and ears open. Since then I have visited eight wars, two revolutions, half a dozen or so local uprisings, a number of third-world election campaigns ... plus any number of places exhibiting garden variety hatred and oppression (the New Hampshire presidential primaries, for instance). I have found them all hilarious."

As Will Rogers puts it: "All I know is just what I read in the papers."

Politics and politicians have always incurred the wrath and the wit of the country's humorists, giving them perhaps their most fertile topic and some of their best lines. Rogers: "With Congress, every time they make a joke it's a law ... And every time they make a law it's a joke."

H. L. Mencken: "A politician is an animal that can sit on a fence and keep both ears to the ground." Art Buchwald: "I always wanted to get into politics, but I was never light enough to make the team."

It would be nice to say that these practitioners of journalistic wit have always used their skills to right wrongs, to topple the bad guys, to defend the weak. But that is not the case. Often the noble and the lowly are vilified with a vengeance equal to that of the corrupt and powerful. In his days as the "Wickedest Man in San Francisco," Ambrose Bierce takes on robber barons, crooks and politicians with a pen so sharp and a wit so pointed he is forced to keep a loaded gun in his desk for his own protection. Yet, he saves his cruelest comments for poets, the deeply religious and "that immortal ass, the average man."

To a poet who seeks his advice, he responds, "Have you tried hanging?"

In his own work, *The Devil's Dictionary*, Bierce may have best described himself: "Cynic, n., a blackguard whose faulty vision sees things as they are, not as they ought to be." Or, "Egoist, n. A person of low taste, more interested in himself than in me."

Humorists are not always happy people. Some are dealt difficult hands. As a child, Art Buchwald lives in foster homes and orphanages. Fanny Fern turns to writing in the 1800s to support herself after fleeing a bad marriage.

— Courtesy Mark Twain Home and Museum/Alex Jamison photo

Above: Mark Twain's corncob pipe: Yes, he can smoke and write at the same time.

Bierce serves in the Civil War and is tormented by the carnage he witnesses and by the memory of his own wounds, including a bullet to the head.

They are often motivated by anger, resentment or revenge. "I'm getting even," says Buchwald. "I am constantly trying to avenge hurts from the past."

Mercurial personalities, they will turn on anyone — the "do-gooder" pol, the annoying child, their colleagues — even the ones who are singing their praises.

"Nothing I've ever written fits the definition of 'distinguished commentary,'" writes Dave Barry. "The Pulitzer is judged by people who are undergoing two extremely stressful things at the same time. One, they're in New York City; and two, they are reading Pulitzer Prize entries ... [which] makes them really hostile toward journalism in general. ... One of my entries was a vicious and unfair attack on New York City and the other was a vicious and unfair attack on the Pulitzer Prizes. So they gave me the prize for distinguished commentary."

What makes these people funny is anybody's guess. Some appeal to sophisticated tastes, some are lowbrow. Some are subtle; some, jackhammer loud.

"Two very different strands run through American humor," says Russell Baker. "And while I refuse to stoop to saying, 'Never the twain shall meet,' the truth is that they usually don't. Defining them to a graduate student's satisfaction would produce ten yards of academic prose ponderous enough to buckle a mule's knees, so I won't try it. The distinctions may be easier to grasp if we keep in mind why Mark Twain and *The New Yorker* would not have made a happy marriage."

At the root of it all, though, is the observation of the obvious: the reportorial witnessing of events, whether the wars and calamities of O'Rourke's notebooks or the mundane matters of the heart or the seemingly trivial details of everyday life.

"I think humor is just real, real personal," writes Erma Bombeck. "It just ferrets down and gets underneath. ... I've done columns just for laughs. There is nothing redeeming about them at all. ... Most of them I like to think get down deeper and do tell the truth about people."

Called "the Socrates of the Ironing Board," Bombeck regularly finds her truths in ordinary matters and workaday lives. "Want a mother to fall apart before your eyes?" she writes. "Just watch her when she asks a child what he is doing and he answers, 'Nothing. ...' Children usually do 'nothing' in a room where the door is shut, a dog is barking, water is running under the door, a sibling is begging

> 'Humor is just real, real personal ... it just ferrets down and gets underneath.'
>
> — ERMA BOMBECK

for mercy, there is a strange odor of fur burning and there is the sound of a thousand camels running in place."

Twain himself might have answered "Nothing!" if asked what he was doing as he scribbled away in his study. "I have had a 'call' to literature of a low order — i.e. humorous," he admits. "It is nothing to be proud of, but it is my strongest suit."

Fanny Fern

1811–1872

Proper women don't leave unhappy marriages. And they don't write for newspapers. Sara Willis Parton does both as "Fanny Fern," a columnist who surveys with biting humor the status of women. "The way to a man's heart," she writes, "is through his stomach." Her writing is so sharp, readers assume Fanny Fern is a man. Her columns make a best-selling book, *Fern Leaves*. For 17 years, she writes about social issues — even taboo subjects such as venereal disease and birth control — for the *New York Ledger*, never missing a deadline.

In the Jan. 26, 1867, New York Ledger, Sara Willis Parton wonders if New York's women are getting what they need:

'Between squalor and splendor'

Nowhere more than New York does the contrast between squalor and splendor so sharply present itself. Particularly is this noticeable with regard to its women. Jostling on the same pavement with the dainty fashionist is the care-worn working girl. Looking at both these women, the question arises, which lives the more miserable life — she who the world styles "fortunate," whose husband belongs to three clubs, and whose only meal with his family is an occasional breakfast, from year's end to year's end ... Or she, this other woman, with a heart quite as hungry and unappeased.

Mark Twain

1835–1910

At Virginia City, Nevada's *Territorial Enterprise,* Samuel Clemens hones the writing genius that makes him Mark Twain. Reporting is "awful slavery for a lazy man," Twain says, so he cooks up hoaxes. But "to write a burlesque so wild that its pretended facts will not be accepted in perfect good faith by somebody, is very nearly an impossible thing to do." A critic calls him a "liar, a poltroon and a puppy." Twain demands a duel, but then flees. His fiction blooms in California in 1865 with "The Celebrated Jumping Frog of Calaveras County."

In the Territorial Enterprise, *Mark Twain reveals the secrets of newspapering:*

'Our duty'

Our duty is to keep the universe thoroughly posted concerning murders and street fights, and balls, and theaters, and pack-trains, and churches, and lectures, and school-houses, and city military affairs, and highway robberies, and Bible societies, and hay-wagons, and a thousand other things which it is in the province of local reporters to keep track of and magnify into undue importance for the instruction of the readers of this great daily newspaper.

Ambrose Bierce

1842–1914

San Francisco Examiner columnist Ambrose Bierce calls his own newspaper "frankly rotten." Still, he writes for the *Examiner* 22 years. Bierce earns the right to "sell abuse" by fighting and surviving the Civil War. His famed fiction includes *Occurrence at Owl Creek Bridge* and *The Devil's Dictionary* (which defines birth as "the first and direst of all disasters" and a saint as "a dead sinner revised and edited"). Bierce wears his moniker, "Wickedest Man in San Francisco," as a badge of honor. He lives by the motto "Nothing Matters," and dies in revolution-worn Mexico fighting with Pancho Villa.

LIBRARY OF CONGRESS

Early press critic Ambrose Bierce tells his fellow journalists "the public buys my rebuking at twice the price your sycophancy earns." And more:

'A badge of disgrace'

We are proud to confess that we have more in common with the average San Francisco jackass than the average San Francisco journalist. You have never seen a jackass lick the feet of his master. You have never seen him wear his owner's collar, knowing it to be a badge of disgrace. These things a jackass had never done; and these many a San Francisco journalist has done, and does.

Will Rogers

1879–1935

Vaudeville cowboy Will Rogers brings his homespun wit to the national stage in 1922 with a new medium, radio. His back-fence philosophizing — "Well, all I know is just what I read in the papers" — makes him a Hollywood star and pithy columnist syndicated in at least 400 newspapers. America's "poet lariat" is quoted almost as often as Shakespeare and the Bible.

In 1932, he falls asleep at the Democratic National Convention and finds himself nominated for president. "If elected," he says, "I promise to resign."

LIBRARY OF CONGRESS

Will Rogers serves up Depression-era tonic in these undated excerpts:

'A few words'

When I started out to write and misspelled a few words, people said I was plain ignorant. When I got all the words wrong, they declared I was a humorist. ... When I die, my epitaph, or whatever you call those signs on gravestones, is going to read: "I joked about every prominent man of my time, but I never met a man I didn't like." ...(About his support of Mussolini: "Dictatorship is the best government in the world provided you have the right dictator. ... I will take Roosevelt for mine.")

James Thurber

1894–1961

Humorist James Thurber calls himself "one of the defenders of the immutable American headline" during his years as a newspaper "drudge." Thurber joins the upstart *New Yorker* magazine in 1927. His essays, cartoons and slices of urban life help establish the young magazine's literary appeal. His Walter Mitty character, the congenitally dreamy American male, enters the language as a classic American personality.

UPI/CORBIS-BETTMANN

In The Years With Ross, *James Thurber describes* The New Yorker's *founding editor, Harold Ross:*

'A genius and a plodder'

Ross was at first view, oddly disappointing. No one, I would think, would have picked him out of a line-up as the editor of *The New Yorker.* Even in a dinner jacket he looked loosely informal, like a carelessly carried umbrella. He was meticulous to the point of obsession about the appearance of his magazine, but he gave no thought to himself. ... He had no Empire Urge, unlike Henry Luce and a dozen other founders ... he was a one-magazine, one-project man. ... He was a visionary and a practicalist, imperfect at both, a dreamer and a hard worker, a genius and a plodder, obstinate and reasonable, cosmopolitan and provincial, wide-eyed and world-weary. There is only one word that fits him perfectly, and the word is "Ross."

Ann Landers and Abigail Van Buren

1918–

In the *Chicago Sun-Times,* Esther Pauline Lederer serves up advice as "Ann Landers." Typical of her 1955 syndicated column: To a mom whose grown-up son lives at home, she writes, "Since Missouri is the 'Show Me' state, I suggest your son show you about 25 percent of his paycheck." Ann calls in experts when common sense fails. Her twin, Pauline Esther Phillips, starts a rival column, "Dear Abby," in the *San Francisco Chronicle.* Together, they say they reach 200 million readers, often using humor to get at difficult subjects. Nothing, Ann says, "is too bizarre, too idiotic or too risky to be real."

ANN LANDERS, LEFT, AND ABIGAIL VAN BUREN, UPI/CORBIS-BETTMANN, COURTESY PHILLIPS-VAN BUREN, INC.

In an interview for the 1987 book Dear Ann Landers, *the syndicated columnist describes what she has learned:*

'Areas I had never thought of'

The column has taken me into areas I had never thought of before. Incest, genetic diseases, rape, drug abuse, schizophrenia, battered wives (and husbands), donating organs for transplantation, women who do their housework in the nude, what happens to missing socks. ... I view the column as an opportunity to educate.

Adds Abby:
I don't write my column for entertainment. I write it primarily to inform, but I like to give advice with a chuckle whenever possible.

Art Buchwald

1925–

Satire artist Art Buchwald writes his first column, "Paris after Dark," in 1948 for the *New York Herald Tribune*. After 14 years in Europe, he moves to Washington, D.C. His creative columns, full of made-up characters and larger-than-life truths, are syndicated nationally. But why humor? In his 1994 memoir, Buchwald explains: "Getting even. I am constantly trying to avenge hurts from the past."

THE ASSOCIATED PRESS

In his April 26, 1973, Washington Post column, Art Buchwald imagines God talking to President Nixon:

'Why didn't you tell me, God?'

"Richard, I tried to warn you that you had sinful people working for you."

"When, God?"

"Just after the Committee to Re-Elect The President was formed. When I saw the people you had selected ... I was shocked."

"Why didn't you tell me, God?"

"I tried to, but Ehrlichman and Haldeman wouldn't let Me talk to you on the phone."

Erma Bombeck

1927–1996

Dayton, Ohio, housewife and mother Erma Bombeck starts a humor column on house-wifery in 1965 for a neighbor-hood newspaper. *The Dayton Journal-Herald* snares her. Before long, Bombeck, some-times called "Socrates of the Ironing Board," appears in 900 newspapers. Why her "Wit's End" humor rings so true: "Doing the laundry keeps you humble," she says. "I spend 90 percent of my time living scripts and 10 percent writing them."

In a May 1974 "At Wit's End" column, Erma Bombeck touches hearts as well as funny bones:

'Fiddling around'

When the good Lord was creating mothers, he was into his sixth day of overtime when the angel appeared and said, "You're doing a lot of fiddling around on this one."

The Lord said, "Have you read the specs on this order?

"She has to be completely washable, but not plastic;

"Have 180 moveable parts ... all replaceable;

"Run on black coffee and leftovers;

"Have a lap that disappears when she stands up ...

"And six pairs of hands ..."

Andy Rooney

1919–

Since 1978, Andy Rooney is the popular CBS pundit on *60 Minutes*. When an Associated Press TV critic suggests he retire, Rooney airs the critic's phone number — 7,000 call in Rooney's defense. The key to his success? Tackling subjects people take for granted. "We're so busy analyzing the obscure," says Rooney, "that we haven't realized that we really haven't mastered the commonplace."

CBS, INC.

Andy Rooney doesn't always kid around. Here, on 60 Minutes, he comments on the 1986 Challenger space shuttle explosion:

'Genuine heroes'

Those seven astronauts ... were genuine heroes, really brave men and women. It isn't brave if you're too dumb to know what the danger is or you don't give a damn about your life. They knew exactly how dangerous their adventure was, and they cared about their lives, too. But they did it, anyway. I suppose that if no one ever died doing a brave and dangerous thing, the quality of bravery would cease to exist. These seven people have reestablished the credentials of bravery. Maybe the best thing to say on an occasion like this is that we can all be prouder to be human beings because of what they were.

Herb Caen

1916–1997

Herb Caen meets San Francisco: love at first sightem. The monitor of California lifestyles holds forth for six decades in the *San Francisco Chronicle*. Inspired by Walter Winchell, Caen starts his three-dot column in 1938 ... Soon, it's required reading, even the foggy Sunday love poems to his "Baghdad by the Bay." ... His secret? Names are news — use them. "People love to see their names in print." Caen's name? "Mr. San Francisco." ... In 1997, readers flock to the waterfront by the thousands for his send-off, along the waterfront's Herb Caen Way.

SAN FRANCISCO CHRONICLE

Herb Caen celebrates his column's 20-year anniversary in the July 5, 1958, San Francisco Chronicle:

'Items, tritems, sightems'

Twenty years. A long time to stand in the corner of a newspaper scrawling inanities. ... Twenty years of unflagging devotion to items, tritems, sightems, slightems, and even frightems; to the highly forgettable fact ... the flash that didn't pan out, the fallen arch remark; to the flopsam and jetsam, the abjectrivial and the three-dotty ephemera of a city's day-by-daze.

Russell Baker

1925–

Watching the 1960 Kennedy-Nixon TV debate, *New York Times* reporter Russell Baker observes "that night television replaced newspapers as the most important communications medium in American politics." Within two years, Baker trades his reporter's notebook for an editorial-page column. His mission: to use humor as "an antidote to the heavy tone of the news." But what makes him laugh? "Very little," Baker says. "When you get to be old and gray, you think the world is going to hell."

THE ASSOCIATED PRESS

In an April 16, 1978, Pulitzer Prize–winning column in The New York Times, *Russell Baker writes about inflation:*

'No way of treating a dollar'

I used to send the dollar to the grocery with orders to bring back a pound of coffee. I figured this would teach it humility. Instead, it went into a severe depression which psychiatry couldn't cure because it has no way of treating a dollar unless accompanied by 34 others, which I didn't have at the time.

Molly Ivins

1944–

After a career that leads to *The New York Times*, Molly Ivins returns to Texas as a political humorist for the *Fort Worth Star-Telegram*. The Lone Star State is made for her, she says. "There is no place more sexist." So she describes herself as a "female chauvinist" with a passion for the little guy and an eye for the absurd. The secret to her biting humor? "God gave me Texas politics to write about. How can I not be funny?"

FREEDOM FORUM

In her 1991 book, Molly Ivins Can't Say That, Can She? *the author explains Texas:*

'Harmless perversion'

I love the state of Texas, but I regard that as a harmless perversion on my part and would not, in the name of common humanity, try to foist my pathology off on anyone else. …The reason the sky is bigger here is because there aren't any trees. The reason folks here eat grits is because they ain't got no taste.

P. J. O'Rourke

1947–

When it comes to foreign lands and national debates, P. J. O'Rourke, *Rolling Stone*'s resident misanthrope, is hell-bent on the "solemn business of mockery." The former editor at the *National Lampoon* hits a neo-conservative nerve in best-selling books like *Give War a Chance*. He champions the "Republican Party Reptile," a jolly breed opposed to things like "Kennedy kids" and "busing our children anywhere other than Yale. ..."

BOB WAGNER/ATLANTIC MONTHLY PRESS

P. J. O'Rourke finds a way to thank Rolling Stone *magazine in his 25-year anniversary collection,* Age and Guile Beat Youth, Innocence and a Bad Haircut, *1995:*

'Trouble spots'

I wanted to go to various of the world's trouble spots and make fun of them — combining the silliness of foreign correspondence with the solemn business of mockery and slander. There were magazines willing to let me do this, but they didn't have the money to send me overseas. Other magazines had the money but thought my project was, as one (okay, more than one) editor put it, "stupid."

Dave Barry

1947–

Syndicated *Miami Herald* columnist Dave Barry is a one-man humor industry. His popular column wins a Pulitzer Prize in 1988. His life is the basis for a TV comedy. His books — on everything from guys to cyberspace — fill store shelves. The secret to his success? Barry says he's "trapped in a world almost totally devoid of reason." When Barry sees his picture in the Newseum, he says, "What I really like is the blank space after 1947-   ."

MIAMI HERALD

In a Feb. 22, 1987, Pulitzer Prize–winning column in The Miami Herald, *Dave Barry explains the Internal Revenue Service:*

'How to Fill Out Your Tax Forms'

To quote from Official IRS Information Pamphlet Number 2893-C, "How to Fill Out Your Tax Forms So You Don't Get Caught": "Taxpayers should ... make up numbers that look like they might be real, such as $1,407.62. ..." This is important, taxpayers. If you write a number like "$500," you might just as well add: "Go ahead and audit me, scuzzballs!"

CHAPTER 5

War Reporters

> 'Don't you men salute officers?" "We're not men," Page said. "We're correspondents.'
>
> — MICHAEL HERR

VICKSBURG, MISSISSIPPI, 1863 —

HOW DOES IT FEEL TO LOOK INTO THE MOUTH OF A cannon? Exhilarating and terrifying. Like the "jaws of death" in Tennyson's classic poem of battle, *The Charge of the Light Brigade.* That's how reporter Albert D. Richardson describes it for *New York Tribune* readers in a dispatch from the eye of the biggest story yet in the nation's history, the American Civil War.

"How the great sheets of flame leaped up and spread out from the mouths of guns!" Richardson scrawls from the Siege of Vicksburg.

In a matter of days, Richardson is captured and thrown into a Confederate jail. Erroneous word filters back to Gen. William T. Sherman's camp that Richardson and two fellow reporters are dead. "Good!" Sherman says. "Now we shall have news from hell before breakfast."

Richardson represents a new breed of reporter: the eyewitness war correspondent, no longer the part-time soldier or military mouthpiece, but independent chronicler of battlefield events.

And so, thorn in the side of the war wagers.

"Buzzards of the press," Gen. Sherman calls them; "spies and defamers" who cause "more bloodshed than 50 times their number of armed rebels."

Thus begins the vilifying and stroking, muzzling and chafing, the odd coexisting of reporter and soldier. From the beginning, the news media have helped rally nations to war. During the American Revolution, journalists were soldiers by day, writers of patriotic prose by night. But by the Civil War, they had become more critical and so, to the mind of the military, more dangerous.

Is the press good and the military bad? Vice versa? The questions aren't so black and white. They are, rather, gray as gray gets. For example: Who should have access to what information in wartime? And should information be "news" if its circulation threatens troop safety, national security or even public mood? Whose truth should the news reflect? And what if they gave a war and no reporters came?

From bayonet to smart bomb, the stories down the decades ring familiar.

When a Union general bans correspondents from camp, Albert Richardson complains to his editor: "This is so eminently a People's War that if you deny the People the right — not the privilege — of a medium of information between them, & their sons & brothers & husbands in the army, what may you not deny them?"

Frederick Palmer, veteran of 50 years of war reporting, calls World War I's official program of censorship the beginning of the end of real war news: "The war correspondent as a news-bearer is dead," he writes in 1914. "He survives only as a writer who can give human expression to what the military staff utters in its laconic and matter-of-fact way."

Persian Gulf War correspondent John J. Fialka describes that war's singular lack of combat access, in a book aptly titled *Hotel Warriors:* " ... the invisible barrier, a kind of plastic bag or cocoon of controls that the military preferred to keep around reporters in this war. While some of us managed to get out of the hotels, most of us never escaped the cocoon."

And CBS-TV correspondent Morley Safer touches the heart of the matter in a memoir about his reporting tour in Vietnam: "The only truth in war, I decide, is the one offered by Senator Hiram Johnson in 1917: 'The first casualty [when war comes] is truth.' "

More than any other stripe of reporter, the war correspondent cuts a romantic image in popular thought. Here's the American sex symbol dodging bullets in epaulets (or fatigues or flak jackets). Here are the men (and women) getting shot at "without shooting back," as Frederick Palmer says, "in order that the world may know how the war is going."

Part of that romance, at least, is rooted in the late 19th- and early 20th-century exploits of Richard Harding

— Courtesy The Albuquerque Museum/Alex Jamison photo

Above: With this typewriter, Ernie Pyle reports from the front during World War II.

Davis, dashing chronicler of numerous wars (and putative role model of correspondent Ernest Hemingway), whose style was showing up at camp with portable bathtub and dinner jacket in case the general invited him to dine. (It is not romantically insignificant that Tennyson's *Charge of the Light Brigade* was based on a Crimean War dispatch by Britain's William Howard Russell, considered patriarch of the modern Western correspondent.)

It may be true, as Gen. Sherman so famously put it, that "war is hell." But it may also be true, for the reporter, that war is the biggest story of a lifetime. The landscape is grander, the stakes higher, the moments of drama more infused with what famed Korean War correspondent Marguerite Higgins calls "the human closeness and magnificence of character that danger sometimes provokes."

Then there's the thrill of it.

"Inclination joined with duty in impelling us to accompany the expedition," Albert Richardson tells his readers. "We wanted to learn how one would feel looking into the craters of those volcanoes as they poured forth sheets of flame and volleys of shells."

Here is Civil War photographer Mathew Brady describing his need to be near the battlefield: "A spirit in my feet said 'Go,' and I went."

World War II legend Ernie Pyle feels a similar pull: "I'm going simply because I've got to, and I hate it."

Korea's Marguerite Higgins says this: "I have known since childhood that if there was to be a war I wanted to be there to know for myself what force cuts so deep into the hearts of men."

And Peter Arnett, chronicler of Vietnam, the Persian Gulf and other conflicts: "I believe that the armpits of the world have to be covered no matter how dangerous they are, because it's important to know what's going on there. And yes, I love a good story, and what is more dramatic than the clash of arms in exotic locales?"

The politics may differ from war to war, but the dramatic clashing of arms is strangely the same. War, as seen by veteran correspondent Martha Gellhorn, is "a horrible repetition."

Here, Richard Harding Davis, in the Greco-Turkish War, 1897, writes of bullets that sound like so many "humming-birds on a warm summer's day."

Here is Gellhorn, in 1937, from Spain: "At first the shells went over: you could hear the thud as they left the Fascists' guns, a sort of groaning cough; then you heard them fluttering toward you."

And Morley Safer, in a 1966 essay about Vietnam: "In battle men do not die with a clean shot through the heart;

> 'The armpits of the world have to be covered … it's important.'
>
> — PETER ARNETT

they are blown to pieces. Television tells it that way."

Part of the war reporter story is how journalists have angered generals more than they have the men in the field. Perhaps that's because a dead correspondent is just as dead as a dead soldier.

In 1965, when combat reporter-photographer Dickey Chapelle steps on a land mine in Vietnam, she sums it up. "I guess it was bound to happen," she says. It's the last thing she ever says.

Paul Revere

1735–1818

Riding ahead of the British troops, Paul Revere delivers the most urgent news bulletin of the American Revolution: "The Regulars are coming out!" Later, patriot riders carry an official "alarm letter" detailing the Lexington and Concord battles. A silversmith and engraver, Revere produces early news illustrations. He depicts the Boston Massacre by etching images of coffins for colonial newspapers and creating a hand-colored news broadside, "Bloody Massacre."

MUSEUM OF FINE ARTS, BOSTON

A Sept. 4, 1774, letter (including misspellings) written by Paul Revere to a New York compatriot:

'Tories are giving way'

The Spirit of Liberty never was higher than at present. ... By reason of some late movements of our friends in the Country ... our Justices of the courts, who now hold their commissions during the pleasure of his Majesty, or the Governor, cannot git a jury to act with them, in short the Tories are giving way everywhere in our Province.

Isaiah Thomas

1749–1831

At 21, Isaiah Thomas founds the *Massachusetts Spy,* a weekly that sets a colonial circulation record of 3,500. A staunch patriot, Thomas does not see his readers as British subjects. He begins his story on the first Revolutionary War battle with a single, telling word: "AMERICANS!" Later, Thomas creates the American Antiquarian Society and writes the first history of the American press.

In the May 3, 1775, Massachusetts Spy, *Isaiah Thomas writes his eyewitness account of the Battle of Lexington:*

'Thirst for blood!'

AMERICANS! forever bear in mind the BATTLE OF LEXINGTON! — where British Troops, unmolested and unprovoked, wantonly, and in a most inhuman manner fired upon and killed a number of our countrymen, then robbed them of their provisions, ransacked, plundered and burnt their houses! nor could the tears of defence-less women, some of whom were in the pains of childbirth, the cries of helpless babies, nor the prayers of old age, confined to beds of sickness, appease their thirst for blood! — or divert them from their DESIGN of MURDER and ROBBERY!

Albert D. Richardson

1833–1869

Intrepid *New York Tribune* reporter Albert Richardson will do almost anything to get a story. Part of a new breed of independent war correspondents, he dons a disguise for a trip through the South, climbs a tree to watch Union troops attack Fort Henry, even tries to run a blockade at Vicksburg. Confederates capture him. But after a year and a half, he gets away. His wire describes his escape: "Out of the jaws of death; out of the mouth of Hell."

In a May 1863 edition of the New York Tribune, *Albert D. Richardson writes from Vicksburg, Miss.:*

'Jaws of death'

I ascertained to my fullest satisfaction how it felt to look into the mouth of a cannon. How the great sheets of flame leaped up and spread out from the mouths of guns! How the shells came screaming and shrieking through the air! How they rattled and crashed, penetrating the sides of the barges or exploding on board in great fountains of fire! ... [E]very time I glanced at that picture, Tennyson's lines rang in my ears: "Boldly they rode and well, Into the jaws of death, Into the mouth of hell."

Thomas Morris Chester

1834–1892

Philadelphia *Press* reporter Thomas Morris Chester is the only African American to cover the Civil War for a major, general-circulation daily. He writes about the black Union soldier, fighting to win not only freedom for his race, but recognition as "a patriot ... a man who offers himself a willing sacrifice upon his country's altar." Chester migrates to Africa to edit the *Star of Liberia*. He studies law in England, then tries politics in Louisiana. In 1892, bitter over the unequal treatment of African Americans, he returns to Harrisburg, Pa., where he dies from a heart attack and is buried in a segregated cemetery.

UNIVERSITY ARCHIVES, CHEYNEY UNIVERSITY OF PA

Thomas Morris Chester rides into Richmond with black Union troops seizing the Confederate capital. The sight of slaves greeting Union soldiers, he writes, is "not only grand, but sublime." From The Press *of Philadelphia , April 4, 1865:*

'Tears of joy'

Along the road ... batches of negroes were gathered together testifying by unmistakable signs their delight in our coming. Officers rushed into each other's arms. ... Tears of joy ran down the faces of the more aged. The citizens stood gaping in wonder at the splendidly-equipped army marching along under the graceful folds of the old flag. Some waved their hats and women their hands in token of gladness. The pious old negroes, male and female, indulged in such expressions: "You've come at last!"

Winslow Homer

1836–1910

Boston illustrator Winslow Homer is hired by *Harper's Weekly* in 1861 as a "special artist" with the Union Army of the Potomac. Quiet tableaus, such as his "Thanksgiving in Camp," set him apart from the Civil War illustrators who prefer bloody battle scenes and military heroics. By 1875, Homer leaves journalism to paint idyllic landscapes and tumultuous seacoasts, becoming a seminal figure in American art.

BOWDOIN COLLEGE MUSEUM OF ART, BRUNSWICK, MAINE. GIFT OF THE HOMER FAMILY

NEWSEUM COLLECTION

In a Feb. 19, 1896, letter to a friend, Winslow Homer explains the origin of his Civil War drawing, "The Sharpshooter":

'A camp follower & artist'

I was not a soldier — but a camp follower & artist, the above [sharpshooter sketch] struck me as being as near murder as anything I could think of in connection with the army & I always had a horror of that branch of the service.

Stephen Crane

1871–1900

Novelist Stephen Crane never sees the Civil War he describes in *The Red Badge of Courage*. But he covers the Spanish-American War for the New York *World* and other publications. Crane feels a "thrill of patriotic insanity" charging with the Rough Riders, "the best moment of anyone's life." The literary journalist dies at 28 from a fever that he may have contracted in Cuba.

COLLECTION OF STANLEY AND MARY WERTHEIM

In the February 1899 McClure's, *Stephen Crane reports on the Spanish-American War:*

'Bullets began to snap'

Then the bullets began to snap, snap, snap, at his head, while all the woods began to crackle like burning straw. I could lie near and watch the face of the signalman, illumined as it was by the yellow shine of lantern-light, and the absence of excitement, fright, or any emotion at all on his countenance was something to astonish all theories out of one's mind.

James Creelman

1859–1915

In 1898, William Randolph Hearst sends James Creelman to Cuba to cover the Spanish-American War. Creelman leads a charge against a Spanish blockhouse at El Caney. He is shot during surrender talks. Hearst, by then in Cuba, files Creelman's story for his *New York Journal*. "The newspaper man must be in the very foreground of battle," Creelman says, "if he would see with his own eyes the dread scenes that make war worth describing."

CULVER PICTURES

In his memoirs, James Creelman describes getting shot at El Caney:

'Sorry you're hurt'

Some one knelt in the grass beside me and put his hand on my fevered head. Opening my eyes, I saw Mr. Hearst ... a straw hat with a bright ribbon on his head, a revolver at his belt, and a pencil and notebook in his hand. ... Slowly he took down my story of the fight. Again and again the tinging of Mauser bullets interrupted. But he seemed unmoved. The battle had to be reported somehow. "I'm sorry you're hurt, but," — and his face was radiant with enthusiasm — "wasn't it a splendid fight? We must beat every paper in the world!"

Richard Harding Davis

1864–1916

Dashing war correspondent Richard Harding Davis wears a uniform "as cool as a golf jacket" to cover World War I. As the Germans take Brussels, he writes one of the war's most vivid reports to *The New York Herald Tribune*: "What came ... is not men marching, but a force of nature like a tidal wave, an avalanche, or a river flooding its banks." Davis penetrates German lines, tries for Paris, gets arrested, then released. He writes plays and novels about his experiences, including *Soldiers of Fortune*.

PACH/CORBIS-BETTMANN

Covering what would become the Spanish-American War, Richard Harding Davis writes on a Spanish execution of a Cuban outside of Santa Clara:

'The young Cuban'

As I fell in at the rear of the procession and looked back, the figure of the young Cuban, who was no longer part of the world of Santa Clara, was asleep in the wet grass, with his motionless arms still tightly bound behind him with the scapular twisted awry across his face, and the blood from his breast sinking into the soil he had tried to free.

Peggy Hull

1889–1967

Kansas farm girl Peggy Hull starts in journalism by delighting department store owners as an "advertising columnist" in Cleveland's *Plain Dealer.* In 1916, the military buff joins the women's auxiliary of the Ohio National Guard and accompanies Brig. Gen. John J. Pershing as a free-lancer on his expedition to Mexico. Her lively columns on military camp life manage to weave in the names of advertisers. The military brass likes her. Two years later, she becomes the first female war correspondent accredited by the War Department and goes on to cover two more wars.

PEGGY HULL DEUELL COLLECTION, KANSAS COLLECTION, UNIVERSITY OF KANSAS LIBRARIES

In the June 6, 1919, Cincinnati Post, *Peggy Hull reports on a Russian recruiting expedition to Siberia:*

'Beaten with whips'

A punitive expedition from Vladivostok visited a village near here ... to draft the sons of the peasants into the new Russian army. ... All the young men ran away into the hills and when their fathers and grandfathers denied knowledge of their whereabouts 11 were taken from their homes, beaten with whips and rifle butts and then taken to an attic, where they were tortured.

Ernie Pyle
1900–1945

On April 18, 1945, soldiers plant a sign on the Pacific island of Ie Shima: "At this spot the 77th Infantry Division lost a buddy." The sign marks the spot where a Japanese sniper ends the life of Ernest Taylor Pyle, who wrote about GIs, their socks and field rations, their letters home, their deaths. Pyle's Scripps-Howard column, written from the foxholes with a "worm's eye" point of view, has real-people appeal. Says President Truman: "No man in this war has so well told the story."

UPI/CORBIS-BETTMANN

From Ernie Pyle's Pulitzer Prize–winning column, "The Death of Captain Waskow":

'I sure am sorry'

The man looked down into the dead captain's face, and then he spoke directly to him, as though he were alive. He said: "I'm sorry, old man." Then a soldier came and stood beside the officer, and bent over, and he too spoke to his dead captain, not in a whisper but awfully tenderly, and he said: "I sure am sorry, sir." Then the first man squatted down, and he reached down and took the dead hand, and he sat there for a full five minutes, holding the dead hand in his own and looking intently into the dead face, and he never uttered a sound all the time he sat there. And finally he put the hand down, and then reached up and gently straightened the points of the captain's shirt collar, and then he sort of rearranged the tattered edges of his uniform around the wound. And then he got up and walked away down the road in the moonlight, all alone.

Mary Marvin Breckinridge

c. 1905–

A Vassar graduate, filmmaker and free-lance photographer, Mary Marvin Breckinridge is in Europe when the Nazis invade Poland. In 1939, Edward R. Murrow signs her up in London as the first female correspondent for CBS. She reports from World War II Europe on "the human side of war." When she leaves radio a year later to marry diplomat Jefferson Patterson, newspapers describe the newswoman, by then in her mid-30s, as a "society girl photographer and broadcaster" struck by "Dan Cupid's arrow."

THE ASSOCIATED PRESS

In a Feb. 8, 1940, CBS Radio World News Roundup, Mary Marvin Breckinridge outwits Nazi censors, slipping a story about the death of press freedom right under their noses. Censors cut the first two sentences of the following dispatch, but didn't understand the last three sentences and let them through:

'Freedom and Bread'

The German papers never carried many ads even before the war. This paper is supported by a prosperous publishing firm which does a lot of official business, and in which Hitler and other government leaders have large interests. The motto of this important official paper is Freedom and Bread. There is still bread. We return you now to Columbia [Broadcasting System], New York.

Bill Mauldin

1921–

Dogface soldiers Willie and Joe live in the Army newspaper *Stars and Stripes*. Created by cartoonist William H. Mauldin, the boys bemoan their grimy GI lot with irony and insight. Says Mauldin: "I understand their gripes." Gen. George Patton objects, asking the cartoonist to cut it out. But Patton's boss, Gen. Dwight Eisenhower, laughs along. The cartoons stay. Mauldin wins journalism's top honors and goes on to draw for the *St. Louis Post-Dispatch* and the *Chicago Sun-Times*.

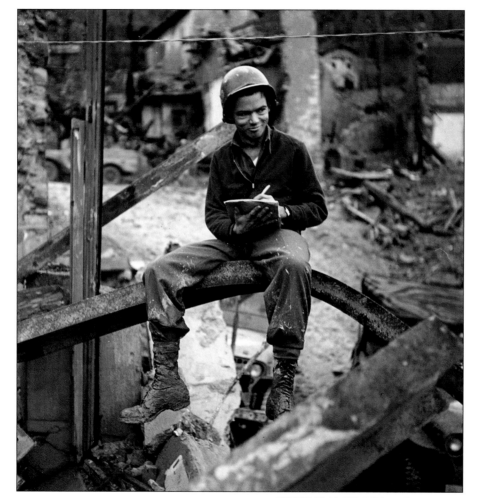

JOHN PHILLIPS, COURTESY NATIONAL PORTRAIT GALLERY

Bill Mauldin explains why he draws soldiers the way he does:

Dry mud and hot coffee

I don't make the infantryman look noble, because he couldn't look noble even if he tried. Still there is a certain nobility and dignity in combat soldiers. ... With dirt in their ears ... They wish to hell they were someplace else. ... They wish to hell the mud was dry and they wish to hell their coffee was hot.

John Hersey

1914–1993

In *The New Yorker* magazine, John Hersey awakens America to the horror of the atomic bomb. The magazine fills an entire August 1946 issue with *Hiroshima*, reporting the devastation wrought Aug. 6, 1945, when the U.S. drops the world's deadliest weapon on Hiroshima, Japan. Says Hersey: "The problem of how to deal with such a massive event was very, very ... difficult to figure out." Thornton Wilder's novel, *The Bridge of San Luis Rey*, gives him an idea: Tell the story of a small group of people united by one terrible event. Reaction to *Hiroshima* is overwhelming. Journalists report Albert Einstein orders 1,000 copies of the magazine.

From John Hersey's Hiroshima, *published in* The New Yorker, *Aug. 31, 1946:*

'The atomic age'

Everything fell, and Miss Sasaki lost consciousness. The ceiling dropped suddenly and the wooden floor above collapsed in splinters ... the bookcases right behind her swooped forward and the contents threw her down, with her left leg horribly twisted and breaking underneath her. There in the tin factory, in the first moment of the atomic age, a human being was crushed by books.

Marguerite Higgins

1920–1966

An Army general orders veteran *New York Herald Tribune* war correspondent Marguerite Higgins to leave Korea because she's a woman. Higgins appeals to Gen. Douglas MacArthur. She stays and wins a Pulitzer Prize. "It is best," she writes, "to tell graphically the moments of desperation and horror endured by an unprepared army so that the American public will demand it does not happen again." Higgins vows to marry any man "as exciting as war." In 1952, she marries Lt. Gen. William Hall. As a *Newsday* columnist in Vietnam, she contracts a rare, fatal disease.

UPI/CORBIS-BETTMANN

In the Sept. 18, 1950, New York Herald Tribune, *Marguerite Higgins reports the landing at Inchon, Korea:*

'Pinned down by rifle'

In the sky there was good news. A bright, white star shell from the high ground to our left and an amber cluster told us that the first wave had taken their initial objective, Observatory Hill. But whatever the luck of the first four waves, we were relentlessly pinned down by rifle and automatic weapon fire coming down on us from another rise on the right.

David Halberstam

1934–

New York Times correspondent David Halberstam questions military claims of progress in the Vietnam War. An upset President Kennedy asks Halberstam's editors to bring him home. Later, President Johnson calls him "a traitor." But Halberstam stays. His dispatches fuel debate over a long, controversial war. Halberstam comes to believe Washington is ignoring reports from the field. "The more you saw," he says, "the more you realized it just didn't work."

NEW YORK TIMES PICTURES

David Halberstam writes about the early lessons of Vietnam in the February 1965 issue of Harper's:

'The enemy was good'

The first lesson that an American advisor in Vietnam learned was that the enemy was good; then if he stayed on a little longer, he learned that this was wrong; the enemy was very good ... they made few mistakes, and in sharp contrast to the government forces, they rarely repeated their mistakes.

Morley Safer

1931–

In 1965, CBS correspondent Morley Safer and a camera crew film U.S. Marines torching a Vietnamese village. His report on the burning of Cam Ne riles U.S. military officials, becoming a watershed for television war reporting. "To a ... peasant whose house means a life of backbreaking labor," Safer tells viewers, "it will take more than presidential promises to convince him that we are on his side." Five years later, Safer becomes a correspondent for *60 Minutes*.

CBS, INC.

Morley Safer recounts the burning of Cam Ne in his book, Flashbacks:

'Torch it'

"We heard voices from that hootch," a private says. The lieutenant empties a magazine from his automatic rifle into the house, and bits of dried mud and thatch go flying. Now the voices are very clear, but not like human voices at all. A wailing sound, high and clear, followed by a chorus of keening and the rattling sound of a baby crying, but it is almost an animal sound. "Torch it," the lieutenant says.

Peter Arnett

1934–

In Vietnam, Associated Press reporter Peter Arnett quotes a U.S. major saying, "We had to destroy the town to save it." Arnett spends the next three decades defending the accuracy of the "immortal quote." In the 1990s, the battlefield veteran camps out in Baghdad for the Persian Gulf War. For the first time, Americans watch their bombs falling — *live* — from the point of view of those being bombed. Arnett battles censors, interviews strongman Saddam Hussein, redefines the term Global Village. Are there any stories worth dying for? "No," he says. "But there are plenty of stories worth risking your life for."

THE ASSOCIATED PRESS

In the fall 1996 issue of the Media Studies Journal, *Peter Arnett defends reporting during the Persian Gulf War:*

'A diplomat and educator'

As the Information Age and its portable communications technology transform the world, the old "whose side are you on" accusation once hurled at the reporters of the Vietnam War is becoming increasingly irrelevant. Today, we're on everyone's side, or no one's, depending on your point of view. ... The once gung ho war correspondent has become a diplomat and educator in addition.

Christiane Amanpour

1958–

CNN's international correspondent Christiane Amanpour confronts President Clinton about his Bosnia policies in a "Global Forum." Some complain that journalists like Amanpour have too much influence, that her work personifies the so-called "CNN effect" — the role TV plays in shaping U.S. foreign policy in the Global Village. Amanpour calls that a "lazy" conclusion by officials who have no policy ideas of their own. "When there's a policy vacuum," she says, "then something's going to fill that vacuum. And in this case, it's been the media coverage of the war."

COURTESY CNN

An excerpt from Christiane Amanpour's 1994 live interview with President Clinton:

'The West ... held hostage'

It's a privilege to address you from Sarajevo. ... Why, in the absence of a policy, have you allowed the U.S. and the West to be held hostage to those who do have a policy — the Bosnian Serbs — and do you not think that the constant flip-flops of your administration on ... Bosnia set a very dangerous precedent?

Replies President Clinton: "No, but speeches like that may make them take me less seriously than I'd like to be taken. There have been no constant flip-flops, Madam. I ran for president saying that I would do my best to limit ethnic cleansing, and to see the United States play a more active role in resolving the problem in Bosnia, and we have been much more active than my predecessor was, in every way, from the beginning."

Media Moguls

HAVANA, CUBA, 1898 —

DISPATCHED HERE TO REPORT ON SPANISH ATROCITIES for the *New York Journal*, illustrator Frederic Remington and correspondent James Creelman find themselves at a loss for material.

So the illustrator sends a cable to the boss, William Randolph Hearst:

EVERYTHING IS QUIET. THERE IS NO TROUBLE HERE. THERE WILL BE NO WAR. WISH TO RETURN. REMINGTON

Intent on exploiting the nation's growing sense of Manifest Destiny — to say nothing of boosting his news-paper's circulation — Hearst thunders back:

PLEASE REMAIN. YOU FURNISH THE PICTURES AND I'LL FURNISH THE WAR. HEARST

Creelman swears the story of the telegrams is true. Hearst denies it. But war does come, and Hearst does help provide it. Within weeks, the battleship *USS Maine* mys-teriously sinks. New York's headline-hungry newspapers — especially Hearst's *Journal* and Joseph Pulitzer's New York *World* — whip Americans into a frenzy by blaming Spain. Hearst sells 3 million copies of his newspaper in three days. "How do you like the *Journal's* War?" it asks. Nearly 80 years later, a Navy study makes the case that an internal explosion — not a mine — sunk the Maine.

Is the press too powerful?

On the contrary, Pulitzer thinks, it isn't powerful enough. Pulitzer's will creates a Graduate School of Journalism at Columbia University and the Pulitzer Prizes, "to make the newspaper profession a still nobler one — by raising its character and standing, by increasing its power and prestige."

A century after the Spanish-American War, nearly a million people annually walk the grounds of Hearst's vast estate at San Simeon, Calif., some paying as much as $25 apiece to marvel at the accumulated opulence of one of America's richest men. Glowering down on the Pacific from its landscaped hilltop, Hearst's castle rises, too, as a monument to the power of the press.

From Benjamin Franklin to Rupert Murdoch, media moguls use their business acumen — often gleefully — to amass fortunes and power for purposes great and small. They crusade for civic progress, influence regulation and legislation, promote political agendas, acquire even more power and wealth. They can make presidents and squash competitors.

"Puff Graham," says Hearst, and his editors respond from coast to coast with glowing stories about the Rev. Billy Graham.

Even the best do not shy away from using their position. Ben Franklin turns the fortune made from the sale of *The Pennsylvania Gazette* into silent partnerships in several colonial newspapers — and then, as postmaster general, decrees the post office shall function as collection agent, charging delivery fees for newspapers and forwarding the fees to printers.

Pulitzer, who dedicates his New York *World* "to the cause of the people," exhorts immigrant families to send their pennies and nickels to finance the foundation of the Statue of Liberty. This, from the publisher whose editorial platform is: "1. Tax Luxuries. 2. Tax Inheritances. 3. Tax Large Incomes. 4. Tax Monopolies. 5. Tax the Privileged Corporations."

How much power is too much? Should a line be drawn?

Says Thomas Jefferson: "Were it left to me, to decide whether we should have a government without newspapers, or newspapers without government, I should not hesitate for a moment to prefer the latter."

Freed by the First Amendment, *New York Herald* publisher James Gordon Bennett asks, "what is to prevent a daily newspaper from being made the greatest organ of social life?" Flying into the electronic age, David Sarnoff observes that "there is no reason why, when we send out a radio signal ... that power should not travel over the

Inset: The Pulitzer Prizes award a gold medal for "meritorious public service."

entire universe."

But as quickly as moguls bestow great power on their mass media, they deny they have much themselves.

Katharine Graham, whose *Washington Post* in the early 1970s helps bring down a U.S. president, is "especially bothered by being talked about as 'powerful.' " She's referred to in headlines and stories as " 'The Most Powerful Woman in America,' making me feel like some kind of weight lifter or bodybuilder. Actually, I was amazed at this perception relating to power, and confounded by how absurd it was to be singling me out as more 'powerful' than Punch Sulzberger or Bill Paley, for example, who controlled more powerful companies but were men."

Ask William Paley, who builds CBS from a small radio network into a huge broadcast organization, bringing news into millions of homes, about his power over the news division and he says, "it's independent ... a self-policing operation run by professional people." Ask CBS' Frank Stanton how powerful the news division is, and during most of his career he tells you the FCC's Fairness Doctrine is a "straitjacket" on broadcast journalism, stripping it "of both the right and responsibility of news judgment."

Try Oprah Winfrey, who with a single televised review can turn a book into a best seller. Did her remark that mad cow disease "stopped me cold from eating another burger" really slash beef prices? When cattlemen sue, Oprah says her personal opinion doesn't sway public opinion. "If I had that kind of power, I'd go on the air and heal," she tells the jury. "I believe the people I speak to are intelligent enough to make decisions for themselves."

But don't we make decisions based on the fact and opinion flowing through the news stream? "A newspaper's power for good is unlimited," says publisher Frank E. Gannett, for the simple reason that "newspapers can create public opinion. There is no limit to what public opinion can do." John S. Knight says newspaper editors should be leaders: "I'm not obligated to anyone, to any political party, to any bankers or politicians or leaders. I'm just Knight." Edward Scripps, father of the modern newspaper chain, builds a turn-of-the-century empire by catering to "that large majority of people who are not so rich in worldly goods and native intelligence as to make them equal, man for man, in the struggle with the wealthier and more intellectual class."

Whether or not moguls tout their power may depend on what they do with it. "Many, many people," admits publisher Otis Chandler, "look at a large company that owns television stations and newspapers and magazines and books, and are astounded at the so-called opportunity you

> 'If I had that kind of power, I'd go on the air and heal.'
>
> — OPRAH WINFREY

have to do either good or evil." Running the *Los Angeles Times*, he says, is a lot better than a "temporary" job in politics. "Four years as governor ... six years as a senator and you're gone. A newspaper goes on and on and on." (It also makes it easy to get your picture in the paper: When Robert Maxwell buys the New York *Daily News*, his photo gets in 40 times during the first three weeks.)

Thanks to technology, the power of the press is being vested increasingly in the hands of anyone with a personal computer and a point of view. So now, media moguls and heirs of old (continued high profit-margins make them 10 percent of the Forbes 400 list of America's richest people) are joined by Global Villagers like Bill Gates, whose software empire is a springboard into mass communications, and entertainment titan Michael Eisner, whose company, Disney, owns ABC News. What do the New Age moguls worry about? Eisner: "All of us live in an age of overcommunication, in which people everywhere are bombarded endlessly with thousands of pieces of information ... as this bombardment continues to grow, people more and more tend to turn to the brands they know and trust. The name, Disney, has become one of the single most powerful brands around the globe."

Whether this new, larger group of media moguls will match the swashbuckling style of their forebears remains to be seen. Some have taken the people to their bosom in a way even Pulitzer could not have matched. Philanthropy is in. Gates donated $20 million to Cambridge University and pledged $200 million to help public libraries. CNN's

Ted Turner has pledged $1 billion to humanitarian programs administered by the United Nations. Just by giving away such sums, they meet the criteria for becoming genuine media moguls unwittingly set down by Franklin. The man who invented the lightning rod and then became one advised his contemporaries: "Either write things worth reading or do things worth the writing."

Franklin, like all true moguls who followed, did both.

Benjamin Franklin

1706–1790

Benjamin Franklin is a newspaper prodigy. At 12, he's apprenticed as a printer to brother James at *The New England Courant.* By 23, he controls *The Pennsylvania Gazette* and turns it into the colonies' most successful paper. The civic leader, diplomat and scientist also helps found a chain of colonial newspapers, including British North America's first foreign-language newspaper, the German *Philadelphia Zeitung.*

Ben Franklin explains his newspaper in the first issue of The Pennsylvania Gazette, *Sept. 25, 1729:*

'A good News-Paper'

We are fully sensible, that to publish a good News-Paper is not so easy an Undertaking as many People imagine it to be. The Author of a Gazette (in the Opinion of the Learned) ought to be qualified with an extensive Acquaintance with Languages, a great Easiness and Command of Writing and Relating Things clearly and intelligibly, and in a few words; he should be able to speak of War both by Land and Sea; be well acquainted with Geography, with the History of the time, with the several Interests of Princes and States, the Secrets of Courts, and the Manners and Customs of all nations. Men thus accomplish'd are very rare in this remote Part of the World; and it would be well if the writers of these Papers could make up among his Friends what is wanting in himself.

James Gordon Bennett

1795–1872

Jobless at 40, James Gordon Bennett vows to become "the genius of the newspaper press." He succeeds. Bennett scrapes up the cash to start *The New York Herald,* his third try at a daily. The innovative newspaper sends out reporters to cover courts, sports, business and more. By 1860, the *Herald*'s aggressive, factual reporting gives it sales of 77,000 daily, largest in the world.

NEWSEUM COLLECTION

From an Aug. 19, 1836, editorial in The New York Herald:

'Greatest organ of social life'

What is to prevent a daily newspaper from being made the greatest organ of social life? Books have had their day — the theatres have had their day — the temple of religion has had its day. ... A newspaper can send more souls to Heaven, and save more from Hell, than all the churches and chapels in New York — besides making money at the same time.

Edward Wyllis Scripps

1854–1926

A hard-drinking "people's champion," Edward Wyllis Scripps develops the first newspaper chain, with dailies in Cleveland and Cincinnati. Eventually, Scripps owns shares of 34 papers in 15 states and the United Press news service. The liberal Scripps builds a $50 million fortune. By the late 20th century, almost all U.S. dailies belong to newspaper groups.

SCRIPPS-HOWARD

Edward Wyllis Scripps writes his editors:

The 'people's champion'

The first of my principles is that I have constituted myself the advocate of that large majority of people who are not so rich in worldly goods and native intelligence as to make them equal, man for man, in the struggle with the wealthier and more intellectual class.

Charles H. Dow

1851–1902

With partners Edward Jones and Charles Bergstresser, business journalist Charles H. Dow launches *The Wall Street Journal* in 1889. For two cents a copy, the paper promises to provide "a faithful picture of the rapidly shifting panorama of the Street." It does, and by 1982 sales top 2 million, the highest in the nation. Dow is the brains behind the idea of averaging stock prices to show trends. Starting with 12 stocks, he creates what becomes the Dow-Jones Industrial Average in 1896, the most closely watched stock market index in the world.

COURTESY DOW JONES & COMPANY

Charles Dow's turn-of-the-century stock market advice, in a Wall Street Journal *editorial:*

'Everybody is stronger than anybody'

In the game called the tug-of-war a score of men, an equal number being at each end ... pull against each other to see which party is stronger. In the game called stock exchange speculation, the speculators are at liberty to take sides and the side which they join invariably wins because, in stock exchange parlance, "everybody is stronger than anybody."

Joseph Pulitzer

1847–1911

Hungarian-born Joseph Pulitzer makes his fortune as an American publisher. Editors everywhere imitate his colorful, crusading "New Journalism." For a time, Pulitzer's New York *World* is the world's best-selling daily. His secret: "Put it before them briefly so they will read it, clearly so they will appreciate it, picturesquely so they will remember it and, above all, accurately so they will be guided by its light." He funds Columbia University's journalism school and the Pulitzer Prizes for journalism, including the gold medal for public service.

BROWN BROTHERS

Joseph Pulitzer on his journalism philosophy:

'Rise above the mediocre'

Every issue of the paper presents an opportunity and a duty to say something courageous and true; to rise above the mediocre and the conventional; to say something that will command the respect of the intelligent, the educated, the independent part of the community; to rise above fear of partisanship and fear of popular prejudice.

William Randolph Hearst

1863–1951

Son of a silver baron, William Randolph Hearst rescues the *San Francisco Examiner* with zing and a flair for exaggeration. A few years later, his *New York Journal* steals the staff of archrival Joseph Pulitzer. Rivals accuse him of starting the Spanish-American War to edge Pulitzer in a circulation war: In the middle of it, he goes to Cuba, finds his war reporter "bloody and bandaged" and writes a story for him. Hearst builds a multimedia empire: magazines, news services, radio. "To rule rightly," he says, people "must be informed correctly." Hearst is a model for the ego-driven magnate in the film *Citizen Kane.*

On May 26, 1898, William Randolph Hearst asks foreign correspondent James Creelman to get ready to do battle against Spain:

'Necessary preparations'

I wish you would make necessary preparations, so that in case the Spanish fleet actually starts for Manila, we will be prepared to buy or charter some English tramp steamer on the Eastern end of the Mediterranean and take her to some narrow and inaccessible portion of the Suez Canal and sink her where she will obstruct the passage of the fleet. I do not know that we will want to do this, but we may, in case the American boats from San Francisco have not reached Dewey and he should be placed in a critical position by the approach of the Spanish vessels.

Adolph Ochs

1858–1935

The New York Times is struggling in 1896 when Adolph Ochs buys a controlling interest for $75,000. Ochs establishes the credo, "All the News That's Fit to Print." In the next 25 years, the *Times* makes $100 million. How? Ochs shuns sensationalism, investing in high-quality news coverage. The *Times* becomes one of the nation's most respected newspapers.

NEW YORK TIMES PICTURES

On Aug. 19, 1896, Adolph Ochs states the philosophy of The New York Times:

'All the news'

It will be my earnest aim that *The New York Times* give the news, all the news, in concise and attractive form, in language that is parliamentary in good society, and give it as early, if not earlier, than it can be learned through any other reliable medium; to give the news impartially, without fear or favor, regardless of any party, sect or interest involved; to make the columns of *The New York Times* a forum for the consideration of all questions of public importance, and to that end to invite intelligent discussion from all shades of opinion.

Henry Luce

1898–1967

In 1923, publisher Henry Luce co-fathers *Time*, the first modern newsmagazine. Luce's empire later expands to include *Life, Fortune* and *Sports Illustrated*. Son of a Presbyterian missionary in China, Luce brings a zeal to publishing: "People are uninformed because no publication has adapted itself to the time which busy men are able to spend on simply keeping informed." *Time* does.

YALE UNIVERSITY ARCHIVES

Time *magazine's mission statement:*

Keeping 'busy men' informed

Although daily journalism has been more highly developed in the United States than in any other country in the world — although foreigners marvel at the excellence of our periodicals ... people in America are, for the most part, poorly informed. This is not the fault of the daily newspapers; they print all the news. It is not the fault of the weekly "reviews;" they adequately develop and comment on the news. To say with the facile cynic that it is the fault of the people themselves is to beg the question. People are uninformed because no publication has adapted itself to the time which busy men are able to spend on simply keeping informed.

Robert McCormick

1880–1955

Chicago Tribune publisher Robert McCormick and cousin Joseph Medill Patterson help set the tone of the 1920s with their New York *Daily News*. The tabloid — easy to read on crowded subways — snares working-class readers with big pictures, brash headlines and snappy stories. By 1924, the *Daily News* sells 750,000 copies a day, tops in the nation. In Chicago, McCormick's *Tribune* grows into a giant that champions conservative and free-press causes.

TRIBUNE ARCHIVES, MCCORMICK RESEARCH CENTER, WHEATON, ILLINOIS

An excerpt of a Jan. 1, 1936, Chicago Tribune *editorial, where Robert McCormick declares war on New Deal Democrats.*

'Turn the rascals out'

There is a new plank this morning in the *Tribune*'s Platform. It is probably the most imperative of them all for the year 1936: "Turn the rascals out." ... The people can vote the rascals out of office, out of Congress, out of alphabetical administrations, out of important missions, boards and commissions, and out of the affairs of the nation.

John H. Johnson

1918–

In 1942, John H. Johnson creates *Negro Digest*, borrowing $500 to start America's most influential and profitable black-owned media company. In 1945 he founds *Ebony* magazine, a coffee-table standard for middle-class African Americans. Johnson offers "positive images of blacks in a world of negative images." *Ebony*'s circulation climbs to nearly 2 million.

JOHNSON PUBLISHING COMPANY

John H. Johnson writes about his dream of building his own business in the December 1993 issue of Ebony:

The 'impossible dream'

All my life, ever since I was a poor, barefooted boy walking in the Mississippi River mud ... I had dreamed of ... achieving what was then an impossible dream for a Black American. ... people told me it couldn't be done ... [my mother] told me, "You can, if you will."

David Sarnoff

1891–1971

In 1912, broadcast pioneer David Sarnoff, a Russian immigrant and one-time New York newsboy, is one of the telegraph operators who relays the message: "Titanic ... sinking fast." Sarnoff later goes on to head RCA, which makes millions selling radios. He founds the nation's leading broadcast network, NBC, and introduces the United States to television at the 1939 World's Fair.

UPI/CORBIS-BETTMANN

Here's how David Sarnoff introduces television to Americans at the 1939 New York World's Fair:

'A new industry'

Today we are on the eve of launching a new industry ... a new art so important in its implications that it is bound to affect all society. It is an art which shines like a torch of hope in a troubled world. It is a creative force which we must learn to utilize for the benefit of all mankind.

William S. Paley

1901–1990

Television is "a business of ideas," says William S. Paley, towering patriarch of CBS for nearly half a century. Paley builds radio then TV news departments that make the network tops in the business. By 1934, CBS, with 94 affiliates, is on its way to dominating the airwaves. "Broadcasting was an absolutely new, unique, fascinating, complicated and much misunderstood business in those early days," Paley writes in a memoir. "There really were no precedents and no limits."

THE ASSOCIATED PRESS

In his memoir, As It Happened, *William S. Paley writes about his first experience with radio:*

'Music out of the air'

The first radio I ever saw was a primitive crystal set. A friend clamped the earphones on me and I was dumbfounded. It was hard to believe that I was hearing music out of the air. ... I quickly found someone to build such a set for me. ... As a radio fan in Philadelphia, I often sat up all night ... listening and marveling.

S. I. Newhouse

1895–1979

The son of tenement immigrants, Samuel I. Newhouse buys control of a newspaper before he's 30. In 1922, *The Staten Island Advance* becomes the first link in what will be one of the largest U.S. publishing chains. Newhouse stresses the bottom line. "Only a newspaper which is a sound business operation," he says, "can be a truly free, independent editorial enterprise." In 1964, Newhouse establishes a school of communications at Syracuse University.

THE ASSOCIATED PRESS

In a 1928 conversation, Samuel I. Newhouse tries to convince a top employee not to leave The Staten Island Advance:

'Stick With Me'

You're making a mistake. I'm going to own a lot of newspapers. I take broken-down papers and make them pay. If you stick with me, you'll be a lot better off.

Frank E. Gannett

1876–1957

At 29, Frank E. Gannett buys into New York's *Elmira Gazette,* starting what will become the nation's largest newspaper group. Newspapers, he says, "must be clean ... honest ... fair to all ... and fight injustice always." His papers are independent, even when Gannett runs for president. In 1935, he donates $100,000 in stock to launch the Frank E. Gannett Newspaper Foundation, now The Freedom Forum.

Frank E. Gannett explains why his Hartford Times *and* Rochester Times-Union *supported different presidential candidates in 1932:*

'Contrary to my views'

Frequently, the editorial policy of the *Times* has been directly contrary to my own personal views. I believe that this is a wholesome situation. It would be a sad day for America if all our newspapers expressed only one view, or if they were owned by one person who insisted on expressing only his opinions.

Walter Annenberg

1908–

One of the world's great philanthropists, Walter Hubert Annenberg is 34 when he inherits Triangle Publications, his father's debt-ridden empire. In a few years, the company — whose holdings include *The Philadelphia Inquirer* — is making money. In 1953, Annenberg founds *TV Guide,* which becomes the largest-circulation magazine in the United States. He sells Triangle in 1988 for $3.2 billion.

UPI/CORBIS-BETTMANN

In an Oct. 12, 1987, interview with Fortune *magazine, Walter Annenberg explains the reason for philanthropy:*

'Like pigs in the slaughterhouse'

Capitalists have a fundamental responsibility to operate with respect for the citizenry. If we get too greedy, we're going to end up like pigs in the slaughterhouse.

John S. Knight

1894–1981

After inheriting the Akron, Ohio, *Beacon-Journal* in 1933, John S. Knight buys *The Miami Herald,* flagship of his newspaper group. Knight doesn't like the phrase "newspaper chain" because that implies links of iron, and "we try to maintain each paper's individuality." Valued are quality, leadership, independence. *Time* magazine calls the group, which later becomes Knight-Ridder, "the chain that doesn't bind."

In an April 9, 1967, Miami Herald *Pulitzer Prize–winning editorial, John S. Knight writes about two generations' views of war:*

A tale of two wars

If the young people of today are different from those of us who accepted the gauntlet without question, it is because they dare to investigate the causes of war and examine its immorality. Vietnam is no blithe adventure, nor is it being fought for a cause which all Americans can conscientiously defend.

Otis Chandler

1927–

In 1960, *Los Angeles Times* publisher Norman Chandler turns the conservative paper over to his 33-year-old son, Otis. The younger Chandler's response: "Wow!" Under his 25-year stewardship, the *Times* grows into a giant, with a 50-person Washington bureau and sterling foreign press corps. It forms the cornerstone of one of the nation's largest media companies, Times Mirror Corp.

THE ASSOCIATED PRESS

In a Poynter Institute oral history, Otis Chandler describes the public's perception of media giants:

'Do ... good or evil'

A media corporation probably has an unduly amount of impact, much greater than its size. ... Many, many people — politicians, educators, people of all walks of life — they look at a large company that owns televisions and newspapers and magazines and books, and are astounded at the so-called opportunity you have to do either good or evil.

Jann Wenner

1946–

In 1967, 20-year-old college dropout Jann Wenner borrows $7,500 to start *Rolling Stone,* the first national magazine dedicated to rock 'n' roll culture. "Rock 'n' roll," Wenner says, "is now the energy core in American life." *Rolling Stone* moves from San Francisco to New York, but doesn't lose its irreverence for politics. By the 1990s, Wenner's media empire — including a whole group of magazines — is worth $200 million.

On the fourth anniversary of Rolling Stone, *Jann Wenner writes:*

'Bills to pay'

As long as there are printing bills to pay, writers who want to earn a living by their craft, people who pay for their groceries, want to raise children and have their own homes, *Rolling Stone* will be a capitalistic operation.

Katharine Graham

1917–

Washington Post president Katharine Graham, one of the first women to run a major media company, makes her newspaper a powerhouse. In 1972, Attorney General John Mitchell threatens her, saying she'll "get her tit caught in a big fat wringer" if the *Post* reveals Watergate illegalities. The story runs. Mitchell goes to prison. Graham's friends give her a necklace that features a small gold breast and a wringer. She tells the story in her biography, which in 1998 wins a Pulitzer Prize.

THE ASSOCIATED PRESS

Katharine Graham, on Oct. 5, 1994, looks back on Watergate:

'The best years'

It was exactly like wading into a river and finding yourself waist deep and choosing to go forward, not back. There's really not much choice. ... Was I scared of what the administration could and did do to us? Of course I was. They were attacking us daily and cutting off our White House sources. I consider I had one of the great privileges of our profession to be there in those times that were, perhaps, the best years for the news business.

Oprah Winfrey

1954–

In 1986, Oprah Winfrey becomes the first African-American woman to host a national TV talk show. Within just a few years, she's one of the richest and most powerful women in entertainment history. Borrowing talk-TV pioneer Phil Donahue's format, *The Oprah Winfrey Show* adds her frank but earthy interview style and goes on to alter daytime TV. She calls her show "a ministry." By the 1990s, she can put a book on the best-seller list just by mentioning it.

THE ASSOCIATED PRESS

In an August 1987 interview with Essence *magazine, Oprah Winfrey reflects on her success:*

'Bridges I crossed'

I am where I am because of the bridges that I crossed. Sojourner Truth was a bridge. Harriet Tubman was a bridge. Ida B. Wells was a bridge. Madame C.J. Walker was a bridge. Fannie Lou Hamer was a bridge.

Michael Eisner

1942–

In 1984, The Walt Disney Company is foundering. Profits are down. Enter Michael Eisner, new company chairman and CEO. He lures top executives, bolsters Disney's filmmaking, expands its theme parks. The result: one of the biggest corporate turnarounds in history. In 1995, Disney buys Capital Cities/ABC Inc., becoming the nation's second largest media company. Eisner's secret: "Don't try to second-guess the audience."

THE ASSOCIATED PRESS

In a 1987 interview with Parade *magazine, Michael Eisner talks about the entertainment business:*

'Stupid is just stupid'

To me, the familiar is boring, excessive violence is anti-social, and stupid is just stupid. In this business, the script is the base of the pyramid. I'd rather hire 10 good writers than one big name star. And it's self-defeating to be obsessed with any one star or director. If you can't get Steven Spielberg — well, there's another Spielberg coming of age in Columbus, Ohio, or someplace. (In 1995, on company growth, he adds: "I don't think we have too much power. What we have is enough size, enough leverage, to be able to afford to do quality programming.")

Sleuths

NEW YORK, 1903 —

CURL UP WITH THIS MONTH'S GREAT, GRIMY READ: Little oil men wrestle with John D. Rockefeller, who gets caught cheating in a real-life game of Monopoly. Or maybe you'd like to know about the crooked Minneapolis mayor who takes payoffs from gamblers, the deals recorded in a ledger and reprinted here for all to see.

This is *McClure's Magazine*, whose circulation soars to 500,000 with exposés on corrupt city government, squalid slums, dirty business practices, social ills that just keep oozing as America's cities struggle with unwieldy growth.

The investigating writers, sometimes working for months or years on a single story, earn loyal readers, personal fame, and a nickname that lives for generations: The Muckrakers.

President Theodore Roosevelt names them after the *Pilgrim's Progress* character, the Man with the Muckrake, who is so mired in the filth below that he can't see the heavens above. While Roosevelt means it as a put-down — poking around in other people's dirt is akin to moral depravity — the name takes on a certain cachet. Modern investigative reporters, hardly the same stripe of social reformer as their early counterparts, take pride in their link to the muckraking tradition of *McClure's* writers Lincoln Steffens, Ida Tarbell and friends.

Tarbell, who spends years ferreting out the court records and secret railroad logs that undo Rockefeller and Standard Oil, hates the "muckraker" name. For one thing, it draws to her door every radical reformer who ever wanted to level an attack on anything. Tarbell describes her role as "that of a journalist after the fact ... rarely that of a reformer, the advocate of a cause or a system." But the requests keep coming.

Lincoln Steffens, exposer of "shame" in turn-of-the-century cities, says he never set out to be one, but now that he is, his muckraking reminds him of his gardening, "when I lift a stone to expose a lot of sow bugs scuttling away for cover."

Muckrakers. Investigative reporters. News sleuths. Should they be seen, as they often are, as *reformers*, in effect, activists out to rid society of danger and the bad guys? Or should they be seen, as muckrakers often see themselves, more like scientific researchers — foraging through files, combing the fine print for the one fact, or the thousand facts, that will nail a story down? Is the news they bring "negative," or simply the harsh, objective truth?

For Nina Totenberg, National Public Radio investigative reporter, it's more of a science. She can spend months chasing a story, only to throw it all away when the hard evidence isn't there. "I've had more good stories ruined by facts," she says. For I. F. Stone, one of the few reporters to take on anti-Communist Sen. Joseph McCarthy in the 1950s, the job means activism. "For me," he says, "being a newspaperman was a cross between ... Hearst and Galahad, because you're always going and rescuing maidens in distress."

The famed Lincoln Steffens is labeled "a reformer," but calls himself a "graft philosopher" who conducts scientific studies on patterns in his reporting on government corruption: "Bribery is not a mere felony, but a ... process which was going on in all our cities," he says in his autobiography. "If I could trace it to its source, I might find the cause of political corruption and — the cure. But first, to make sure that the process was identical everywhere, I must go and make a study of the police corruption of Minneapolis, to compare it with that of New York."

For author Jessica Mitford, whom *Time* dubs "Queen of the Muckrakers" in the 1960s, the job is one part science, one part activism, and one part good old-fashioned hell-raising: "I just don't like people who do rotten things."

A strange thing happens to American muckraking in the 1970s, when *Washington Post* reporters Bob Woodward and Carl Bernstein help topple the president of the United States.

In the wake of the story known as Watergate, staff

— Courtesy Mrs. Celia Gilbert/Max Reid photo

Above: I. F. Stone uses this magnifying glass to pore over several newspapers daily.

and cabinet members in Richard M. Nixon's White House end up in jail. Nixon himself becomes the first president in U.S. history to resign in disgrace. Woodward and Bernstein survive "negative reporter" smears and ride their revelations all the way to a Pulitzer Prize, becoming folk heroes on a scale early muckrakers never could have imagined.

Lost in the Hollywood of it all is the real story behind muckraking — that it is a tedious, thankless pursuit filled with endless locked files, slammed phones, closed doors, accusations of bias, threats of lawsuits and, finally, time and money requirements so high that many newspapers, many reporters, don't even try.

And when they do, it is hardly glamorous.

"It's probably not all that nice," says Seymour Hersh, who uncovers the My Lai massacre and other major stories. "Look what I do for a living. I expose things."

Jessica Mitford on the muckraker's choice of topic: "One does by far one's best work when besotted by and absorbed in the matter at hand. ... I could not warm up to hearing aids as a subject for the kind of thorough, intensive, long-range research that would be needed to do an effective job."

Bob Woodward on Watergate: "Truth *emerges* ... it often takes a great deal of time to assemble those facts, to get a clear picture."

And Carl Bernstein, the other half of the "Woodstein" duo: "We knocked on doors, we talked to people at the bottom, which is to say secretaries and file clerks rather than starting at the top ... there was nothing glamorous about it."

The penalty for shortcuts: Your story is wrong. Be wary, warns longtime Chicago newsman Edward H. Eulenberg: "If your mother says she loves you, check it out."

Add to the tediousness what columnist Jack Anderson calls "an inconstant public sentiment" that the work you do is "of some vague use to society."

As the 20th century dawns, Ida Tarbell is treated as a hero in oil country, Tulsa, Okla., when her investigation of Standard Oil results in antitrust laws. Citizens send a 40-piece band and throw her a parade.

But there are no parades when *Mother Jones*, the muckraking magazine founded in the mid-1970s "to raise hell," exposes sometimes-fatal explosions in rear-end collisions of the Ford Pinto, resulting in more than a million cars being recalled.

Does muckraking, Jessica Mitford wonders, "lead to reforms that merely gloss over the basic flaws of society?"

Does it matter? Or is the story itself enough? "That's what motivates good reporters, I think. Pursuit," says

> 'That's what motivates good reporters, I think. Pursuit.'
>
> — MIKE WALLACE

Mike Wallace of *60 Minutes*. "Most reporters I know are professional skeptics in any case, and so investigation comes with the territory. How much investigation you are drawn to, or are willing to get bogged down in, separates the Woodsteins from the rest."

I. F. Stone calls the work "the best in America's traditions ... in a line that reached back to Jefferson."

And Rachel Carson, whose book *Silent Spring* exposes pesticide pollution, speaks for legions of muckrakers when she says she is bound by a "solemn obligation" to try.

To fail? Always possible.

But not to try? Says Carson: "I could never again be happy in nature."

Ida Tarbell

1857–1944

Ida Minerva Tarbell watches one of John D. Rockefeller's companies force her father out of the oil business. In *McClure's*, Tarbell reveals Rockefeller's ruthless monopolistic practices in *The History of the Standard Oil Company.* The magazine series leads to new antitrust laws. Tarbell is called a muckraker, but doesn't like it. She sees herself as a historian, not a crusader.

LIBRARY OF CONGRESS

Ida Tarbell on muckraking and objectivity:

'Historical study'

I had hoped that the [Standard Oil] book might be received as a legitimate historical study, but to my chagrin I found myself included in a new school. ... This classification of muckraker, which I did not like, helped fix my resolution to have done for good and all with the subject which had brought it on me. But events are stronger than I. All the radical reforming element ... were begging me to join their movements. I soon found that most of them wanted attacks. They had little interest in balanced findings. Now I was convinced that in the long run the public they were trying to stir would weary of vituperation, that if you were to secure permanent results the mind must be convinced.

Lincoln Steffens

1866–1936

Investigative reporter Lincoln Steffens is the best known of the dirt-digging muckrakers. In *McClure's Magazine*, Steffens reveals government corruption in Minneapolis, Philadelphia, St. Louis and elsewhere. His *Shame of the Cities* series aims to spread the "shameful facts" that will "set fire to American pride" and spark reform. He succeeds.

UNIVERSITY OF CALIFORNIA ARCHIVES, BERKELEY

Lincoln Steffens from one of The Shame of the Cities *series titled "Philadelphia: Corrupt and Contented":*

'A disgrace'

Disgraceful? Other cities say so. But I say that if Philadelphia is a disgrace, it is a disgrace not to itself alone, nor to Pennsylvania, but to the United States and to American character. For this great city, so highly representative in other respects, is not behind in political experience, but ahead. ... Philadelphia is a city that has had its reforms. ... The present condition of Philadelphia, therefore, is not that which precedes, but that which follows reforms, and in this distinction lies its startling significance.

Jacob Riis

1849–1914

A Danish immigrant named Jacob Riis becomes an early crusader to clean up New York's slums. A police reporter for the New York *Sun,* Riis turns his investigations into an 1890 book, *How the Other Half Lives.*
His writings are full of stereotypes — "swarthy" Italians is a mild example. But his exposé prompts nationwide reforms. Theodore Roosevelt calls Riis "New York's most useful citizen."

Jacob Riis describes turn-of-the-century New York in How the Other Half Lives:

'A little careful'

Suppose we look into one [tenement]. ... Be a little careful please! The hall is dark, and you might stumble over the children pitching pennies back there. Not that it would hurt them; kicks and cuffs are their daily diet. They have little else. Here where the hall turns and dives into utter darkness is a step, and another, another. A flight of stairs. You can feel your way if you cannot see it. ... The sinks are in the hallway, that all the tenants may have access — and all be poisoned alike by their summer stenches.

Carr Van Anda

1864–1945

Managing editor Carr Van Anda leads *The New York Times* to new heights. In 1923, Van Anda reveals the murder of ancient Egypt's King Tut by spotting forged hieroglyphics in a photo. He catches a math mistake that Albert Einstein makes during a lecture. Envy the editor, Van Anda says, because he decides what "the world will see at the breakfast table."

NEW YORK TIMES PICTURES

Though Carr Van Anda is a managing editor, he maintains a night editor's schedule:

'Never dull'

The man most to be envied is the night editor. The night editor's work, always of world wide scope, is never dull. He is the appraiser of events. He is the keeper of a St. Peter's Ledger of the news of the day. To him the excellence of a newspaper is due. He can make it or mar it. The night editor passes finally on every item. He is the retriever of errors and must always be on the lookout for shortcomings and neglected opportunities. He should be keen, alert and well-informed. He must be sympathetic, imaginative, human. As he sits quietly reading proof slips, it is he who is framing the reflection of itself the world will see at the breakfast table. When you have achieved this post you have reached the highest place in your profession.

I. F. Stone

1907–1989

Son of a Russian immigrant, Isador Feinstein Stone becomes a liberal legend at his one-man *I.F. Stone's Weekly.* With a magnifying glass, he scours newspapers and official reports, exposing cover-ups like the Atomic Energy Commission's attempt to hide underground nuclear testing. Before that, he reports for *The Philadelphia Inquirer,* the *New York Post* and *The Nation.* Conservatives attack him as everything from a Communist propagandist to KGB agent. Stone hopes to live long enough to "graduate from a pariah to a character, and then ... a public institution." He does.

UPI/CORBIS-BETTMANN

I. F. Stone analyzes the meaning of President Kennedy's assassination in the Dec. 9, 1963, issue of I.F. Stone's Weekly:

'Murder in their hearts'

The first problem that has to be faced is the murder itself: Whether it was done by a crackpot leftist on his own, or as the tool of some rightist plot ... the fact is there are hundreds of thousands in the South who had murder in their hearts for the Kennedys ... because they sought in some degree to help the Negro.

Rachel Carson
1907–1964

Biologist and science writer Rachel Carson brings world attention to "the chain of evil" of the earth's pollution in her 1962 book, *Silent Spring.* Magazines reject *Silent Spring* for fear of losing advertisers. The chemical industry tries to block it. "There would be no peace for me if I kept silent," Carson says. Her groundbreaking exposé leads to bans on certain pesticides and herbicides, and helps create the environmental movement.

LIBRARY OF CONGRESS

An excerpt from Silent Spring:

'Chain of evil'

The most alarming of all man's assaults upon the environment is the contamination of air, earth, rivers, and sea with dangerous and even lethal materials. This pollution is for the most part irrecoverable; the chain of evil it initiates not only in the world that must support life but in living tissues is for the most part irreversible. In this now universal contamination of the environment, chemicals are the sinister and little-recognized partners of radiation in changing the very nature of the world — the very nature of its life.

Seymour M. Hersh
1937–

Free-lancer Seymour M. Hersh makes his name with a story no one wants to print. In 1969, Hersh reveals the My Lai massacre: A U.S. Army officer is charged with ordering 109 Vietnamese civilians killed — "hard news," says Hersh, and "written as such." But only tiny Dispatch News Service will buy and distribute the story that eventually wins journalism's top honors and helps sway a nation against a war. Later, for *The New York Times,* Hersh uncovers widespread FBI wiretaps and illegal domestic CIA snooping.

UPI/CORBIS-BETTMANN

Seymour M. Hersh describes the My Lai massacre in his 1972 book, Cover-Up:

'Macabre forms of murder'

Within weeks the operation had degenerated and the pilots, instead of "snatching" civilians, were deliberately killing them sometimes by running them down with their helicopter skids. Other pilots devised even more macabre forms of murder, including a process in which a lasso was used to stop a Vietnamese peasant attempting to flee.

Jessica Mitford

1917–1996

Jessica Mitford inspires a generation of inquisitive reporters with her 1963 exposé of the funeral industry, *The American Way of Death.* After her investigation, some mortuaries reform their "hard-sell" practices of pushing high-priced funerals on grieving relatives. Born a British aristocrat, she chronicles the U.S. prison system, U.S. birth practices and her own life as social reformer and early Communist. "Enemies," she says, "are as important as friends in my life."

UPI/CORBIS-BETTMANN

Jessica Mitford comments on the funeral industry in her book Poison Penmanship:

'Cheap funerals'

In England, the name Mitford is no doubt associated ... with my sister Nancy's novels and biographies. In America ... our name has suddenly become synonymous with cheap funerals. ... At a New York cocktail party a woman related her conversation with the undertaker. ... "We want the plainest and the least expensive funeral available," whereupon he replied, "Oh, you mean the Mitford style?"

Bob Woodward

1943–

He may not like it, but he's a celebrity. *Washington Post* reporter Bob Woodward is one of America's most famous newspaper journalists. After he co-reports the Watergate scandal stories that lead to President Richard Nixon's downfall, Woodward stays at the *Post* as an editor, writing books about the Supreme Court and the CIA. Journalism is "increasingly too superficial," he says. "If stories are underreported ... or not passed through the powerful instincts of a great editor, we'll become irrelevant to readers."

THE ASSOCIATED PRESS

Bob Woodward's relationship with his mysterious anonymous source, Deep Throat, is explained in his 1974 book, All the President's Men, *written with Carl Bernstein:*

'Strong-arm takeover'

His friendship with Deep Throat was genuine, not cultivated. Long before Watergate, they had spent many evenings talking about Washington, the government, power. On evenings such as those, Deep Throat had talked about how politics had infiltrated every corner of government — a strong-arm takeover of the agencies by the Nixon White House.

Carl Bernstein

1944–

THE ASSOCIATED PRESS

In 1973, Washington Post *Managing Editor Howard Simons nominates his reporters for a Pulitzer Prize:*

'To report and to be right'

Carl Bernstein and Robert Woodward worked against enormous odds — secrecy; implicit Administration intimidation of potential sources; explicit verbal attack upon the reporters' credibility and that of the newspaper, its owner, and its editors. But in spite of the attacks, subtle and blatant; in spite of carefully worded denials; in spite of a silent majority in the rest of the media, Bernstein and Woodward continued to investigate and to report and to be right. ... "Watergate," as a euphemism, is now more than just wiretapping and breaking and entering. It is political espionage and sabotage, reaching into the highest echelons of government. And it was *The Washington Post,* Bernstein and Woodward ... who brought this to the American attention and the American conscience.

Jack Anderson

1922–

Pulitzer Prize–winning investigator Jack Anderson exposes political corruption in his syndicated columns. He ridicules J. Edgar Hoover's investigative methods by rummaging through the FBI director's trash and publishing the findings. Presidents don't like Anderson. "Only the press," he says, "can stand as a true bulwark against an executive branch with a monopoly on foreign policy information." Editors and publishers don't always like him, either: "They usually belong in the same social world as the people we're exposing."

THE ASSOCIATED PRESS

Jack Anderson's Pulitzer Prize–winning column reveals that the United States is headed for a showdown with India because President Richard Nixon favors Pakistan in the developing India-Pakistan war:

'The hush-hush group'

The President has made no attempt to hide his favoritism for Pakistan. ... Mr. Nixon has ordered his crisis team, known formally as the Washington Special Action Group, to find ways short of direct intervention to help Pakistan. The hush-hush group, headed by presidential policymaker Henry Kissinger, has been meeting almost daily in the White House's fabled secret Situation Room.

Dave Mitchell

1943–

Cathy Mitchell

1944–

In 1975, Dave and Cathy Mitchell buy the ailing *Point Reyes Light,* weekly circulation 1,700, "convinced we would make it *The New York Times* of West Marin," California. Their investigation of Synanon, a drug rehabilitation center turned "corporate cult," wins the 1979 Pulitzer Prize. Dave says the *Light* "would not be afraid of angering readers, only of boring them." They sell the newspaper. Later, Dave returns; Cathy goes on to teach.

THE ASSOCIATED PRESS

Dave and Cathy Mitchell describe Synanon in their book, The Light on Synanon — How a Country Weekly Exposed a Corporate Cult — and Won the Pulitzer Prize:

The 'punk squad'

The children were often led to believe they were going to an avant-garde program in which they would enjoy life in the country. ... Many were shocked by what they found. Synanon placed juvenile newcomers in a "punk squad" more military than avant-garde. The children learned it would be months, if not years, before they could enjoy such pleasures as horseback riding.

Mike Wallace

1918–

Mike Wallace tries radio, quiz shows and adventure shows before discovering, on a TV program called *Night Beat,* his rare talent. Wallace can ask the tough questions. By 1968, he's a founding co-editor of *60 Minutes,* pioneering investigative reporting on TV. After an investigation clears Coors of discrimination allegations, the beer company runs a full-page ad with the headline: "The Four Most Dreaded Words in the English Language: MIKE WALLACE IS HERE."

CBS, INC.

From a 1976 Mike Wallace interview on 60 Minutes about a clinical lab in Chicago running Medicaid kickback operations (filmed through a one-way mirror):

'I heard you right here'

LAB REP: Well — wait a minute. You look familiar to me.

WALLACE: Yeah. Tell me something: How much in the way of kickbacks and rebates do you get involved with, and why?

LAB REP: I — I don't give — I don't give kickbacks.

WALLACE: You just — I heard you right here. You offered 25 percent in a rebate to these two gentlemen.

LAB REP: Well, I — I didn't mean it that way. I think I better not say anything now.

Ed Bradley

1941–

When Ed Bradley goes to a job interview, he goes prepared. In 1967, he gets a job at WCBS in New York by grabbing a tape recorder and going out into the streets to report a story. Bradley becomes one of the most successful African-American TV journalists. He joins the CBS network as a reporter in 1971, covering Vietnam, the 1976 presidential race and the White House. A lifetime of being prepared earns him a spot on the network's top-rated *60 Minutes*.

THE ASSOCIATED PRESS

In a Jan. 13, 1995, interview with the Palm Beach Post, *Ed Bradley talks about the success of* 60 Minutes:

'They'll learn something'

We don't live or die by the interview of the moment, the hot interview of the week. I think people feel on any Sunday they'll learn something. We don't always hit a home run, but we get on base every Sunday.

Edna Buchanan

1939–

Miami Herald police reporter Edna Buchanan becomes a celebrity with the gritty style she uses to cover Miami's underbelly. The one-time factory worker wins a Pulitzer Prize in 1986 for crime reporting. In her eyes, any good reporter is an investigative reporter. A typical Buchanan lead: " 'What are you going to do, kill me?' he asked, and handed her a gun. 'Here, kill me,' he challenged. She did."

An excerpt from Edna Buchanan's memoir, The Corpse Had a Familiar Face:

'Smell the blood ... hear the screams'

At a fresh murder scene you can smell the blood and hear the screams; years later, they still echo in my mind. Unsolved murders are unfinished stories. ... The face of Miami changes so quickly, but the dead stay that way. I feel haunted by the restless souls of those whose killers walk free.

Eugene Roberts

1932–

Even the owner of *The Philadelphia Inquirer* calls the newspaper "unqualifiedly awful" before Eugene Roberts is named editor in 1972. Roberts, a former top reporter, leads the newspaper to 17 Pulitzer Prizes, including one for exposing shortcomings in the nation's blood banks. "Take care of our communities by covering them well," Roberts says, "and they will take care of us." He returns to *The New York Times* as managing editor, then goes on to lead a national effort to promote quality journalism.

THE PHILADELPHIA INQUIRER

In a Spring 1996 Media Studies Journal *article, Gene Roberts talks about the future of newspapers:*

'Increasing profits'

With a few exceptions, the talk at the high levels of newspapers these days is of the increasing profits. ... To talk of increasing coverage or newshole or staff on most newspapers now would be tantamount to confessing lunacy. And that is a tragedy — because sound, readable, dependable news coverage *is* our future.

Donald L. Barlett

1936–

James B. Steele

1943–

As investigative reporters for *The Philadelphia Inquirer*, Donald Barlett and James Steele pore over roomfuls of documents to demystify complex issues. In their 26 years with the paper, they win two Pulitzer Prizes. What always amazes them, Steele says, "is how much is out there." Their 1991 series becomes the best-seller *America: What Went Wrong.* The book, which brings the reporters acclaim as Lincoln Steffens-caliber "muckrakers" for the '90s, describes a system run by "the lawmakers in Washington and the dealmakers on Wall Street," allowing the wealthy to flourish and the middle class to shrink. Critics dispute them, but the book influences the 1992 elections. In 1997 Barlett and Steele join Time, Inc.

THE ASSOCIATED PRESS

Donald Barlett and James Steele describe the American middle-class view of President George Bush's vaunted economic recovery, in America: What Went Wrong:

'Beyond your reach'

You might have a different view. Especially if you were one of the 74,000 workers destined to lose their jobs at General Motors. ... You might also have a different view if you are a member of America's disappearing middle class. ... And you especially might have a different view if you are one of the millions of Americans seeking to attain a middle-class status that you now find beyond your reach. But that's because you have a skewed vision. You are on the bottom rung looking up.

Those in charge, on the other hand, are on the top looking down. They see things differently. Call it the view from Washington and Wall Street.

CHAPTER 8

Barrier Breakers

> 'I owe my momma and daddy ... I owe Jackie Robinson ... the NAACP ... the black church ... the black press ... that's how I got to ABC.'
>
> — MAL GOODE

NEW YORK, 1918 —

AMERICAN WOMEN CAMPAIGN FOR THE RIGHT TO vote. They call for birth control, equal education and pay. They've been doing this now for 70 years. But big-city newspapers, as big as they are, don't cover the story well. The campaign is waged in small, specialized journals that give voice to the women that press giants ignore or consign to the fringe.

Editor-columnist Alice Stone Blackwell, for one, brings suffrage news to women for 35 years in *Woman's Journal,* a paper once edited by her famous mother, suf-

fragist Lucy Stone. *Woman's Journal* provides news to other papers. Blackwell herself writes it up, folds the envelopes and sends them off in the mail.

In 1920, the work pays off. The 19th Amendment grants women the right to vote. This gigantic political barrier didn't just break; it's worn down with small bumps and steps along the way, from the day in 1848 when women meet to start a movement in Seneca Falls, New York.

As a young girl in grammar school, Blackwell quivers delivering the valedictory address, but survives triumphant, and comes home to write a prescient line in her journal:

It's perhaps the first, but I don't mean it to be the last old fence I shall break through.

Barrier breakers are disparate folk from disparate worlds who share a common lot. They break through old fences. They forge new ideas. They push the boundaries, press the status quo, expand the horizons of news.

Sometimes, they are the very first, or at least the most visible first: The *first* woman foreign correspondent for a U.S. newspaper (Margaret Fuller, 1840s). The *first* African-American network newscaster (Mal Goode, early 1960s). The *first* successful "metro-burban" tabloid (Alicia Patterson's *Newsday*, 1940s). Yet the true contribution of the barrier breakers is the width of trail they make — wide enough so others may follow.

"The country's greatest achievements came about because somebody believed in something, whether it was in a steam engine, an airplane or a space shuttle," writes Robert C. Maynard, the first African American to own a major general-circulation newspaper, the *Oakland Tribune*. "Only when we lose hope in great possibilities are we really doomed. Reversals and tough times sometimes inspire people to work harder for what they believe in."

What K. W. Lee believes in, as founder of *Koreatown*, the first national Korean-American newspaper: "a need to make the invisible world visible."

Adds anchor-interviewer Barbara Walters, the first network anchor to earn a million dollars a year: "I didn't wave the flag and didn't burn my bra. I just kept on working and stayed close to women on and off the camera. ...

In retrospect, maybe having to prove myself saved me."

A century and a half before Walters and Maynard and Lee, in 1827, John B. Russwurm and Samuel Cornish co-found *Freedom's Journal*, the first African-American newspaper. The editorial in their maiden issue speaks for all manner of news barrier breaker:

Too long have others spoken for us.

What does it sound like to speak for oneself? It can sound like Margaret Fuller, who helps set up the Seneca Falls convention by explaining how men can't have it both ways:

Those who think the physical circumstances of Woman would make a part in the affairs of national government unsuitable, are by no means those who think it is impossible for negresses to endure field work, even during pregnancy.

Or like young editor Bernard Kilgore, who takes over the narrow-focus *Wall Street Journal* just after the Great Depression to create a true national newspaper by redefining what news is, and who an audience is:

If you are publishing in Elkhart, Indiana, you have got to edit for the Elkhart reader. The [national] business community is our Elkhart.

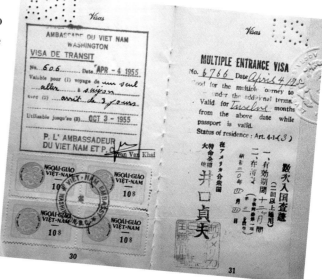

— Courtesy Carl Rowan/Max Reid photo

Above: Carl Rowan's passport isn't the only thing that takes him places.

Award-winning radio and TV correspondent John Hockenberry, reporting from a wheelchair after an accident leaves him a paraplegic, sometimes sees himself as a barrier, a bulky obstacle on oversized wheels blockading narrow spaces and checkout lines:

I could go away or push ahead. Going away was always a defeat.

Hockenberry mines "crip humor" because, as he tells it, disabled folks need to laugh and vent as much as anyone else:

In the crip world, there are jock jobs, crip jobs, and then there are real jobs. Jocks get a lot of attention in their sporty wheelchair basketball chairs or their tennis outfits. ... Crip jobs are "for crips." Like the little blind midget who sells magazines at the State Capitol building, or the taxi dispatcher in a wheelchair, these jobs are crip-designated. They are the "Oh, it's so nice that he has a job" jobs. ... Real jobs are ones that are not crip-designated, that take on humanity at large. Quad-riplegic lead dancer for the New York City Ballet. The armless pitcher. Deaf Beethoven, blind Stevie Wonder. If Helen Keller had been a waitress instead of a professional role model she could have qualified.

And this is Carl Rowan, the first African-American columnist distributed by a mainstream syndicate, about the path he hopes to tread:

There were virtually no Negro role models in any field of communications for a black youngster in 1946. No more than a handful of Negroes worked as reporters on white daily newspapers, and none was close to being a household name. The great magazines had no Negro staff editors and rarely ran anything written by a black person. Richard Wright had made a monumental breakthrough six years earlier when his Native Son *was published and again in 1945 when* Black Boy *came out. Still, most publishers were not clamoring for black authors. ... So what was I doing on this journey? I believed that I could change things.*

Then the voice of Randy Shilts, among the first openly gay reporters for major metropolitan newspapers, who pioneered AIDS reporting:

People died while scientists did not at first devote appropriate attention to the epidemic because they perceived little prestige to be gained in studying a homosexual affliction. ... People died and nobody paid attention because the mass media did not like covering stories about homosexuals and was especially skittish

> 'People died ... the mass media did not like covering stories about homosexuals.'
>
> — RANDY SHILTS

about stories that involved gay sexuality. Newspapers and television largely avoided discussion of the disease until the death toll was too high to ignore and the casualties were no longer just outcasts.

Tim Giago, Lakota Sioux founder and publisher of *Indian Country Today*, recalls Whitman when he hears America singing:

I read William Raspberry. I read Ellen Goodman. I read George Will. All of these opinions give you an idea of what America is all about. The Indian view ... should be included.

Says Margaret Fuller:

Let every arbitrary barrier be thrown down.

In 1962, not long after Mal Goode joins ABC-TV, the network receives a letter from a South Carolina viewer, who adds her voice to the mix:

I think that was a colored man I saw reporting all day long on the Cuban missile crisis. And although I am white, and although he is a colored man, I want to thank him and thank ABC because this is America, and that's the way it ought to be.

Mary Katherine Goddard

1738–1816

The quarrelsome William Goddard starts *The Providence Gazette, The Pennsylvania Chronicle* and *The Maryland Journal.* Each time he launches a newspaper, his mother, Sarah, and sister, Mary Katherine, have to step in to save it. Editor Isaiah Thomas singles out Mary Katherine as "an expert" in running colonial newspapers who has "ably conducted the printing house of her brother."

A statement credited to "Sarah Goddard and Company" from the first Providence Gazette, *Aug. 9, 1766:*

'For the benefit of mankind'

The former Printer has left us an elegant and complete Assortment of Materials and Utensils of every Kind, necessary for that Use [printing a newspaper]; not only that a moderate Family, with whom he is connected, might be supported by it, but for the Benefit of Mankind in general.

John B. Russwurm

1799–1851

John B. Russwurm is the second African American to graduate from a U.S. college — Bowdoin. In 1827, he and Samuel Cornish start the first African-American newspaper, *Freedom's Journal,* in New York. Russwurm wants black people to return to Africa. Cornish disagrees. The dispute kills the newspaper. Russwurm edits the *Liberia Herald* in the African nation founded by former slaves.

On March 16, 1827, a statement of purpose in the first issue explains Freedom's Journal:

'Our own cause'

We wish to plead our own cause. Too long have others spoken for us. Too long has the publick been deceived by misrepresentations, in things which concern us dearly, though in the estimation of some mere trifles; for though there are many in society who exercise towards us benevolent feelings; still (with sorrow we confess it) there are others who make it their business to enlarge upon the least trifle, which tends to the discredit of any person of colour; and pronounce anathemas and denounce our whole body for the misconduct of this guilty one.

Samuel Cornish

c. 1790–c. 1859

Presbyterian minister Samuel Cornish campaigns against slavery in the newspaper he co-founds, *Freedom's Journal,* and later in *The Colored American.* "We were born free and equal," he says. "Let us contend for all the rights guaranteed to us by the Constitution of our native country." His themes — self-help, education and equality — influence future African-American leaders.

SCHOMBURG CENTER FOR RESEARCH IN BLACK CULTURE, NEW YORK PUBLIC LIBRARY

In the Feb. 18, 1837, Weekly Advocate, *Samuel Cornish explains why an African-American press is needed:*

'By and with us'

Coloured Americans must support, as an organ, their own [press] or never be free men. If our press live not and flourish not among us, and by and with us, we cannot live in America, neither morally, intellectually or civilly — we shall only stay.

Margaret Fuller

1810–1850

A feminist and a gifted writer, Margaret Fuller is the first female journalist hired by a major U.S. daily, the *New York Tribune*. Yet the literary critic and social-issue reporter doesn't actually go to the newspaper. She works out of Horace Greeley's home. Fuller's book, *Woman in the Nineteenth Century,* starts a national drive for women's rights. In 1846, she reports from Europe as America's first female foreign correspondent. Returning, she drowns with her husband and two-year-old son in a shipwreck off Fire Island.

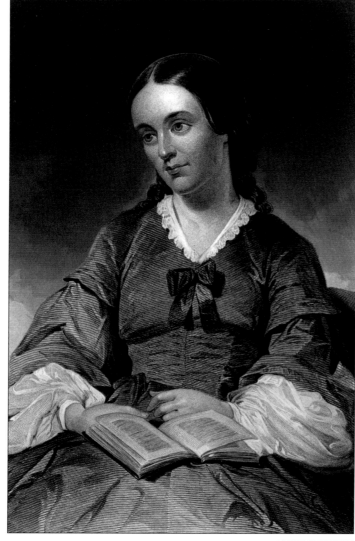

LIBRARY OF CONGRESS

Margaret Fuller writes from Italy in the Jan. 22, 1848, New York Tribune:

'Lured into combat'

This morning came the details of infamous attempts by the Austrian police to exasperate the students of Pavia. The way is to send persons to smoke cigars in forbidden places, who insult those who are obliged to tell them to desist. These traps seem particularly shocking when laid for fiery and sensitive young men. They succeeded: the students were lured into combat, and a number left dead and wounded on both sides. The University is shut up; the inhabitants of Pavia and Milan have put on mourning; even at the theater they wear it. The Milanese will not walk in that quarter where the blood of their fellow-citizens has been so wantonly shed. They have demanded a legal investigation of the conduct of the officials.

Alice Stone Blackwell

1857–1950

For 35 years, Alice Stone Blackwell edits the *Woman's Journal,* America's leading women's rights newspaper. "Make the world better," her mother tells her, and she does. Alice takes over editing the weekly *Journal* from her mother, Lucy Stone, and devotes it totally to the campaign that ultimately brings women the right to vote. That job done, Blackwell retires from the *Journal* to crusade for racial equality and against fascism.

LIBRARY OF CONGRESS

In an 1879 letter to a friend, Alice Stone Blackwell describes her mother, Lucy Stone:

'Heavy load'

It is a heavy load for poor Mamma — the *Journal* every week, the general supervision of the suffrage cause in Massachusetts, and the care of this big place, indoors and out — planning what we are to eat three times a day. ... I should think she would go cracked; but she ... shows no sign of breaking down.

Kyutaro Abiko

1865–1936

Many see Japanese immigrants as visitors earning money to send home. Not Kyutaro Abiko. His *Nichibei Shimbun* urges the "issei" to establish roots as U.S. citizens. Abiko fights immigration limits, prodding the "nisei" — second-generation Japanese Americans — to build bridges between the two cultures. In the 1920s, sales of his San Francisco Japanese-language daily top 25,000. After Abiko's death, his wife, Yonako, keeps it going. In 1942, the U.S. closes the paper and whisks Japanese Americans into relocation camps. But after World War II, the *Nichibei Times* appears, edited by Kyutaro's son, Yasuo Abiko.

SAN FRANCISCO PUBLIC LIBRARY

In a speech (c. 1909), Kyutaro Abiko talks about Japanese immigration to the United States:

'People who misunderstand'

Among the Americans, there are people who misunderstand the Japanese, and who think that the Japanese live on a low level, and are laborers who are satisfied with low wages. This is a misunderstanding. Naturally, while the Japanese are in Japan, they eat poorly and are satisfied with low salaries, but when they go to the United States and adapt, the Japanese will only accept high wages, and their standard of living becomes higher. There is also the point that white laborers greatly profit as a result of the Japanese immigrating and performing certain types of work.

If these circumstances were researched, it would completely eliminate such misunderstandings. ... Among certain scholars, there are people who say that the culture of Japan and their own culture do not agree, but there is no race that can assimilate easier than the Japanese ... instead of excluding the Japanese immigrants, the day is coming when they will be welcomed.

W.E.B. DuBois

1868–1963

In 1910, Harvard-educated sociologist W.E.B. DuBois founds *The Crisis,* a magazine of African-American news, opinion and literature. His editorials attack the Ku Klux Klan and oppose discrimination in housing, education, the military and elsewhere. The magazine's name, he says, reflects that this is "a critical time" in history. The magazine represents an organization DuBois co-founds, the NAACP.

UPI/CORBIS-BETTMANN

W.E.B. DuBois' statement of purpose in The Crisis:

'Critical time in history'

[To] set forth those facts and arguments which show the danger of race prejudice, particularly as manifested today toward colored people. It takes its name from the fact that the editors believe that this is a critical time in the history of the advancement of men.

Mary Baker Eddy

1821–1910

In 1908, Mary Baker Eddy starts *The Christian Science Monitor* as an alternative to the era's sensational dailies. The newspaper plays down violence and sex in favor of news analysis. Under Eddy (founder in 1879 of the Church of Christ, Scientist), The *Monitor* pioneers solution-seeking journalism, its circulation growing to more than 200,000. Its credo: "To injure no man, but to bless all mankind."

NEW YORK PUBLIC LIBRARY/THE ASSOCIATED PRESS

Mary Baker Eddy tells her readers how The Christian Science Monitor *fits in with her general publishing scheme, in the editorial in the first edition of* The Christian Science Monitor, *Nov. 25, 1908:*

'To spread ... the Science'

I have given the name to all the Christian Science periodicals. The first was the *Christian Science Journal*, designed to put on record the divine Science of Truth; the second I entitled *Sentinel*, intended to hold guard over Truth, Life and Love; the third, *Der Herold der Christian Science*, to proclaim the universal activity and availability of Truth; the next I named *Monitor*, to spread undivided the Science that operates unspent.

Ignacio E. Lozano

1886–1953

Press visionary Ignacio E. Lozano starts the Spanish-language daily *La Prensa* in 1913 with $1,200. Lozano's San Antonio–based newspaper dominates the Latino market in the Southwest, reaching even into his native Mexico. In 1926, he expands by launching Los Angeles–based *La Opinión*, the nation's second longest-lived Spanish-language daily after New York's *El Diario La Prensa*.

LA OPINION ARCHIVES

In a June 19, 1913, address, Ignacio Lozano promotes newspaper independence:

'Government funded newspapers'

Do not read a government funded newspaper, because its news will be influenced by the funds it receives from the government ... by practicing a form of journalism which seeks to twist its public's criteria. Also, do not read a newspaper that is openly anti-government because its news is equally misleading and almost always inspired by spite.

Claude A. Barnett

1889–1967

Chicago Defender reporter Claude A. Barnett starts the Associated Negro Press in 1919, a news service that serves major black newspapers. His vision: "a well-trained correspondence man in every strategic part of the country whose sole business it would be to get news to us." Starting with 80 subscribers, ANP reaches 112 by 1945. By 1959, it includes subscribers in Africa. But the 1960s bring competing news services, and ANP fades away.

CHICAGO HISTORICAL SOCIETY

Claude A. Barnett describes the mission of the Associated Negro Press in a 1920 testimony before the Chicago Commission on Race Relations:

'National importance'

We handle only items that are of national importance because we are a national news service. ... If there is anything that affects the interests of the country at large, which also has an indirect or direct influence on our group, we feature it, but as a rule, most of the news we gather is about things which particularly affect colored people.

Lorena Hickok

1893–1968

THE ASSOCIATED PRESS

Lorena Hickok's story on the death of the baby of famed aviator Charles Lindbergh, published in the May 13, 1932, New York Herald Tribune:

'No more hope'

The land where the baby was found is known as the "old John Van Dyke property" and is owned by St. Michael's Orphanage of Hopewell. The 500 children at the orphanage had been praying daily that the kidnapped child might be left unharmed at the door of the institution. In their anxiety to speed the return of the child, the orphans and the nuns in charge hurried to the orphanage steps every morning. This morning the children will learn there is no more hope that their prayers will be answered.

Alicia Patterson

1906–1963

Granddaughter of a *Chicago Tribune* publisher and daughter of a *New York Daily News* publisher, Alicia Patterson polishes her writing at *Liberty* magazine. In 1940 she creates the innovative *Newsday* on Long Island, N.Y. "Our first, second and final object," she writes, "is to present the news ... honestly." Patterson bucks trends. A Republican, she attacks Sen. Joseph McCarthy. Her newspaper features quality news in a tabloid format and metropolitan-style reporting in suburbia. *Newsday* booms.

UPI/CORBIS-BETTMANN

Alicia Patterson writes in the first edition of Newsday:

'Present the news'

Our first, second and final object is to present the news. That is why "Newsday" is our slogan as well as our name. If we present the news honestly, we know we will have readers. If we have readers, it will be profitable for advertisers to use our columns whether they agree with our policy or not.

Lisa Ben

1921–

Her pseudonym — Lisa Ben. The real name of the "founding mother" of the contemporary gay and lesbian press isn't publicly discussed. In 1947, she types out the first issue of her magazine for lesbians. The first carbon-copy "press run" of *Vice Versa:* 12 copies. Despite its small size, the magazine makes a heroic impact. "To every newspaper I ever read," she says, "we were the unspeakables." Unscrambled, her pen name, Lisa Ben, spells lesbian.

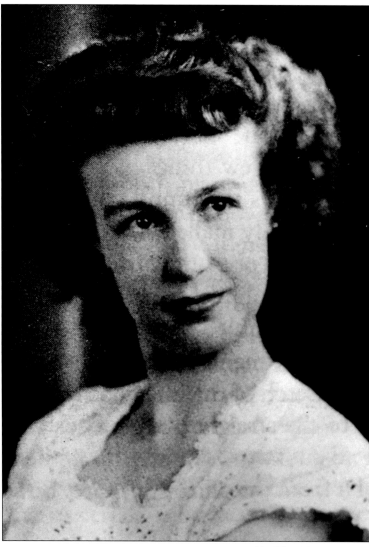

COURTESY RODGER STREITMATTER

In a c. 1948 article in Vice Versa, *Lisa Ben tells a tale of a homophobic drunk waking up in a world of gays and lesbians:*

'Call the cops!'

Harry Runk suddenly felt himself spun around. ... An irate girl with jet black hair and flaming green eyes faced him. "I heard what you called my friend. Take that, you unspeakable outrage of nature!" Runk picked himself up off the floor. Two husky ladies in skin-tight bolero suits pinioned his arms to his sides. "Somebody call the cops!" shrilled one.

Mal Goode

1908–1995

The grandson of slaves, Mal Goode is hired by ABC in 1962 as the nation's first African-American network television reporter. "There was never a day," he says, "that something didn't come up and remind me I was black." Executives give Goode out-of-the-office assignments — such as covering the United Nations — because they fear the white staff and visitors in the main studio will object to his presence there. Goode becomes a role model for people of color in broadcasting.

CAPITAL CITIES/ABC, INC.

In an October 1986 address to the National Black Media Coalition, Mal Goode talks about his road to success:

'Fight isn't over'

I owe my momma and daddy, who are in the grave. I owe Jackie Robinson. I owe the NAACP. I owe the black church. I owe the black press ... I owe them. That's how I got to ABC. I didn't get there by myself. ... The fight isn't over by a long shot.

Bernard Kilgore

1908–1967

Editor Bernard Kilgore turns the staid *Wall Street Journal* into the country's biggest newspaper and a national institution. Circulation soars from 33,000 in 1941, when he becomes managing editor, to 1.1 million by 1967. Kilgore's secret? Clear writing. "If I see 'upcoming' slip into the paper once again," he warns colleagues, "I'll be downcoming and someone will be outgoing."

Bernard Kilgore explains exchange rates in his "Dear George" column in The Wall Street Journal:

'Cheaper to ship the gold'

Dear George ... I told you foreign exchange rates — i.e., the value of one currency in terms of others — were determined within certain limits by supply and demand for foreign funds. These certain limits, in the case of currencies based on gold, are the points at which it becomes cheaper to ship the gold itself than to buy credit abroad.

Carl T. Rowan

1925–

In 1951, Carl T. Rowan exposes how the South has legalized bigotry in a *Minneapolis Tribune* series, "How Far From Slavery?" His goal: "to tell hard truths." Rowan breaks barriers all his life — as civil rights reporter, ambassador, head of the United States Information Agency, the first nationally syndicated African-American columnist. In the 1990s, when he discovers corruption in the NAACP, he's urged to cover it up. "I'll go to hell," he says, "before I'll accept that." Outside journalism, Rowan raises millions in "Project Excellence" scholarships for black students.

UPI/CORBIS-BETTMANN

Carl T. Rowan's first syndicated column in 1965 in the Chicago Daily News *begins:*

'I have come to inform'

I am a stranger on your doorstep today. Good manners require that I explain my presence and my purpose. I have come to inform, to provoke, to prod, to inspire — to become a factor in that great process through which the people of a democracy make the decisions that spell life or death for nations, and even civilizations.

K. W. Lee

1928–

COURTESY K.W. LEE

In the May 5, 1996, Sacramento Bee, K. W. Lee writes about the media's role in the riots that sweep South Central Los Angeles after the first Rodney King verdict acquits police officers of brutality:

'Into the Roman arena'

Even before Korean and African Americans had a chance to get to know each other through their common struggles and sorrows, both groups watched themselves tearing each other apart. ... Instead of fighting together their No. 1 tormentors — crime and poverty — they were dragged into the Roman arena [by] ... media managers in pursuit of ever higher ratings.

Barbara Walters

1931–

In 1976, ABC News offers popular NBC *Today* show host Barbara Walters an unheard-of million-dollar salary. She takes it — and becomes American TV's first regular network anchor-woman. (Later, she confides, "I would probably do this for much less.") Her pairing with Harry Reasoner doesn't last, but Walters becomes a celebrity with her evocative interviews on the magazine show *20/20*: "With the grace of God and a good lighting director, I plan to stick around for a good long time."

THE ASSOCIATED PRESS

Barbara Walters talks to Les Brown of The New York Times *in the newspaper's May 2, 1976, edition:*

I don't worry about being able to do the job at ABC but only whether people will accept a woman on the news at night, and whether they feel a woman can have the proper authority.

People tend to go to male doctors. We still have to learn whether they can accept the idea of going to a female. …

I know now that I'm totally professional and good at what I do. I may not be great at ABC, but I know I won't be terrible. This is the kind of confidence that men have always known but women are only just beginning to get. If I make it, there'll be other women in these anchor jobs all over the country. This was why I wanted Sally Quinn to succeed at CBS, but few people understood that.

Randy Shilts

1951–1994

San Francisco Chronicle reporter Randy Shilts is one of the first openly gay journalists at a major daily. In 1982, he reveals "baffling diseases hitting primarily gay men." His AIDS investigation leads to a newspaper series and a best-selling book, *And the Band Played On,* about bungled government attempts to deal with the disease. Shilts, too, is infected, but tells only friends: "I didn't want to end up being an activist. I wanted to keep on being a reporter."

JANET SILVA/ABC

Randy Shilts writes an early story about Acquired Immune Deficiency Syndrome in the May 13, 1982, San Francisco Chronicle:

'Baffling diseases'

"Every time I see a new spot I think I'm a step closer to death," said Jerry, a former waiter. "I don't even look in the mirror anymore." Jerry is a victim of one of a series of baffling diseases hitting primarily gay men. ... Scientists have lumped the various illnesses together under the acronym GRID — for gay-related immuno-deficiency diseases.

Tim Giago

1935–

Editor-publisher Tim Giago, a Lakota Sioux and press freedom champion, believes the Native-American press is not free because most papers are tribally owned. In 1981, he starts the *Lakota Times* (later, *Indian Country Today*) — the first successful independent Indian newspaper, and in his words, "the only way we are going to get a voice in America."

USA TODAY

In a 1993 editorial, Tim Giago celebrates Indian Country Today's *12 years of independent publication:*

'Powerful enemies'

News stories about corruption in tribal government, or challenging an organization that believed it was not accountable to the Indian people ... [have] made me several powerful enemies. ... For years a scandal sheet filled with filth about me made the rounds. ... If that is the price one must pay in order to bring freedom of the press to Indian country, then that is the price I must pay.

Bob Maynard

1937–1993

Nancy Maynard

1946–

Washington Post editorial writer Robert C. Maynard and *New York Times* reporter Nancy Hicks Maynard leave good jobs to co-found the Institute for Journalism Education and push for newsroom diversity. From 1983 to 1992, the Maynards are the first African Americans to own a major metropolitan daily, the *Oakland Tribune*. Revamped into "an instrument for community understanding," the newspaper wins hundreds of awards, including a Pulitzer Prize. "The country cannot be the country we want it to be if its story is told by only one group of citizens," Bob says. "Our goal is to give all Americans front-door access to the truth."

Nancy Hicks Maynard writes in the summer 1995 Media Studies Journal:

'The emerging world'

Those who interpret America's story everyday should reflect the demographic make-up of our society. But in a nation that grows browner by the day, those who report and edit the news are still overwhelmingly white. ... Now, opportunities for minority journalists are exploding ... in the emerging world of niche markets to serve a growing, educated population too often ignored in traditional mass media. ... Niche marketing takes away the need for sweeping generalizations about people based on great big numbers and no real facts. ... This boon for the market may result in lousy social policy if it causes enclaves to dominate our political structure to the exclusion of a common national vision.

John Hockenberry

1956–

In 1980, a report on the Mount St. Helens eruption by free-lancer John Hockenberry leads the news on National Public Radio. His editors call his reports "incredible stuff." Only when he misses a deadline do his editors learn that his legs have been paralyzed since a car accident at age 19. The problem? He couldn't fit his wheelchair into a phone booth. Hockenberry's 1995 memoir *Moving Violations* describes his award-winning journalistic adventures. "I like being on the edge of change," he says. In 1996, Hockenberry joins NBC, and later gets his own show on MSNBC.

THE ASSOCIATED PRESS

In Moving Violations, *John Hockenberry talks about covering the Palestinian uprising:*

'Plenty of ramps'

I had been assured that Israel would be more accessible than most places. The Arab-Israeli wars had produced thousands of crips, American Jews told me. I would find Israel with plenty of ramps. The geopolitical barbarity that had made Israeli society terrified and bellicose for much of its existence was supposed to make me feel right at home.

Photographers

NEW YORK, 1928 —

The tabloids are at war. The *Evening Graphic* races ahead with front-page "composographs" — made-up photos of such scenes as Caruso meeting Valentino in heaven. But the *Daily News* finds something better — reality. When Ruth Snyder is strapped into Sing Sing's electric chair, photographer Tom Howard is there. Secretly, he lifts his pant leg and takes a picture with a hidden ankle-camera. The *Daily News* sells a million extra newspapers with "the most sensational picture in the history of photojournalism." A few years later, the *Evening Graphic* is dead.

Flash back to another war, the Civil War. Alexander Gardner walks the field near Gettysburg. He unloads a big box camera from his wagon, its shutter speed so slow he can photograph only the dead. Gardner drags a Confederate soldier's body 40 yards into better light. He sets it behind a rock wall. He places a spent artillery shell near it, arranges a rifle across its legs, keeps a dismembered hand vividly out front. This is "Home of a Rebel Sharpshooter," Gardner's most celebrated photo, showing the "dreadful details" symbolizing the "fearful struggle," complete with fictitious caption.

Is seeing believing? Yes, says Oliver Wendell Holmes, looking at Civil War photographs in Mathew Brady's New York gallery. "Let him who wishes to know what war is, look at these."

Flash to another war, another place: 1945, Dachau, Germany. The outside world understands nothing of the horrors as Lee Miller steels herself to photograph the just-liberated concentration camps of World War II. Holocaust victims, little more than skeletal corpses stacked in bunks, die even as she focuses the lens. Her work awakens the world with stark, undeniable images projecting a power far beyond words. "I implore you to believe this is true," she cables her *Vogue* magazine editors. They do.

The elusive goal of the photojournalist: proving the unthinkable true. But often, truth is in the eye of the photographer. "Utter truth is essential," says Margaret Bourke-White, who flies in fighter planes to find it. *Life*'s W. Eugene Smith, father of the photo-essay, calls his truth "perspective that penetrates the superficial." And Gardner's posed Civil War pictures? Says his one-time boss, Mathew Brady, "Accepted by posterity with an undoubting faith." Since the first photo published in a newspaper — "direct from nature," in the *New York Daily Graphic*, 1873 — editors have praised the realism of photojournalism. But for Gordon Parks, the camera is a tool, like a pen, like a paintbrush — "my weapon against poverty and racism." Parks worries about being caught up in "the anguish of objectivity." At Martin Luther King, Jr.'s funeral, Moneta J. Sleet, Jr., the first African-American photographer to win a Pulitzer Prize, has no doubt of his role: "I wasn't there as an objective reporter. I had something to say. My mission was ... to show the side that was the right side."

Some photojournalists are driven by the adventure, some by the story, others by a sense of right and wrong. "Our work is a never-ending source of inspiration," says David Turnley. "You're on the stage, along with the actors," points out James Nachtwey, making a "connection on a human level." Chasing murder and mayhem through New York's night streets, Weegee sums it up: "It's exciting. It's dangerous. It's funny. It's tough. It's heartbreaking. It tears the guts right out of you. But I love it." And it doesn't hurt for a photojournalist to be as brash as early Hollywood photographer George Watson, who yells to the king of Belgium: "Hey, king, take off your hat!" For an instant, the king did just that.

The one look, the perfect moment, the serendipitous, split-second confluence of subject, light, shadow; camera, shooter, history; the right place, the right time — this is a photojournalist's quest.

— Newseum/Max Reid photo

Inset: George Watson snaps Hollywood's rising stars with this camera.

Eddie Adams, of The Associated Press, presses the shutter precisely when a bullet fired by a South Vietnamese policeman smashed into the head of a captured Viet Cong terrorist. "I thought he was going to threaten him," Adams recalls of the microsecond. "When he fired, I fired." It is a moment, Adams will say later, "that ruined that guy's life. ... I'm sorry I took the picture. I don't like talking about that picture."

And the AP's Joe Rosenthal — anticipation spurred by a "kind of inside radar" — struggles up a steamy hillside near the end of a battle in which 6,821 U.S. Marines died, clambers atop a rockpile, swings his Speed Graphic and snaps in a fraction of a second the most-remembered image of World War II, the flag-raising on Iwo Jima's Mount Suribachi. "There's only one right moment," he says. It is a moment that becomes a bond poster, a postage stamp and the Marine Corps Memorial monument in Washington, D.C.

In the adrenaline of the chase, photographers can follow the moment anywhere. Combat photographer Robert Capa lives by this refrain — "if your pictures aren't good enough, you aren't close enough" — and he dies by it, too, in Vietnam. "After a while," Nachtwey says, "you tend not to think about the danger."

As the Soviet Union breaks apart in regional uprisings, newspapers show two men carrying a Chechen woman out of a firefight to safety. They're photojournalists Peter Turnley and Christopher Morris. "We've never been motivated by bravado," Turnley observes, "but it's also about having respect for the person in front of the lens."

There are some things too horrible to photograph. In Vietnam: "We had pictures we never released," Adams remembers. "To be sure it wasn't used," Parks destroys a negative of a gang member holding a smoking gun. In Haiti, *The Washington Post*'s Carol Guzy sees "far too much death, too many wives wailing in grief, too much poverty, too much suffering, too much pain." Even Weegee has his limit: "I never photographed a dive [out of a window]. I would drive by."

Perhaps the camera never blinks. But a photographer can. Even a photograph that seeks the truth can lie. And the better the technology, the more illusive the manipulation. During the Civil War, Gardner took his Civil War photos on plates that required exposure times of 10 long seconds. Like a painter, he created a posed "sentimental composition." Capa and Rosenthal spend years explaining why their best shots are not similarly staged. Miller's smoky abstracting of wartime scenes weave life and art into what admirers call a "precarious balance between

> 'If your pictures aren't good enough, you aren't close enough.'
>
> — ROBERT CAPA

reality and nonreality." Parks emphasizes "a mood, a flash, a flavor" as he imagines "things as being more beautiful than they actually are." Smith is a darkroom artist who believes "humanity is worth more than a picture of humanity." And in the days of digital photography, critics notwithstanding, newspapers like *The Orange County Register* can zipper a boy's pants without a trace.

"I'm optimistic about my photography," says Yunghi Kim, "but I think photojournalism is in a transition stage. I think photojournalism is going to become an art form."

Alexander Gardner

1821–1882

Early battlefield photographer Alexander Gardner splits from the famed Mathew Brady to open his own studio in Washington, D.C. Unlike Brady, Gardner often spends most of his time in the field. Gardner's photographs of dead soldiers — the "dreadful details," as he calls them — help change the romantic vision Americans have of war. The pictures are seen in studios and through parlor-room stereoscopes: Newspapers lack the technology to print them.

D. MARK KATZ COLLECTION

Alexander Gardner writes in his 1865 Photographic Sketch Book of the War *about the importance of recording the war:*

'Ever be held sacred'

Localities that would scarcely have been known, and probably never remembered, save in their immediate vicinity, have become celebrated, and will ever be held sacred as memorable fields, where thousands of brave men yielded up their lives, a willing sacrifice for the cause they had espoused. Verbal representations of such places, or scenes, may or may not have the merit of accuracy; but photographic presentments of them will be accepted by posterity with an undoubting faith.

Frances Johnston

1864–1952

Frances Johnston is dubbed "photographer of the American court" for her photos of political leaders, but she also covers the Spanish-American War, a world's fair, Pennsylvania miners and rural Southern life. She studies art in America and Europe, but rebels against the art world's Victorian norms. In this self-portrait, for example, she drinks a beer, smokes and shows off her stockinged leg.

In an 1897 series in the Ladies' Home Journal, *Frances Johnston describes what makes a good female photographer:*

'Good common sense'

The woman who makes photography profitable must have ... good common sense, unlimited patience to carry her through endless failures, equally unlimited tact, good taste, a quick eye, a talent for detail, and a genius for hard work.

George Watson

1892–1977

Photographer George Watson chronicles the rise of Hollywood in all its eccentricity: Albert Einstein arm in arm with Charlie Chaplin; 18 starlets high-kicking on an airplane wing. Watson, first full-time photographer for the *Los Angeles Times,* even shouts at the visiting king of Belgium: "Hey king, take off your hat!" The king takes off his hat. *Click.*

DELMAR WATSON PHOTOGRAPHY ARCHIVES, INC.

George Watson talks about the skill of the news photographer in a 1977 interview:

'Have lots of guts'

A photographer has to have a lot of guts, and he has to know how to use a camera properly. A camera to a photographer is like an easel to an artist or a typewriter to a writer. ... A news photographer must have an instinct for the news and then must develop that instinct. It can't be learned from a book.

Robert Capa

1913–1954

Photographer Robert Capa shoots to fame when *Life* magazine prints his 1936 picture of a Spanish Republican soldier spilling backward onto Spanish soil "the instant he is dropped by a bullet." But questions arise about its authenticity. Is it staged? Capa insists it is not. Eventually, his story is accepted. Capa's advice to photographers: "If your pictures aren't good enough, you aren't close enough." He dies in Vietnam when he steps on a mine.

GEORGE RODGER, MAGNUM PHOTOS, INC.

In a Sept. 1, 1937, interview with the New York World Telegram, *Capa defends the authenticity of his famous photo, "Falling Soldier":*

'The best propaganda'

No tricks are necessary to take pictures in Spain. You don't have to pose your camera [subjects]. The pictures are there, and you just take them. The truth is the best picture, the best propaganda.

Weegee

1899–1968

They call him Weegee. Arthur Fellig shows up before competitors, even before police, to record accidents, murders and fires. Typical caption: "A truck crash with the driver trapped inside ... " Fellig gets his nickname from the Ouija board. He seems to be able to read the future, always there with his four-by-five Speed Graphic. Weegee's secret: He sleeps with a radio tuned to police bands. Fellig raises the gritty street picture to an art form. His collection, *Naked City,* becomes the basis for a Hollywood movie.

UPI/CORBIS-BETTMANN

"Weegee the Famous" explains how he sells his free-lance pictures:

'Good meaty story'

There had to be a good meaty story to get the editors to buy the pictures. A truck crash, with the driver trapped inside, his face a crisscross of blood ... a just-shot gangster lying in the gutter, well dressed in his dark suit and pearl hat, hot off the griddle, with a priest, who seemed to appear from nowhere, giving him the last rites.

Joe Rosenthal

1911–

Associated Press photographer Joe Rosenthal captures the single most celebrated image of World War II: Marines and a Navy corpsman struggling to raise the American flag on Iwo Jima's Mount Suribachi. The photograph of the day's second flag-raising is reproduced in dozens of forms — as stamps, cards, posters — even as the U.S. Marines Corps Memorial. Says Rosenthal of the shot: "There's only one right moment."

Joe Rosenthal describes the most famous photograph of World War II, the U.S. flag-raising on Iwo Jima's Mount Suribachi:

'Inside radar'

Most news photographers sort of build up some kind of an inside radar which reacts, like shooting at a football play. It's only one right moment ... 10th of a second, 25th of second ... I shot it the moment I did [and] I hope that the first picture that I shot — one single picture — would come out the way that I saw it.

W. Eugene Smith

1918–1978

For *Flying* magazine, photographer W. Eugene Smith takes dramatic black-and-whites of World War II troops under fire. He pioneers the photo-essay, telling a complex story with a series of pictures. Smith perfects the form at *Life* magazine before quitting in a dispute over an Albert Schweitzer photo-essay. For the next quarter century, free-lancer Smith flies solo.

CENTER FOR CREATIVE PHOTOGRAPHY, UNIVERSITY OF ARIZONA

W. Eugene Smith takes these notes for his Albert Schweitzer photo-essay, which runs in the Nov. 15, 1954, issue of Life:

'Goodness and wisdom'

Having accepted this man in his weakness, then his towering strengths begin to reassert their values of goodness and wisdom, and the fact of his greatness does return; and the viewer, once more viewing in [a] perspective that penetrates the superficial is still aware of the ragged edges but does not allow their raggedness to delude.

Margaret Bourke-White

1904–1971

Photojournalist Margaret Bourke-White insists on "utter truth" in her work, "how it looks, how it meshes." She snaps *Life* magazine's first cover, a New Deal dam. During World War II, as the first woman to fly on combat missions, she takes photos from bombers. She photographs world leaders, liberated concentration camp survivors, even her own torpedoed ship.

CULVER PICTURES

Margaret Bourke-White describes how it feels to be a war photographer:

'A protecting screen'

It is a peculiar thing about pictures of this sort. It is as though a protecting screen draws itself across my mind and makes it possible to consider focus and light values. ... This blind lasts as long as it is needed — while I am actually operating the camera. Days later, when I developed the negatives ... I could not bring myself to look at the films.

Gordon Parks

1912–

Photographer-trainee for the Farm Security Administration, Gordon Parks meets a black custodian with a poignant life story. He poses her with broom and mop in front of a U.S. flag and snaps his most famous photo, the 1942 classic "American Gothic." In 1948, Parks becomes the first African-American photographer for *Life*. What propels his life and work? "I wouldn't let bigotry stand in my way." As well as photographer, Gordon Parks is a composer, film director, painter and author of a 1963 novel, *The Learning Tree*, based on his childhood.

UPI/CORBIS-BETTMANN

In a 1996 Parade *magazine interview, Parks describes his "American Gothic" photo of Ella Watson, a custodian whose grandfather was lynched, husband accidentally shot, and baby daughter lost in childbirth. Watson mops floors to raise her grandchildren.*

'Impulse of despair'

I made it in innocence, in an impulse of despair. It was a strike against intolerance. But I have come to realize that you don't put everyone in that same pit.

Lee Miller

1907–1977

She's a fashion photographer, but she wants to shoot a war. So Lee Miller talks *Vogue* magazine into sending her to Europe for World War II. She captures images of blitz-torn London and the unspeakable murder of Jewish prisoners in Nazi concentration camps. The death photos arrive in New York with Lee's cable: "I implore you ... believe this is true." *Vogue* prints the pictures — some of the most famous images from the war — with the headline "Believe it!"

LEE MILLER ARCHIVES

Lee Miller writes of her arrival at the concentration camp in Dachau, Germany, on April 30, 1945:

Prisoners of Dachau

The crematorium was out of fuel for long enough to pile up two rooms of bodies. The gas chambers look like their titles, written over the doors, "SHOWER BATHS" ... men ... lay in bed, too weak to circulate the camp in victory ... they mostly grinned and cheered ... in the few minutes it took me to take my pictures, two men were found dead, and were unceremoniously dragged out and thrown on the heap outside the block. Nobody seemed to mind except me. The doctor said it was too late for more than half the others.

Eddie Adams

1933–

In Saigon, Associated Press photographer Eddie Adams freezes the moment when a South Vietnamese officer shoots a prisoner point-blank in the head. The 1969 Pulitzer Prize-winning photo defines the war's brutality and alters life for photographer and executioner alike: "I destroyed his life," says Adams. Executions happen in wars, "but rarely is a photographer there to record the act." Adams goes on to become a top portrait photographer and mentor for rising photojournalists. "A great picture," he says, "just rips your heart out."

THE ASSOCIATED PRESS

Eddie Adams describes the scene of his Saigon execution photo in the April 15, 1985, Newsweek:

'All an accident'

As soon as [South Vietnamese police chief] Loan raised his pistol, I raised my camera. Later on, the U.S. military studied the picture ... and it turned out that the moment he pushed the trigger, I pushed the shutter on my camera. It was all an accident. I just took the picture because I thought he was going to threaten him.

Moneta J. Sleet, Jr.

1926–1996

In 1968, photographer Moneta J. Sleet, Jr., shoots the funeral of the Rev. Martin Luther King, Jr. "I must say, I wasn't there as an objective reporter," he says. "I had something to say." His picture, of Coretta Scott King tearfully clasping daughter Bernice, wins a Pulitzer Prize, and makes Sleet the first African American to win journalism's highest honor.

SCHOMBURG CENTER FOR RESEARCH IN BLACK CULTURE, NEW YORK PUBLIC LIBRARY

In an Oct. 19, 1986, interview with The New York Times, *Moneta Sleet talks about his photographic philosophy:*

'Don't mind waiting'

You've got to know when to intrude and when not to intrude and when to pull back. You have to be very patient. ... I have a lot of patience and don't mind waiting — the thing is to get the editors to wait.

Jim Nachtwey

1948–

Time magazine photographer James Nachtwey travels the world, gets wounded, caught in cross fire and reported dead. In one year, 1995, he also wins photojournalism's three highest honors: the Robert Capa Gold Medal, Magazine Photographer of the Year and World Press Photo of the Year. "I've seen things," he says, "that make every bone in my body hurt."

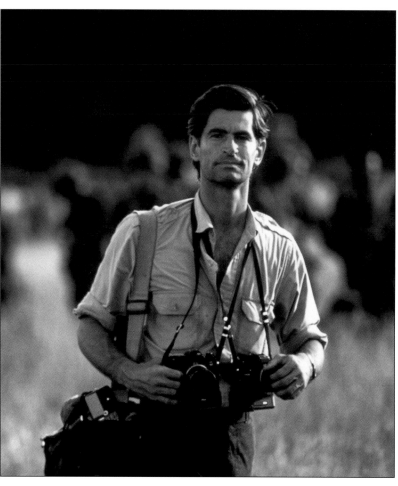

BLACK STAR

Magnum Photos, Inc.

In 1996, James Nachtwey drives around Kabul, Afghanistan, in a beat up Toyota taxi. He sees a woman mourning at the grave of her brother, the victim of a rocket attack in a nation still debased by civil war.

On photography:

I believe in what I'm doing. I believe in the free press, in communication, and that by appealing to people's best instincts, something might happen. And that's what gets me through -- it's an act of faith and having trust in people.

Why he went to Afghanistan:

I thought it had dropped out of America's consciousness. ... More has to be done about the humanitarian situation. Those people should not be forgotten.

David and Peter Turnley

1955–

Twins David and Peter Turnley live parallel lives. They are both award-winning photojournalists — David for *The Detroit Free Press,* Peter for *Newsweek.* They cover the fall of the Berlin Wall, the Tiananmen Square uprising and Somalia. They collaborate on books and photo exhibits. Do they compete? Says Peter: "We have a chance to witness events that make history. The challenge of communicating them through photography is just so superior to competition with anybody else."

DAVID TURNLEY, LEFT. PETER TURNLEY, RIGHT. BLACK STAR

In this June 26, 1996, interview with The New York Times, *David Turnley talks about the inspiration for his work:*

'Source of inspiration'

The most important part is the emotional side. Making sure that the work doesn't make you jaded, hardened. What keeps you young, I think, is that you witness such incredible things: courage, generosity, resilience. Our work is a never-ending source of inspiration.

Carol Guzy

1956–

In 1986, *Miami Herald* photographer Carol Guzy develops an "obsession" with Haiti, how it "reaches into your soul." Guzy moves to *The Washington Post* and nearly 10 years later wins her second Pulitzer Prize — for covering the Haitian crisis and its aftermath. Her first Pulitzer: chronicling the devastation caused by the eruption of a Colombian volcano. In the 1990s, the former registered nurse is one of the world's most renowned photographers. Her motto: "Try to open your mind a little bit and see differently than the standard picture."

THE WASHINGTON POST

Carol Guzy describes her affection for Haiti in the July/August 1995 issue of the Columbia Journalism Review:

'Touched by the Haitian spirit'

I had been covering the situation in Haiti on and off since Duvalier left in 1986. In that time I had seen far too much death ... too much pain. ... But also, beyond the hardships, I had been touched by the Haitian spirit. It reaches into your soul and moves you in a way hard to describe. I wanted to believe peace would come to this troubled land, but my heart was reluctant. Then came a whisper of hope. ... Whether this tenuous calm is only a temporary respite ... remains to be seen.

Yunghi Kim

1962–

South Korea-born Yunghi Kim comes to the United States at age 10. She finds English difficult and soon discovers photography as "an easy way of expression." By the 1990s, Kim is one of the nation's most acclaimed young photojournalists, winning awards for her coverage of Somalia, South Africa and Rwanda. She shoots for *The Boston Globe* for seven years, leaving in 1995 to free-lance. Kim returns to Korea to cover the "comfort women" — Koreans forced during World War II to have sex with Japanese soldiers. "Look to see what else is there," she advises young photojournalists, "other countries, other styles of photography."

YUNGHI KIM WITH HER NIECES. ©1998 KENNETH LAMBERT. ALL RIGHTS RESERVED.

In U.S. News & World Report, *Yunghi Kim describes shooting "comfort women":*

'Then silence'

Artillery fire. An aircraft's drone. The moans of the wounded. These are the sounds of combat most World War II veterans recall. For Korean grandmother Son Pon Nim, lured from her impoverished village at age 17 and forced into the Japanese Imperial Army's "comfort corps," life in the trenches left a far different aural imprint: the impatient jostling of soldiers queued before her cubicle in a Borneo military brothel, the ripping of clothing, her stifled sobs as her body was pounded raw — often more than 20 times a day. And then silence. For nearly five decades, no one spoke of the ordeal fact finders later would call "unmitigated misery" and "living hell."

CHAPTER 10

Literary Journalists

'Journalism is actually the last great unexplored literary frontier.'

—TRUMAN CAPOTE

KERN COUNTY, CALIFORNIA, 1936 —

JOHN STEINBECK SCOURS THE LANDSCAPE. HE FINDS rusted cars full of kids and rotting blankets. He finds migrant campsites like city dumps, houses made of weeds and a curious look he later identified as the terror of starving.

Then he writes it in the newspaper.

Steinbeck's stories of the "harvest gypsies," dust bowl refugees roaming California from crop to crop, first surface in October 1936 in a series of articles for *The San Francisco News*. "With the first rain," he writes, "the care-fully built house will slop down into a brown, pulpy mush." And: "The father is vaguely aware that there is a culture of hookworm in the mud along the river bank."

The words are true to life. Readers, even politicians, sit up and take note. They even talk some about the need for reform. But Steinbeck wants the stories even truer. So he goes back and scours the landscape again. And three years later, in 1939, the harvest gypsies roll into the ages as the fictional Joad family in the classic American novel *The Grapes of Wrath*.

Journalism, says the poet Matthew Arnold, is "litera-ture in a hurry." Literature, says the poet Ezra Pound, is "news that stays news." Somewhere in the middle lies the shifting place where journalism and literature meet, Siamese-twin disciplines, distinct, yet joined at their truth-seeking core.

Steinbeck sees it as clearly as anyone. "You can write anything in the morning paper so long as it happened," he writes to a friend. "The fiction writer wouldn't dare do this. What he writes must ... not only have happened but must continue to happen."

He could well have been speaking for Stephen Crane, Carl Sandburg, Langston Hughes, Margaret Mitchell, Tom Wolfe, poets, novelists, essayists — scores of the most celebrated from the American literary pantheon who once did time, like Hildy Johnson in *The Front Page*, writing for newspapers.

Enter Ernest Hemingway.

Even now, decades after his death, the reporter-turned-novelist is invoked as Patron Saint of the Possible by endless writers of the news whose odd desk drawer holds the half-written manuscript that might one day deliver them from the indignities of the newspaper city room.

Just what are the indignities? Here, Hemingway recalls reporting for *The Kansas City Star:* "It was regular newspaper work: Who shot whom? Who broke into what? Where? When? How? But never Why, not really Why."

Here, novelist-newspaperman Mark Twain describes an editor talking about his reporters: "Jones will be here at three — cowhide him. ... Ferguson will be along about four — kill him. ... If you have any odd time, you may write a blistering article on the police." And here is poet-newsman Walt Whitman ranting in *The Brooklyn Daily Eagle* about American newspapers in general: "Why are our editors so ... superficial? Why do they so rarely bring what they write to bear on the light of great principles and truths?"

The message from these lions of literature unsettles the writerly soul. The very nature of news, they suggest — fast, reckless, oddly predictable — first can humble, then humiliate, maybe even suck the life from the reporter who dreams of writing the kind of prose that rolls into the ages. "We have the newspaper," says Ralph Waldo Emerson, "which does its best to make every square acre of land and sea give an account of itself at your breakfast table."

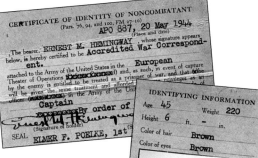

The "hack-work" of newswriting, as Truman Capote says, is seen as "literary photography ... unbecoming to the serious writer's artistic dignity."

But, at the same time, the very nature of reporting — mining the world to get at the truth — informs, enriches, indeed, engenders the best works of the imagination.

Hemingway again: "The more [the writer] learns from experience the more truly he can imagine. If he gets so he can imagine truly enough people will think that the things he relates all really happened and that he is just reporting."

— Courtesy John F. Kennedy Presidential Library/Ben Lourie photo

Above: During World War II, Ernest Hemingway uses this certificate of identity as a press pass.

Just reporting. The phrase suggests (though its author would argue) that reporting is somehow the province of drones, and imagining the province of angels.

"Writers like to think that, after all, it's not the material that is responsible for their genius, but their brilliant imagination," says literary journalist Tom Wolfe.

In the 1960s and 1970s, Wolfe and a cadre of others push at the edges of journalism by exploring the use of literary techniques to bring purer meaning to nonfiction. The movement is called "the New Journalism." But it isn't completely new.

Editor Clay Felker, champion of the "new" journalists, once read volumes of Horace Greeley's *New York Tribune* from a century before anyone had ever heard of Wolfe, Talese or Capote. He finds the writing dramatic, fresh and new, full of "all of the classical literary techniques of storytelling, narrative flow." Says Felker: "I began looking for writers who could write that way."

The other side to the same story: *New Yorker* writer Lillian Ross includes among the greatest writer-reporters the novelists Defoe and Turgenev.

In the end, or perhaps, the beginning, the real — the touched and felt and seen — makes imagining possible.

> 'Who shot whom?
>
> Who broke into What?
>
> Where? When? How?
>
> But never Why …'
>
> — ERNEST HEMINGWAY

"Reporting … gives the imagination something to work with," says Wolfe. "Human imagination isn't that strong; it can't work in a vacuum for very long."

Stephen Crane knows it as well as anyone. In 1895, he writes *The Red Badge of Courage* without ever having seen a battlefield. Perhaps his classic account of the Civil War is a miracle, as some suggested. But before long, Crane is telling friends that his mind could no longer see, he needed to get to a real battlefield and report so he could imagine again.

Most of all, he needed to know that *The Red Badge* was "all right" — that it was accurate, true. So he takes a job for Hearst's *New York Journal* as a war reporter. "From a distance it was like tearing cloth," Crane writes in an early dispatch from the Greco-Turkish war. "Nearer it sounded like rain on a tin roof and up close it was just a long crash after crash. It was a beautiful sound — beautiful as I had never dreamed."

Yes, he did dream it first. But, like Steinbeck and others after him and before, he needed to scour the landscape to make it real again.

William Cullen Bryant

1794–1878

American poet William Cullen Bryant becomes editor-in-chief of the *New-York Evening Post* in 1829 and stays half a century. "The American Wordsworth" gives the *Post* a polished literary style with a Jacksonian-Democrat bent. His editorials leave their stamp on the major social issues of the era, including the crusade to abolish slavery. Asked how a poet can bear the politics, he says: "Politics and a bellyful are better than poetry and starvation."

In the June 13, 1836, New-York Evening Post, *William Cullen Bryant defends tailors convicted of conspiracy for refusing to work at low wages:*

'The flag of slavery'

If this is not SLAVERY, we have forgotten its definition. Strike the right of associating for the sale of labour from the privileges of a freeman, and you may as well at once bind him to a master, or ascribe him to the soil. In 1857, Bryant condemns the Dred Scott decision, which declares slaves non-citizens: "Hereafter, wherever our flag floats it is the flag of slavery; it should be dyed black, and its device should be the whip and the fetter."

Edgar Allan Poe

1809–1849

Poet of the macabre, Edgar Allan Poe works for newspapers and magazines to pay the rent. His newspaper hoaxes prove more popular than his literary work. In one, published in the New York *Sun,* Poe describes a fictitious balloon flight across the Atlantic Ocean. Poe sees the future of journalism in magazines. "The magazine in the end," he says, "will be the most influential of all departments of letters." Poems like *The Raven* and tales like *The Tell-Tale Heart* bring Poe renown only in his last lean years.

NATIONAL ARCHIVES

In the April 13, 1844, New York Sun, *Edgar Allan Poe entertains readers with what proves to be a hoax about a trans-Atlantic balloon flight:*

'Crossed in a balloon'

The great problem is at length solved! The air, as well as the earth and the ocean, has been subdued by science, and will become a common and convenient highway for mankind. The Atlantic has been actually crossed in a balloon! And this, too, without difficulty — without any great apparent danger ... and in the inconceivably brief period of seventy-five hours from shore to shore!

Walt Whitman

1819–1892

At 27, Walt Whitman edits *The Brooklyn Daily Eagle,* "chief of the Long Island journals." He opposes slavery. But his bosses favor it, and this "led to rows." After two years, he says, "I lost my place." He tries other newspaper jobs and carpentry. In 1855, *Leaves of Grass* is published, and Whitman becomes America's most celebrated poet.

Walt Whitman writes about newspaper writing in the Sept. 29, 1846, Brooklyn Daily Eagle:

'So flippant, so superficial'

It is a singular fact that while people of the United States are a newspaper-ruled people, we have in reality few, we may almost say no, newspapers that approach even in the neighborhood of the perfect specimens of their kind. We have little fine, hearty, truthful writing in our papers. ... The American people are intellectual in a high degree — their brains are clear, and their penetration eagle-eyed. Why then, does not the press which asks their "patronage" present something like the food we might reasonably suppose would be craved by such a mental appetite? ... Why are our editors so flippant, so superficial, so vague and verbose? Why do they so rarely bring what they write to bear on the light of great principles and truths?

Jack London

1876–1916

Hard-drinking, odd-jobbing child of the Oakland waterfront, Jack London gains fame with his 1903 novel, *The Call of the Wild*. As a reporter he covers everything from the San Francisco earthquake to a championship boxing match he calls "the greatest battle of the century." The longtime socialist writes 40 books, many political manifestos. But celebrity doesn't cure London's depression and alcoholism. He dies at 40.

In 1910, Jack London covers the championship fight between white boxer Jim Jeffries and black boxer Jack Johnson in The New York Herald:

'The story of the fight'

When Jeffries sent in that awful rip of his, the audience would madly applaud, believing it had gone home to Johnson's stomach, and Johnson, deftly interposing his elbow, would smile in irony at the audience, play acting, making believe he thought the applause was for him. ... The greatest battle of the century was a monologue delivered to twenty thousand spectators by a smiling negro, who was never in doubt and who was never serious for more than a moment at a time. It is to be doubted if the old Jeffries could have put away this amazing negro from Texas. ... Johnson is a wonder. No one understands him, this man who smiles. Well, the story of the fight is the story of a smile.

Don Marquis

1878–1937

In 1916, playwright, poet and novelist Don Marquis creates "archy," a poet-philosopher reincarnated into the body of a cockroach. The popular insect and his friend, "mehitabel," a cat who was once Cleopatra, entertain readers of Marquis' *Sun Dial* column in the New York *Sun.* A free-verse poet, archy muses on life, love and letters, jumping up and down on the typewriter keys (only in lower case).

Complains archy:

some of your readers
are always interested in
technical
details when the main
question is
whether the stuff is
literature or not.

LIBRARY OF CONGRESS

In the New York Sun, *Don Marquis fights Prohibition by sending archy the cockroach to interview an Egyptian mummy in the Metropolitan Museum. Says the mummy:*

'Thinking…'

i have been lying here
and there
for four thousand years
with silicon in my esophagus
and gravel in my gizzard
thinking
thinking
thinking
of beer.

Sherwood Anderson

1876–1941

Sherwood Anderson, author of the best-selling novel *Winesburg, Ohio,* is called "the official spokesman for the small town." His popular *Smyth County News* column, "Buck Fever Says," chronicles Marion, Virginia, country life through the fictitious Buck's homespun notes. Buck mines the true meaning of Kiwanis Club meetings, hunting season, moonshining and west end hens. Anderson calls it a "non-materialistic, sincerely human life."

ALFRED STIEGLITZ, COURTESY LIBRARY OF CONGRESS

This dispatch appears in the December 1927 issue of the Smyth County News:

'Buck Fever'

We are in receipt of a letter signed Malaria Fever, who says she is the mother of our ready correspondent, Buck Fever. The letter says: "I wish you would not let my boy Buck write so much for your papers. I am afraid he may become a newspaper writer. It is a low occupation. We Fevers are of an old Virginia Family. I think it is vulgar to be always having our name in the paper. ... Buck Fever's father (and incidentally the husband of Malaria Fever) is a member of the firm of Fever and Ague. They keep a general store at the head of Coon Hollow."

Margaret Mitchell

1900–1949

A decade before her 1936 book *Gone With the Wind* and world fame, author Margaret Mitchell writes about gutsy women for the *Atlanta Journal* Sunday magazine. She meets a "lady axe murderess" and mines Southern history for unsung heroines, all the while barred from the all-male city room. Mitchell's advice for successful storytelling: "Tell it like a woman would tell it."

HARGRETT RARE BOOK & MANUSCRIPT LIBRARY, UNIVERSITY OF GEORGIA

In the May 1923 Atlanta Journal *Sunday magazine, Margaret Mitchell describes an American revolutionary patriot in a story about historic women soldiers:*

'She coolly shot him'

One of them, not knowing Nancy's reputation for sharpshooting, tried to rush her, but she coolly shot him down. Whether the others were unnerved by her suddenness or by the certainty of death at the hands of the Whigs or the incongruity of her cross-eyes that seemed to make each one the object of her ferocious gaze, suffice to say that they made no further resistance.

John Steinbeck

1902–1968

John Steinbeck meets the editor of *The San Francisco News* at the Carmel home of muckraker Lincoln Steffens. The editor invites Steinbeck to do a newspaper series on life in Okie migrant camps. Summer 1936 finds him touring the state in an old bakery truck with one Tom Collins, a Federal Resettlement Administration official. "There is more filth here," he writes. Steinbeck's reporting becomes the basis for his novel, *The Grapes of Wrath,* and draws attention to the plight of farm workers in the Golden State. The California writer goes on to win a Nobel Prize in literature.

NATIONAL ARCHIVES

John Steinbeck writes this account of life in a California farm labor camp for the refugees fleeing drought in Oklahoma's dust bowl, in the Oct. 6, 1936, San Francisco News:

'Full of flies'

There is more filth here. The tent is full of flies clinging to the apple box that is the dinner table, buzzing about the foul clothes of the children, particularly the baby, who has not been bathed or cleaned for several days. There is no toilet here, but there is a clump of willows nearby where human feces lie exposed to the flies — the same flies that are in the tent.

Carl Sandburg
1878–1967

Poet of the American worker, Carl Sandburg writes for Milwaukee newspapers to help feed his family. Like his poetry, his more than 20 years of reporting and editorial writing celebrate the common individual. He quotes Rudyard Kipling: "I will be the word of the people. Mine will be the bleeding mouth from which the gag is snatched." In 1940, Sandburg's renowned Lincoln scholarship wins him the Pulitzer Prize for history. His poetry wins the prize in 1951, making Sandburg the only reporter with two Pulitzers for disciplines other than journalism.

NATIONAL ARCHIVES

In the Aug. 3, 1909, Milwaukee Daily News, *Carl Sandburg writes his first published piece on Abraham Lincoln:*

'Coin of the common folk'

The face of Abraham Lincoln on the copper cent seems well and proper. If it were possible to talk with that great, good man, he would probably say that he is perfectly willing that his face is to be placed on the cheapest and most common coin in the country. The penny is strictly the coin of the common people. At Palm Beach, Newport and Saratoga you will find nothing for sale at one cent. No ice cream cones at a penny apiece there. ... Follow the travels of a penny and you find it stops at many cottages and few mansions. ... The common, homely face of "Honest Abe" will look good on the penny, the coin of the common folk from whom he came and to whom he belongs.

Ernest Hemingway

1899–1961

Nobel Prize–winning novelist Ernest Hemingway first is a *Kansas City Star* reporter. He lives by its stylebook: "Use short sentences ... short first paragraphs ... vigorous English." During World War I, the macho correspondent also is a Red Cross volunteer. Says Hemingway: "I love combat." He trains recruits and even fights in some of the wars he covers. His partisan syndicated dispatches from the Spanish Civil War front become the basis for his novel *For Whom the Bell Tolls*. In 1961, seven years after winning the Nobel Prize in literature, Hemingway kills himself.

THE ASSOCIATED PRESS

In 1937, Ernest Hemingway reports on the Spanish Civil War for the North American Newspaper Alliance:

'Seventeen blocks away'

The window of the hotel is open and, as you lie in bed, you hear the firing in the front line seventeen blocks away. ... The rifles go tacrong, capong, craang, tacrong, and then a machine gun opens up. It has a bigger calibre and is much louder, rong, cararong, rong, rong. Then there is the incoming boom of a trench mortar shell and a burst of machine gun fire. You lie and listen to it and it is a great thing to be in bed with your feet stretched out gradually warming the cold foot of the bed and not out there in University City or Carabanchel. A man is singing hard-voiced in the street below and three drunks are arguing when you fall asleep. In the morning ... they send for someone to repair the gas main and you go in to breakfast. A charwoman, her eyes red, is scrubbing the blood off the marble floor of the corridor. The dead man wasn't you nor anyone you know and everyone is very hungry in the morning after a cold night and a long day the day before up at the Guadalajara front.

Langston Hughes

1902–1967

American poet-playwright Langston Hughes writes a weekly column for *The Chicago Defender.* It begins with conversations with the fictional James B. Semple ("Simple"), a black common man. Simple is created to bolster African-American support for World War II. (Hughes had covered black soldiers in the Spanish Civil War for the *Baltimore Afro-American.*) But Simple becomes a popular character, bringing uncommon wit to almost any subject.

NATIONAL PORTRAIT GALLERY, SMITHSONIAN INSTITUTION

Langston Hughes gives voice to his character "Simple" in The Chicago Defender:

'Nice and peaceful'

This here movie showed great big beautiful lakes with signs up all around: NO FISHING — STATE GAME PRESERVE — but it did not show a single place with a sign up: NO LYNCHING. ... It were nice and peaceful for them fish. ... There ought to be some place where it is nice and peaceful for me, too.

Lillian Ross

1927–

Legendary among *New Yorker* magazine writer-reporters, Lillian Ross pioneers the nonfiction novel. *Picture,* her 1952 portrait of a John Huston film-in-progress, becomes a book, a classic of literary nonfiction. Ross tells serious writers to shun newspapers and newsmagazines. Their trends in style, she says, "have nothing to do with writing to get at the truth."

PHOTOGRAPH BY WILLIAM SHAWN, FROM THE COLLECTION OF LILLIAN ROSS

From Picture, *Lillian Ross's 1952 classic book:*

'Devil to pay'

Huston lay on the bed, his back resting against the headboard, and sketched thoughtfully on a yellow pad as Band read off the lines that were considered objectionable.

"Gawd, he's runnin'," Band said.
"Look, he's runnin'," Huston said in a bored voice.
"It'll be hell to pay," Band read.
"It'll be the devil to pay," said Huston.
"You can't say that," Reinhardt said.
 Huston said, "The hell you can't."

James Baldwin

1924–1987

Novelist and essayist James Baldwin calls himself "witness to the truth" of racial injustice, theme of his fiction and magazine journalism. His motto: "To be an honest man and a good writer." In 1948, frustrated by scant literary recognition in the United States, Baldwin moves to Paris, where he wins international literary fame. Baldwin's essays make him a civil rights hero. He crusades against racial prejudice, but also against black separatism: "Negroes are Americans and their destiny is the country's destiny."

THE ASSOCIATED PRESS

In his 1963 book The Fire Next Time, *James Baldwin talks to his nephew about the roots of racial injustice:*

'Because you were black'

This innocent country set you down in a ghetto in which, in fact, it intended that you should perish. Let me spell out precisely what I mean by that, for the heart of the matter is here, and the root of my dispute with my country. You were born where you were born and faced the future that you faced because you were black and for no other reason.

E.B. White

1899–1985

His elegant essays grace the pages of *The New Yorker* magazine for half a century as he strives to assemble "a reasonable facsimile of the truth." But E.B. White is best known for the writing handbook he co-authors, *The Elements of Style,* and his classic children's books, such as *Charlotte's Web.* Says White: "Television has taken a big bite out of the written word. But words still count with me."

E.B. White describes a wartime gathering of patriotic Americans in the December 1942 issue of Harper's Magazine:

'American occasion'

Here, for a Nazi, was ... all that was contemptible and stupid — a patriotic gathering without strict control from a central leader, a formless group negligently dressed ... a group shamelessly lured there by a pretty girl for bait, a Jew in an honored position as artist, Negroes singing through their rich non-Aryan throats ... a sprawling, goofy American occasion, shapeless as an old hat.

Truman Capote

1924–1984

Novelist and short-story writer Truman Capote becomes a household name with the 1966 book *In Cold Blood. New Yorker* errand boy-turned-elegant stylist claims credit for establishing a new literary form — the nonfiction novel — with his widely-imitated best seller: "I wanted ... the credibility of fact, the immediacy of film, the depth and freedom of prose, and the precision of poetry."

UPI/CORBIS-BETTMANN

Truman Capote explores the murdering psyche in his 1966 best seller, In Cold Blood:

'The setup'

And listening to Dick's conceited chatter, hearing him start to describe his Mexican "amorous conquests," he thought how "queer" it was, "egomaniacal." Imagine going all out to impress a man you were going to kill, a man who wouldn't be alive ten minutes from now — not if the plan he and Dick had devised went smoothly. And why shouldn't it? The setup was ideal.

Gay Talese

1932–

In 1965, reporter Gay Talese breaks away from *The New York Times* and formula-writing to explore fictional techniques in nonfiction. He becomes a best-selling progenitor of 1960s and 1970s New Journalism, a style he describes as the "most reliable reportage, although it seeks a larger truth." In his books, Talese humanizes institutions as diverse as the Mafia and the *Times itself,* "Realism," he says, "is fantastic."

Gay Talese writes about singer Frank Sinatra in an early 1960s Esquire *portrait:*

Portrait of Sinatra

"Oh, yeah," Sinatra said, "well I've seen it, and it's a piece of crap."

"That's strange," Ellison said, "because they haven't even released it yet."

"Well, I've seen it," Sinatra repeated, "and it's a piece of crap."

Now Brad Dexter, very anxious, very big opposite the small figure of Ellison, said, "Com'on, kid, I don't want you in this room."

"Hey," Sinatra interrupted Dexter, "can't you see I'm talking to this guy?"

Joan Didion

1934–

California-born, Berkeley-educated Joan Didion is one of the most celebrated of the "new journalists" of the 1970s. She writes brilliant columns and essays for *The Saturday Evening Post* and *Esquire,* and produces best-selling novels. Didion mixes a fine writer's technique with precise reporting. She delves into everything — from San Francisco's hippies to feminism to U.S. foreign policy fiascoes.

THE ASSOCIATED PRESS

Joan Didion writes about a murder in California in "Some Dreamers of the Golden Dream," an essay in the book Slouching Towards Bethlehem:

'Every voice seems a scream'

This is a story about love and death in the golden land, and begins with the country. The San Bernardino Valley ... is in certain ways an alien place: not the coastal California of the subtropical twilights and the soft westerlies off the Pacific but a harsher California, haunted by the Mojave just beyond the mountains, devastated by the hot dry Santa Ana wind that comes down through the passes at 100 miles an hour and whines through the eucalyptus windbreaks and works on the nerves. October is the bad month for the wind, the month when breathing is difficult and the hills blaze up spontaneously. There has been no rain since April. Every voice seems a scream. It is the season of suicide and divorce and prickly dread, wherever the wind blows.

Tom Wolfe

1931–

In 1962, Tom Wolfe brings a Yale Ph.D. and a distinctive writing style to the *New York Herald Tribune.* Wolfe and other "New Journalism" writers use the techniques of novelists to "get into the heads" of their subjects. Wolfe, whose books include *The Kandy-Kolored Tangerine-Flake Streamline Baby,* is forever linked with the *vroom! vroom!* style that upends American feature writing.

UPI/CORBIS-BETTMANN

From Tom Wolfe's account of the San Francisco hippies who call themselves the Merry Pranksters, in The Electric Kool-Aid Acid Test:

'A creamy groove machine'

The trip back was a psychic Cadillac, a creamy groove machine and they soon found themselves grooving in a group mind. Now they could leave behind all the mind-blown freaky binds and just keep going Further! on the bus.

Sallie Tisdale

1957–

A writer for *Harper's, The New Yorker* and *The New York Times,* Sallie Tisdale turns subjects from sex to salt into award-winning books that mine ethical questions. In her 1987 book *Harvest Moon,* the one-time nurse tells a behind-the-scenes story of life in a troubled nursing home. Tisdale has a "willingness to use myself and everyone else around me as grist to a story's mill."

JEFF LEE PHOTOGRAPHY

Sallie Tisdale writes in Harvest Moon:

'Self-justified worlds'

By their nature nursing homes are self-justified worlds, concerned with problems, crises, and solutions of no concern to the culture at large. They exist precisely because their concerns aren't shared by the culture at large — created to manage those unavoidable concerns abdicated by that same culture. ... Standing apart this way ... the nursing home becomes a kind of tribal village, a place of misfits. It has a language of its own, customs of its own. ... Nursing homes are communities of people incapable of claiming more than they receive, utterly at the mercy of our goodwill.

CHAPTER 11

Radio People

> 'Good evening, Mr. and Mrs. North and South America and all the ships at sea.'
>
> — WALTER WINCHELL

LONDON, 1940 —

"*T*HE SHRAPNEL CLICKED AS IT HIT ... AND *still the German bombers came.*" Edward R. Murrow reports live from blitz-torn Britain. For the first time, turn on your radio — you, like Murrow, are there. Murrow dives for the pavement five times in 10 blocks. The people of London? How do they react? What is it really like? *"That moan of stark terror and suspense cannot be encompassed by words."* So Murrow reaches for the sounds. The screech of the siren, the crack of anti-aircraft guns, the *ack-ack*, the scuffing feet, people walk-ing, not running, to shelters.

For the first time, Americans in far-off living rooms are hearing the sounds of a war as it happens. Poet Archibald MacLeish notes that Murrow's live reports shape the nation's thoughts about the world war brewing in Europe: "You burned the city of London in our houses, and we felt the flames that burned it. You laid the dead of London at our doors and we knew that the dead were our dead ... were mankind's dead."

This is the power of radio. From its earliest days in the 1920s, when the human voice first comes through the airwaves, radio transfixes the American mind. How thrilling, how mysterious, to hear a real voice materialize out of thin air. By 1938, when World War II takes form in Europe, nearly nine out of 10 American homes have radio. One survey shows that owners would rather sell their icebox than give up the talking box in the corner. The radio is not just an appliance. It is a friend.

"I live in a strictly rural community," says E.B. White, "and people speak of 'The Radio' in the large sense, with an overmeaning. When they say 'The Radio' ... they refer to a pervading and somewhat godlike presence which has come into their lives and homes."

Radio delivers a duel magic: immediacy and intimacy. Through radio, a president rallies a nation, a baseball hero hits a homer before a million fans, a king steps down while the world listens. On Dec. 7, 1941, it is a Sunday football game. The Mutual radio network breaks in with the message: *"Japanese planes bomb Pearl Harbor."* In a few seconds, radio alerts a far-flung nation to war in its own backyard. On May 7, 1933, it is a president speaking directly to the American people, frightened by the news of collapsing banks: "My dear friends," says Franklin D. Roosevelt. "I want to talk for a few minutes ... about banking."

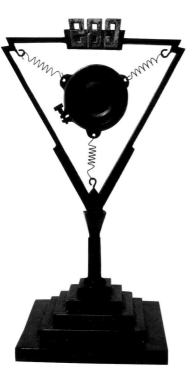

— Max Reid Photo

Newscaster Edwin C. Hill likens Roosevelt's talk to "a wise and kindly father" sitting down to chat "sympathetically and patiently and affectionately with his worried and anxious children." CBS' Harry Butcher labels them "fireside chats." Decades later, National Public Radio's Susan Stamberg describes radio's ability to soothe. "Even more than words, the way the words are said colors the telling. The voice is any story's most important instrument. It's the voice that puts you in the presence of a person and a life."

But if radio can inform in an instant, it can deceive just as fast. An out-of-town baseball game sounds live, when in fact, it is a studio re-enactment. A politician sounds capable and credible, even if he is Adolf Hitler. As Murrow himself says: "The speed of communication is wondrous to behold. It is also true that the speed can multiply the distribution of information that we know to be untrue."

In May 1937, it is the trans-Atlantic flight of the *Hindenburg* airship: *"It's burst into flame! Yes, it's started. Yes, it's started. It's a fire and it's crashing."* In his classic eyewitness account of tragedy in the making, radio correspondent Herb Morrison insists no one can survive. But half the passengers live, and Americans

Inset: Edward R. Murrow brings the London blitz into American living rooms with this microphone.

learn that reporters making spur-of-the-moment judgments can be flat wrong.

On Halloween eve, 1938, it is a "special news bulletin" about Martians invading the earth: *Those strange beings who landed in the Jersey farmlands tonight are the vanguard of an invading army from the planet Mars.*" In truth, it is actor Orson Welles reading a radio drama of *War of the Worlds*, causing mass hysteria. "New York is destroyed!" one woman screams in a church. "It's the end of the world. You might as well go home to die ... I heard it on the radio."

Yet radio endures. Turn the dial forward, to the 1990s. As other electronic media — TV, cable, the Internet — pervade our weeks and our lives, Americans still listen to radio three hours a day. What is new in those radio hours: the participatory opinion-fest of talk radio. "From the day the show began on August 1, 1988 ... people were going crazy over this show," says conservative talk radio personality Rush Limbaugh. "Here, finally, was someone on the radio saying what they felt, what they said to their friends and family." You can talk back to Limbaugh in a way that you could never talk back to, say, Peter Jennings.

As the 20th century comes to a close, 18 percent of Americans get most of their news from radio. And radio is still the most common source of news worldwide. It has staying power, and something more. Says Murrow: "A loud voice which reaches from coast to coast is not necessarily uttering truths more profound than those that may be heard in the classroom, bar or country store. But there they are. You can listen or leave them alone. By turning the dial, you can be entertained, informed or irritated."

Doc Herrold

1875–1948

In 1909, inventor Charles David "Doc" Herrold starts the first regular radio broadcasts with a homemade microphone and a tall antenna on the Garden City Bank Building in San Jose, Calif. Doc broadcasts news by reading items from a local newspaper. His wife, Sybil M. True, has a program, too. Herrold proves radio can work long before the East Coast giants. His pioneering effort evolves into San Francisco all-news station KCBS, which calls itself the nation's oldest radio station.

SAN JOSE HISTORICAL MUSEUM

In a c. 1940 letter, Doc Herrold describes his first days of broadcasting:

'Real broadcasting'

When I opened my school [of radio] I kept some sort of wireless telephone equipment hooked up all the time. The output was always small. ... It was real broadcasting — how do I know? Because I had to make my own audience. I went out through the valley and installed crystal sets so that people could listen to the music.

Harry P. Davis

1868–1931

In 1920, Westinghouse executive Harry P. Davis realizes that radio will draw large audiences. He urges the creation of KDKA, the first commercial radio station in the United States. Instead of "confidential," one-to-one communication, Davis sees radio as a medium of "wide publicity." The Pittsburgh radio station goes on the air Nov. 2, broadcasting the news that a newspaper publisher, Warren G. Harding, has been elected president. The *Pittsburgh Post* supplies the reports.

UPI/CORBIS-BETTMANN

In 1928, Harry P. Davis speaks at Harvard University on the history of broadcasting:

'Open new avenues'

We became convinced that we had in our hands, in this idea, the instrument that would prove to be the greatest and most direct mass communicational and mass educational means that had ever appeared. The natural fascination of its mystery, coupled with its ability to annihilate distance, would attract, interest and open many avenues to bring ease and happiness into human lives.

Pedro J. González

1895–1994

Depression-era radio pioneer Pedro J. González fights the deportation of Mexican workers from the United States. His Spanish-language wake-up show captures a large Los Angeles audience, but angers city officials. In 1934, González is sent to prison on a phony rape charge. Six years later, his accuser admits that police forced her to lie. Even so, González is deported. For the next 30 years, he broadcasts from Tijuana, a hero to Southern California's Latino population.

KPBS-TV

Pedro González recalls his imprisonment during an interview for the video about his life, entitled Ballad of an Unsung Hero:

'Unthinkable things'

When I arrived in San Quentin, I noticed most prisoners were Mexicans. They assigned me the hardest work. I was given punishments used perhaps 500 years ago, when San Quentin was a Spanish prison. Unthinkable things.

Floyd Gibbons

1887–1939

In 1930, NBC launches daily network newscasts with radio pioneer Floyd Gibbons. "Excitement is news," says Gibbons. "I take an incident and try to dramatize it into a human story." The newscaster practices what he preaches. As a young reporter, he cuts a phone line to scoop a competitor and covers an auto race from inside the winning car. Gibbons covers nine wars, losing an eye in one.

THE ASSOCIATED PRESS

In the Feb. 26, 1917, issue of the Chicago Tribune, *Floyd Gibbons writes the World War I story, "German U-Boat Sinks Laconia":*

'Red glare over roaring sea'

It is now a little over thirty hours since I stood on the slanting decks of the big liner, listened to the lowering of lifeboats, heard the hiss of escaping steam and the roar of ascending rockets as they tore lurid rents on the black sky and cast their red glare over the roaring sea.

Lowell Thomas

1892–1981

"So long ... until tomorrow," the baritone sign-off of Lowell Jackson Thomas, is known to millions of NBC and CBS listeners from 1930 to 1976. Thomas profiles T.E. Lawrence in the book *With Lawrence in Arabia,* helping make both men famous. He broadcasts radio travelogues, narrates newsreels and, in 1939, delivers the first regular television newscast in the United States.

UPI/CORBIS-BETTMANN

In his first radio broadcast — carried by NBC in the East, and CBS in the West, on Sept. 29, 1930 — Lowell Thomas doubts Germany could defeat Russia:

'Go ask Napoleon'

There are now two Mussolinis in the world. Adolf Hitler has written a book in which this belligerent gentleman states that cardinal policy of his powerful German party is the conquest of Russia. That's a tall assignment, Adolf. You just go ask Napoleon.

Ora Eddleman Reed

1880–1968

Like a lot of radio pioneers, Ora Eddleman Reed gets her start in print. She's editor of Oklahoma's *Twin Territories: The Indian Magazine* in the 1920s. When Reed moves with her new husband to Casper, Wyo., she starts a Native-American radio talk show. Reed, who is part Cherokee, calls herself the "Sunshine Lady." In her two-hour program, she offers advice and "happiness" commentaries. Her early radio and publishing experiments are cut short by the Great Depression.

ARCHIVES & MANUSCRIPTS DIVISION OF THE OKLAHOMA HISTORICAL SOCIETY

Ora Eddleman Reed celebrates her appointment as editor in the March 1900 issue of Twin Territories:

'Here to stay'

When we started out a year ago, there are some who smiled rather dubiously. Attempts like ours have been made before and have failed utterly, and it was not unnatural to believe we might do the same ... while we have not as yet realized all our ambitions ... one thing is certain: *Twin Territories* is here to stay.

Paul White

1902–1955

Behind reporters are editors; behind broadcasters, news directors. When Paul White joins CBS in 1930, it has no news department. He establishes one that becomes widely respected. The news director stresses objectivity: "The fact that it is difficult ... to attain," he says, "does not ... excuse the broadcaster from a constant and vigilant effort to try for it."

THE ASSOCIATED PRESS

An excerpt of a September 1945 memo written by Paul White to CBS reporters:

'Intensity and good writing'

I listened to a great number of news programs over the weekend. I think we should now cover domestic events like reconversion, the hurricanes, and the Detroit labor troubles with the same intensity and good writing that we cover the collapse of Japan and the meeting of the Big 5 Ministers in London.

Gabriel Heatter

1890–1972

In 1935, Mutual Broadcasting System's Gabriel Heatter reports live the verdict of Bruno Hauptmann, the man accused of killing Charles Lindbergh's baby. His reports are restrained, in vivid contrast to the try-him, convict-him media-circus behavior surrounding Hauptmann's trial. During World War II, Heatter starts each broadcast with "Ah, there's good news tonight." His philosophy: "Even when the news was grim, I tried to find a patch of blue ... on which to hang real hope."

NATIONAL ARCHIVES

Gabriel Heatter reports live during Bruno Richard Hauptmann's execution:

No confession

I am in a hotel room looking at a certain window ... as close as I wish to get to a room in which a man is about to die. ... There will be no reprieve, of that I am certain. ... [I] wonder what's going on in that room. It wouldn't be a confession ... no, that silent fellow, lips pressed together, would not confess.

Herb Morrison

1905–1989

May 6, 1937. Chicago radio reporter Herb Morrison is in Lakehurst, N.J., for the landing of the Hindenburg after its trans-Atlantic flight. Midreport, the German airship bursts into flames. Morrison's eyewitness description — "It's fire, and it's crashing. It's crashing terrible" — airs the next day on NBC networks, the first recorded radio news report NBC airs. Says Morrison: "I was telling something beautiful and then it turned horrible."

DENNIS R. KROMM COLLECTION

From Herb Morrison's eyewitness account of the Hindenburg disaster:

'Oh, the humanity'

It's practically standing still now. They've dropped ropes out of the nose of the ship, and it's been taken ahold of, down on the field by a number of men. It's starting to rain again. The rain had slacked up a little bit. The back motors of the ship are just holding it, uh, just enough to keep it from ... It's burst into flame! Yes, it's started. Yes, it's started ... Oh my, get out of the way, please. It's burning, bursting into flames, and it's falling on the mooring mast. And all the folks ... this is terrible. This is one of the worst catastrophes in the world. Oh, flames going, oh, four to five hundred feet in the sky. And it's a terrific crash, ladies and gentlemen. The smoke and flames now, and the frame is crashing down into the ground, not quite to the mooring mast. Oh, the humanity!

Edward R. Murrow

1908–1965

Everyone who listens to CBS Radio knows Edward R. Murrow (born Egbert Roscoe Murrow). Flying over Berlin during World War II, he describes bombs "bursting below like great sunflowers gone mad." His *Hear It Now* program becomes TV's *See It Now*. The conscience of TV news, Murrow crusades against Sen. Joseph McCarthy's communist witch-hunts, concluding, "The fault, dear Brutus, is not in our stars, but in ourselves." In 1961, he worries television is dissolving into a ratings scramble and quits to head the United States Information Agency.

On Sept. 9, 1940, Edward R. Murrow covers the bombing of London in this CBS Radio dispatch:

'It grew cold'

Before eight, the siren sounded again. We went back to a haystack near the airdrome. The fires up the river had turned the moon blood red. The smoke had drifted down 'til it formed a canopy over the Thames; the guns were working all around us, the bursts looking like fireflies in a Southern summer night. ... Suddenly all the lights dashed off and a blackness fell right to the ground. It grew cold. We covered ourselves with hay. The shrapnel clicked as it hit the concrete road nearby, and still the German bombers came.

Don Hollenbeck

1905–1954

CBS Radio and TV reporter Don Hollenbeck, host of *CBS Views the Press* from 1947 to 1950, kills himself inhaling stove gas in his apartment. *The New York Times* obituary doesn't say why. Hollenbeck, a George Polk Award winner for press criticism, has been pummeled by attacks from sympathizers of communist-baiting Sen. Joseph McCarthy. Friends say the attacks led to his suicide.

CBS PHOTO ARCHIVE

On CBS News of America, *Don Hollenbeck supports Edward R. Murrow's efforts — also on CBS, on the program* See It Now *— to expose the false accusations made by communist-baiting Sen. Joseph McCarthy:*

'What I saw'

I don't know whether all of you have just seen what I saw, but I want to associate myself and this program with what Ed Murrow has just said, and I have never been prouder of CBS.

Ike Pappas

1933–

Just two days after President John F. Kennedy's assassination, New York radio reporter Ike Pappas is covering the jail transfer of suspected gunman Lee Harvey Oswald. Suddenly, nightclub owner Jack Ruby brushes past and shoots Oswald in the stomach. Pappas tells himself: "Don't freeze — talk." His dramatic eyewitness account enters broadcast legend. Pappas moves to CBS News, where he covers Vietnam, presidential campaigns and the space program. His credo: "Truth with honesty, accuracy and, if possible, passion."

IKE PAPPAS (FAR RIGHT); COURTESY IKE PAPPAS

Tape recorder in hand, Ike Pappas relays his eyewitness account of the slaying of Lee Harvey Oswald in November 1963:

'The shot rang out'

Let me see if I can reconstruct it. Lee Harvey Oswald was coming out in the garage in the police headquarters at Dallas. He was being led out by Capt. Fritz who had been interrogating him for two days. He was wearing a black sweater. There were massive reporters and cameramen. We were all lined up. I was directly opposite Oswald and as Oswald came out, I leaped forward and said, "Do you have anything to say in your defense?" Immediately after that, the shot rang out. ... Man wearing a black hat rushing up jamming a gun in his belly firing once. Oswald doubled up, said, "Oh," fell on his knees, and there was tremendous struggle. Here is young Oswald now. He is lying flat. ... He, to me, appears dead.

Dallas Townsend

1919–1995

Forty-four-year CBS News radio veteran Dallas Townsend writes and anchors *The CBS World News Roundup.* He covers every presidential campaign and convention from 1948 to 1980. Townsend can harness the immediacy of radio, but co-workers also admire his fairness and decency. Says one: "If every journalist were like Dallas Townsend, the public wouldn't complain nearly so much about journalism."

CBS, INC.

In an essay in the 1963 book Journalists in Action, *Dallas Townsend muses about the state of television news:*

'Not doing what it should'

The type of news program I have described is not doing what it should be doing. It may be adequate as a means of reporting late developments. (Flourish of trumpets. "And now — NEWS!!! Up to the second — when it happens, where it happens ... brought to you by. ...") But as a vehicle for putting those developments in perspective ... it often falls flat.

Charles Osgood

1933–

In 1967, Charles Osgood joins CBS Radio. By 1972, he's also doing television. Osgood's three-minute radio feature, *The Osgood File*, is a huge hit. In it, he displays his gift for verse — as he does in the title of one of his books, *Nothing Could Be Finer Than a Crisis That Is Minor in the Morning*. In 1994, CBS makes him the host of *Sunday Morning*.

CBS RADIO

Charles Osgood understands how the public feels about the news:

'Like singing in the shower'

Powerful are those who choose
The items that make up the news.
And yet in spite of all that power,
It's much like singing in the shower.
For it is clear from card and letter
That you all think you'd do it better.

Paul Harvey

1918–

He's probably been heard by more radio listeners than anyone in the history of the United States. Paul Harvey starts broadcasting at age 14 and spends more than 50 years on the ABC Radio Network. His 15-minute morning and noon shows reach 21 million. How has radio changed? "My goodness," he says of contemporary talk radio, "nowadays anybody can go on any talk show, anywhere, anytime and swing in all directions."

UNIVERSITY OF MARYLAND

Paul Harvey talks to The Washington Post, *July 7, 1995:*

'Three categories'

When I was first in radio, there were three categories. There was the commentator, the analyst and the reporter. And if you behaved yourself as a reporter ... you were allowed to call yourself an analyst. And if you developed a batting average ... a select few would become commentators. Now all that's blurred. It's utterly meaningless.

Susan Stamberg

1938–

National Public Radio's Susan Stamberg is one of the "founding mothers" of the 1960s experiment, public broadcasting. Early host of the popular *All Things Considered,* Stamberg brings the personal to radio news. She helps NPR become a kind of national diary, looking beyond the headlines into the daily lives of a generation of Americans. "People in powerful positions always have microphones," she says. But regular folk are "what make the country run."

COURTESY NATIONAL PUBLIC RADIO

In an April 1990 discussion about breast cancer, Susan Stamberg interviews Washington Post *fashion writer Nina Hyde:*

'On the cancer'

Nina Hyde's mind — a mind slowed but not dulled by medication — is on the cancer she's been dealing with. ... The woman who'd bounced into our studios in 1983 — her eyes bright, her black hair a lustrous, thick crown around her head — was, on the day we last met, sitting carefully, with a discomfort she fought to disguise.

Nina Totenberg

1944–

In 1991, National Public Radio legal affairs correspondent Nina Totenberg reveals sexual harassment charges against U.S. Supreme Court nominee Clarence Thomas. Totenberg's story leads to dramatic televised hearings that open public debate on sexual harassment. In the end, however, Thomas is confirmed as a high-court justice. Totenberg's girlhood hero? "Nancy Drew," because she always found "the bad guy."

On the Oct. 6, 1991, broadcast of National Public Radio's Weekend Edition, *Nina Totenberg breaks the Clarence Thomas–Anita Hill story:*

'His sexual interests'

The relationship, she said, became even more strained when Thomas, in work situations, began to discuss sex. On these occasions, she said, Thomas would call her into his office to discuss work. ... According to Hill's affidavit, Thomas, after a brief work discussion, would "turn conversations to discussions about his sexual interests. His conversations," she said, "were vivid."

Rush Limbaugh
1951–

In 1994, conservative syndicated radio and TV personality Rush Limbaugh helps fan the anti-government fervor that hands the Republican Party a congressional majority for the first time in decades. The Missouri native starts broadcasting at age 16. He becomes "the most dangerous man in America" in 1988 with a national show and an audience of 17 million. His rabid fans call themselves "Dittoheads" because they agree with Limbaugh's attacks on the "feminazi" and "humaniacs."

E.J. CAMP

Rush Limbaugh's show opener:

'Flawlessly'

Greetings ... this is Rush Limbaugh, the most dangerous man in America ... serving humanity simply by opening my mouth, destined for my own wing in the Museum of Broadcasting, executing everything I do flawlessly with zero mistakes, doing this show with half my brain tied behind my back just to make it fair because I have talent on loan from God.

Don Imus

1940–

Millions follow irreverent radio jock Don Imus. His national talk show — sometimes shocking, always surprising — features guests who are "lying thieving politicians or liberal weenie pundits." During the 1992 presidential campaign, he calls Bill Clinton "my man Bubba." Politicians who respect the influence of non-traditional media line up to get on his show. "It's not *Nightline,* it's not *Meet the Press,*" says Imus. "It gives them an opportunity to reveal their humanity."

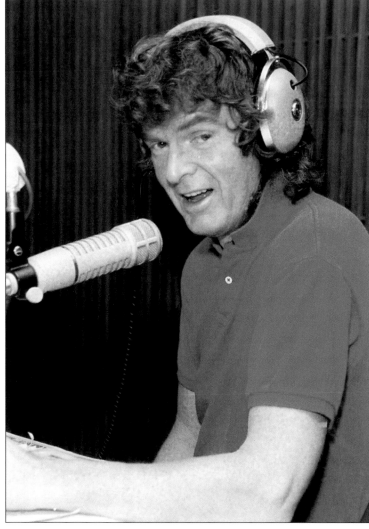

THE ASSOCIATED PRESS

In the June 13, 1994, Broadcasting & Cable, *Don Imus explains that his listeners have at least a high school education:*

'It's just my interests'

I think if you wanted to draw a distinction, for example, between me and Howard Stern, you would at least have to have a GED to listen to me. I have a greater interest in talking to Anna Quindlen or Nina Totenberg or Bob Dole than I do Jessica Hahn or Joey Buttafuoco. That's not to suggest that one's necessarily any more valid in terms of either their interest value or entertainment value, it's just my interests. I don't do this show based on what I think people want to hear. I do it based on what I'm interested in. I've always done it that way.

CHAPTER 12

TV People

> 'Never in the history of humankind has there been a medium with the impact of television. It ... literally has brought the world home in a box.'
>
> — WALTER CRONKITE

NEW YORK, 1963 —

NIGHTLY NETWORK NEWS EXPANDS FROM 15 TO 30 minutes. Within a few years, most Americans list TV as their primary news source. The moving pictures sear the collective memory and begin to shape national thought. President Lyndon Johnson, for one, will soon tune his specially built set to three network newscasts at once to watch the news unfold. By 1972, the title of most trusted American (with a rating of 73 percent) goes not to a president or a minister, but to *CBS Evening News* anchor Walter Cronkite. The broadcast legend's advice to viewers: Read newspapers to be "truly well-informed."

Is television superficial? Sometimes it seems the fledgling medium delivers only flashy pictures, celebrity, skimmed information and the wall-to-wall programming FCC chairman Newton Minow once so famously described as "a vast wasteland."

There is both show and news in this business. At the 1961 presidential gala, Frank Sinatra and Milton Berle honor NBC's "Gold Dust Twins" with a song to the tune of *Love and Marriage:* "Huntley, Brinkley; Huntley, Brinkley ... one is glum and the other quite twinkly." Their producer admits the chemistry between newscasters Chet Huntley and David Brinkley "is a show business thing." Click ahead to the first *CBS Evening News* broadcast that veteran anchor Dan Rather shares with Connie Chung. At sign-off, Chung says, "Good night, Chet." Replies Rather: "Good night, David."

"There's a fine line between show biz and news biz," says famed CBS producer Don Hewitt. "The trick is to walk up to that line and touch it with your toe but don't cross it. And some people stay so far away from the line that nobody wants to watch what they do. And other people keep crossing the line ... but there has to be a line because the line is called truth."

On the one hand, a handful of dramatic images can do more work than thousands of words to bring down Red-baiting Sen. Joseph McCarthy, to advance the cause of Civil Rights, to help change public opinion about the Vietnam War. But only if those images hit the screen. In 1966, CBS News President Fred Friendly quits in disgust when the network refuses to air Senate hearings on Vietnam, opting instead for reruns of *I Love Lucy* and *The Real McCoys*. "We cannot," he says, "in one of the crucial debates of our time abdicate ... responsibility."

On the other hand, the people who bring us the nightly news are, and have been, like it or not, celebrities, sometimes on a par with Hollywood actors. They appear on magazine covers, they get fan mail, their lives help feed the gossip press. Which isn't all bad for the networks. Celebrity newscasters help networks win big audiences,

which draw big advertisers. It is not surprising that TV anchors earn much fatter salaries than their luminary counterparts in print media and radio.

Not all TV newspeople like the trappings. "I'm a newsman. A journalist," says CNN anchor Bernard Shaw. "If I signed autographs, that would make me some sort of celebrity, and I'm not. ... it can be very poisonous ... very seductive. [It can] undercut honest work. ... I'm just a newsman."

Click back to 1948, to early regular newscasts, *CBS News With Douglas Edwards*, and the popular *Camel Newsreel Theater*, hosted by John Cameron Swayze. Viewers play along on "Swayze," the board game. When the show becomes *The Camel News Caravan*, Swayze's on-camera appeal is used to sell cigarettes. The TV host's fame diverts attention from his notable journalistic skills: Swayze can get a last-minute briefing and recite from memory the breaking news of the day, without a script.

At the same time, TV (at least with the right personality in focus) can generate visual intimacy — body language, warm or dramatic expressions — a more sophisticated version of the voice intimacy that makes radio magic.

— Newseum/Max Reid photo

Above: From 1965 to 1981, Walter Cronkite delivers the news in color through these cameras.

"The lens seemed to be so direct and friendly ... almost as if I could see someone there," says Dave Garroway, the affable first host of NBC's morning TV news experiment called *Today.* "I am much more comfortable and more in communication with whoever is at the end of the black hole than I am with someone in person." But Garroway is show biz as well. His co-host: a live chimpanzee named J. Fred Muggs, who inspires a souvenir doll.

Just a few years earlier, during World War II, broadcast means radio. Some of the rules of the radio airwaves, good and bad, spill over to the newer medium, whose three networks, by 1963, deliver news to nine out of 10 Americans. "When listeners hear a woman's voice, they turn off their radios, because a woman's voice just doesn't carry authority," an editor tells Pauline Frederick, who has to "make my own opportunity" to cover TV news. "I was told that there was great objection to a woman being on the air for serious issues, and he had orders not to use me. But he said if by chance, I got an exclusive, he'd have to use me, adding, 'though I'll slit your throat if you tell anyone I gave you this advice.' "

When Huntley and Brinkley start out, TV news is simple. "You just use pictures when you have them and words when you don't, and stop once in a while for a commercial," says Brinkley. "There's no other way to do it." But there is. It comes about as the medium matures. It's "a dimension of anchoring ... live editorial television," says ABC anchor Peter Jennings. "Anchors are expected to ... sit down and talk on the Challenger disaster, the Wall Street crash, the State of the Union, presidential elections, primaries, earthquakes, rape, murder, pillage — at the drop of a hat. You say, 'Thank God for the 30 years I spent on the street.' "

Words or pictures? As better technology brings faster, better pictures, do the words begin to fade? "My preference," says legendary NBC producer Reuven Frank, "has always been for picture reporting." But pictures of what? When on-camera armchairs and anchor small-talk come to New York's WNBC, local news reporter Gabe Pressman, a local legend in his own right, quits for a time in protest. "I believe strongly in hard news coverage," Pressman says. "I believe, too, in the need for more profound investigative reporting." Then comes electronic newsgathering. And with it, action news, eyewitness news, satellite news, bigger, better, faster, more. "The biggest change," says NBC anchor Tom Brokaw, "is that there is more of it on the air ... more competition ... technology ... financial pressures. And they all play against each other. ... We have to work harder at story selection."

There is more than just *more.* Public television offers

> 'You just use pictures when you have them and words when you don't.'
>
> — DAVID BRINKLEY

an alternative, "the variety to satisfy my inner nature," in the words of PBS reporter Bill Moyers, "but usually not enough production money." Cable News Network offers news all the time. While once derided as the experimental "Chicken Noodle Network," CNN keeps viewers front and center during the 1991 Persian Gulf War, with Bernard Shaw speaking to the world "from the center of hell." The decade of the '90s opens up a whirl of "narrowcasted" news, meaning news tailored to an audience, from Spanish language news on Univisión to news geared to young rockers on MTV.

"Out of that hailstorm, will people still want some institution they respect or tolerate, like *The New York Times* or *NBC Nightly News* or *MacNeil-Lehrer?*" says Robert MacNeil, who helps pioneer in-depth TV reporting on PBS. "Do they want them once a day or once a week to pull the world together for them and give them the synthesis that they traditionally relied on and trusted?"

The answer is a definite maybe. Despite the flood of narrowcasted news — and even though the three major networks have lost half their audience — TV news for the moment still belongs to Peter Jennings, Dan Rather and Tom Brokaw, each with five to 10 times the audience of CNN or MSNBC.

A multichannel hailstorm? "We're all better for it," says Brokaw, "if we always keep in mind one fundamental truth: ultimately, information is useful only if you can trust it. Is it factual? What's the source? How does it fit with other information? Technology alone cannot provide those critical tests. Mass media work best when they have intelligent, curious people of independent judgment examining and testing information in a raw, shapeless form before it lands on your television set."

John Cameron Swayze

1906–1995

In 1948, John Cameron Swayze becomes NBC's first television newscaster, on *The Camel Newsreel Theater.* The next year, as host of *The Camel News Caravan,* he recognizes the need for film crews and writers on a TV news program. He also smokes on the air, advising viewers to "sit back, light up a Camel, and be an eyewitness to the happenings that made history." Swayze's final words at the end of each broadcast, "That's the story, folks. This is John Cameron Swayze, and I'm glad we could get together," prompt other newscasters to seek their own patented sign-offs.

In a 1952 speech to the Los Angeles Advertising Club, John Cameron Swayze describes the impact of television on news:

'Brings the story'

Newspapers are necessary if one is to have the complete story of what is going on in the world. ... [But] television ... has the extra dimension of the pictorial to aid it in telling a news story. Television more than any other medium brings the story to the public and lets the viewer make up his own mind.

Lawrence Spivak

1900–1994

In 1947, Lawrence Spivak publishes *American Mercury* magazine. He decides to co-host an NBC talk show, *Meet the Press,* to promote his magazine. Aired only in New York, the show is a hit. NBC takes it national. Viewers tune in to national and international leaders facing tough questions from Spivak. The host's editorial formula, followed by future hosts all the way up to today's Tim Russert: "Learn everything about your guests' positions on the issues — then take the other side!" Spivak moderates *Meet the Press* until 1975, a stint of nearly 30 years.

THE ASSOCIATED PRESS

Lawrence Spivak explains why he grills his guests on Meet the Press:

'Make or break'

Since I wasn't beholden to anybody, I just felt that the questions had to be asked. It just had to be fair and informative and accurate. And sometimes the refusal to answer becomes more significant than the answer. We just [furnished] an opportunity for a guest to make or break himself.

Dave Garroway

1913–1982

He's sometimes called "the founding father of morning television." Dave Garroway is the first host of NBC's "brash experiment" — the *Today* show — premiering in 1952. In the wacky world of morning television, Garroway's co-host turns out to be J. Fred Muggs, a trained chimpanzee. NBC finds Garroway after he's been a disc jockey and the host of *Garroway at Large* in Chicago. He stays with *Today* until 1961. The show becomes a long-lived and widely imitated television format. J. Fred Muggs retires to Florida. The chimp outlives Garroway.

NBC/ GLOBE PHOTOS

Dave Garroway greets viewers of NBC's first Today *show broadcast on Jan. 14, 1952:*

'A new kind of television'

Well, here we are, and good morning to you. The very first good morning of what I hope ... will be a great many good mornings between you and me. Here it is, January 14, 1952, when NBC begins a new program called *Today*, and if it doesn't sound too revolutionary, I really believe this begins a new kind of television.

Pauline Frederick

1906–1990

In the 1940s, Pauline Frederick is the only woman working as a network television reporter. With ABC, she is the first woman to cover the United Nations. In 1976, she's the first woman to moderate a presidential debate on PBS. The most-often asked questions on U.N. tours during the 1960s: "Where did Khrushchev bang his shoe?" and "Do you ever see Pauline Frederick?"

THE ASSOCIATED PRESS

In a 1974 interview with a University of Maryland journalism student, Pauline Frederick recalls her early days in network news:

'I'll slit your throat'

I was told by my editor that there was great objection to a woman being on the air for serious issues, and he had orders not to use me. But he said if by chance, I got an exclusive, he'd have to use me, adding "though I'll slit your throat if you tell anyone I gave you this advice."

Gabe Pressman
1924–

New York's Gabe Pressman pioneers on-the-street broadcast reporting in 1954 when he joins WRCA Radio and TV (later, WNBC). Some call him the "inventor of local television journalism." Pressman spends more than 40 years chasing local stories. He protests the station's move toward fluff and ratings: "I believe strongly in hard news coverage as the essence of television journalism."

THE ASSOCIATED PRESS

In a Feb. 21, 1994, interview with Electronic Media, *Gabe Pressman talks about signing a new contract at age 70:*

'A compulsion'

It's fun. Despite the vagaries of the business and changes in policy, I still love doing it. I have a compulsion to inform the world. ... I think that there's a continuing struggle for the soul of broadcast journalism. Regardless of what decade I'm in, the challenge is there. ... I hope that by giving me a long-term contract they're endorsing what I do. That doesn't mean I agree with everything they do.

Chet Huntley

1911–1974

He's not a celebrity — at first. Chester Robert Huntley is a broadcaster for 20 years, mostly with CBS, before he begins working with David Brinkley at the 1956 political conventions. The deep-voiced Montanan and the skeptical North Carolinian launch *The Huntley-Brinkley Report* on a 14-year run, making millions for their network. In 1960, they move to number one; by 1965, the two are as well-known as John Wayne and the Beatles. The dual-anchor format lasts until Huntley retires in 1970 to his Big Sky estate to do advertisements for American Airlines.

THE ASSOCIATED PRESS

Chet Huntley answers his most frequently asked question: Are you Huntley or Brinkley?

'It's hard ...'

I'm not sure. Sometimes it's hard even for me to keep us straight.

David Brinkley

1920–

In 1956, David Brinkley joins Chet Huntley on *The Huntley-Brinkley Report*, the show that puts their network on top. Their familiar refrain, capping reports from Washington and New York: "Good night, Chet. Good night, David. And good night for NBC News." They break up in 1970 when Huntley retires. Brinkley later takes his sardonic, knowing style to ABC for *This Week With David Brinkley*. He retires from news in 1997 to do an ad campaign for the show's sponsor. About journalism, Brinkley says: "It may be impossible to be objective, but we must always be fair."

NBC/GLOBE PHOTOS

In his memoir, David Brinkley, *the longtime television newsman recalls how his 1956 convention coverage changed his life:*

'Television news pantheon'

Jack Gould, television critic for *The New York Times* ... wrote an intensely flattering column. ... Gould had installed me in the television news pantheon, set like a stone bust in a niche standing alongside Murrow and Sevareid ... it was a stunning and unsettling experience to read that the *Times* thought more highly of me than I ever did.

Reuven Frank

1920–

"The highest power of television journalism is not in the transmission of information but in the transmission of experience," says Reuven Frank, an early innovator in TV news. Frank joins NBC as a writer in 1950. He organizes early political convention coverage and brings together the "Gold Dust Twins" — the Chet Huntley/David Brinkley news duo. Twice, Frank serves as network news president.

NBC/GLOBE PHOTOS

In the winter 1995 issue of the Media Studies Journal, *Reuven Frank discusses changes in how television covers national political conventions:*

'No more news'

There used to be news in fights over the party platform. ... The civil rights struggle and the Vietnam War, the great dramas of recent American history, were played out at the conventions before the cameras. There are no such great dramas these days. There is, in sum, no more news at conventions.

Don Hewitt

1922–

"I assume you gentlemen know each other?" That's what CBS producer Don Hewitt says to Richard Nixon and John Kennedy before the first televised presidential debate in U.S. history. Hewitt's debate debut is just one pioneering move: He produces the first regular CBS newscast in 1948, takes evening news from 15 to 30 minutes in 1963 and launches the widely imitated news magazine, *60 Minutes,* in 1968. "Television is successful," says Hewitt, "when you have a gut feeling about a show."

CBS PHOTO ARCHIVE

Don Hewitt recalls the 1960 presidential debate, after which most radio listeners declare Nixon the winner while most TV viewers give the edge to Kennedy:

'A travesty'

We offered to put some makeup on [Nixon] but he said no because he didn't want people to say he used makeup and Kennedy didn't. ... When the first debate was over, I said, "My God, we don't have to wait for election night." I said, "I just produced a television show that elected a president of the United States." That was a travesty.

Nancy Dickerson

1927–1997

At CBS in 1962, Nancy Dickerson excels at snaring congressional interviews. She often gets interviews that her male colleagues could not. Her first break is an exclusive with camera-shy House Speaker Sam Rayburn. Moving to NBC in 1963, she becomes the first female broadcaster to report from a national convention floor and the first to broadcast from the Senate floor. "There were a lot of firsts," she says.

THE ASSOCIATED PRESS

In her 1976 memoir, Among Those Present, *Nancy Dickerson recalls tough times early in her career at CBS:*

'Jurisdiction'

I suggested every conceivable story idea that wouldn't infringe on the jurisdiction of a male CBS correspondent. Obviously no male correspondent would want to cover a luncheon for the First Lady, so I went. Luckily, it was one of the few times in Mamie Eisenhower's life that she actually made a speech.

Walter Cronkite

1916–

Walter Cronkite's just-the-facts manner earns him the title "the most trusted man in America." Cronkite starts as a *Houston Post* newspaper reporter, going on to cover World War II for United Press. In 1950, Edward R. Murrow brings him to CBS. By 1963, Cronkite is anchoring the nation's first half-hour network newscast, *The CBS Evening News.* "Uncle Walter" shepherds the nation through President John F. Kennedy's assassination, the Vietnam War, the walk on the moon, and more. His famous sign-off: "And that's the way it is."

THE ASSOCIATED PRESS

After North Vietnam's 1968 Tet offensive, Walter Cronkite uses the last minutes of airtime to oppose the Vietnam War:

'An honorable people'

To say that we are mired in stalemate seems the only realistic, yet unsatisfactory conclusion. ... It is increasingly clear to this reporter that the only rational way out, then, will be to negotiate, not as victors, but as an honorable people who lived up to their pledge to defend democracy, and did the best they could.

Bill Moyers
1934–

Prophetically unhappy with President Lyndon B. Johnson's Vietnam policy, White House press secretary Bill Moyers leaves to become publisher of *Newsday*. He jumps to public television, to CBS, then back again. Moyers specializes in idea-oriented reports and interviews, setting himself apart from most television journalists. His view of White House reporters: They "ask bumper-sticker questions to get fortune-cookie answers."

THE ASSOCIATED PRESS

In a January 1997 speech, Bill Moyers talks about commercial television:

'They come over the transom'

You can no more escape the influence of these images coming into your community than you can escape the emissions from automobiles by staying home and leaving your car in the garage. They come in the room when you're not watching. They come over the transom. They come in the window.

Fred Friendly

1915–1998

CBS producer Fred Friendly, working with Edward R. Murrow, produces hard-hitting documentaries in the first decades of television. Friendly resigns his two-year presidency of CBS News in 1966 when the network denies him air time for live coverage of Senate hearings on Vietnam. Instead, CBS goes with sitcom reruns. "The decision not to carry the hearings," he writes, "makes a mockery of ... access to congressional debate."

CBS PHOTO ARCHIVE

A letter Fred Friendly releases to the press after he resigns from CBS:

'I am resigning'

I am resigning because CBS News did not carry the Senate Foreign Relations hearings last Thursday. ... I am resigning because the decision not to carry the hearings makes a mockery of the Paley-Stanton Columbia News division crusade of many years that demands broadest access to congressional debate. ... We cannot, in our public utterances, demand such access and then, in one of the crucial debates of our time, abdicate that responsibility.

Belva Davis

1933–

San Francisco's KPIX-TV hires Belva Davis in 1967, and she becomes the first African-American woman to anchor television news in the western United States. A five-time Emmy winner, Davis is known for probing, issue-based community reporting. Her question for white female journalists in top management jobs: "Will they share their power more than their white male counterparts?"

COURTESY KRON-TV

Belva Davis talks about the subtleties of reporting:

'Get to the personal'

My goal always had been to somehow get to the personal. If there's anything I always tried for, it was to try to get to something that was outside of the hard facts of the story, to some sort of feeling.

Robert MacNeil

1931–

When PBS launches *The MacNeil/Lehrer Report* in 1975, co-hosts Robert MacNeil and Jim Lehrer are pitched as the "thinker's alternative" to nightly network news. Their fans say only the "fourth newscast" provides news without network spiff-and-glitz. Their critics call it staid, even boring. Says MacNeil, who retires to write after a successful 20-year stint: "We have the courage to be boring."

THE ASSOCIATED PRESS

In an article in the summer 1995 Media Studies Journal, Robert MacNeil writes about television's role in society:

'A phenomenon like television'

In medieval Europe, the church was a matrix of thought, the boundary of popular imagination: It explained everything. Today, television sets the boundaries of the popular imagination. ... There has never been a phenomenon like television in its ubiquity, its seductive appeal ... its ability to leap across international frontiers and over the barriers of class and literacy.

Jim Lehrer

1934–

Novelist and one-time *Dallas Times Herald* city editor Jim Lehrer becomes co-anchor with Robert MacNeil in 1975 of *The MacNeil/Lehrer Report* on PBS. The hour-long news program delves deeply into a few stories instead of skimming the surface of many. It finds a niche. "Our ratings are way up," Lehrer says, "because viewers are tired of the screaming school of journalism." When MacNeil retires in 1995, Lehrer becomes solo host of the popular show.

JEANNE MARKLIN

Jim Lehrer tells why he writes novels in a Dec. 30, 1996, interview with Publishers Weekly:

'A paper person'

I'm a written-word person, a page person, a paper person. I love television and I get great satisfaction out of those moments when things go really well. But those moments pass. The moments in books never pass and that's why I write novels.

Tom Brokaw

1940–

Since 1983, Tom Brokaw anchors *NBC Nightly News.* His is one of the best-known faces on U.S. television. Brokaw conducts the first one-on-one interview with Soviet leader Mikhail Gorbachev and is the only U.S. anchor on the scene when the Berlin Wall falls. The South Dakota native says he always has cast his eyes "over the horizon to see what else was going on in the world."

USA TODAY

Tom Brokaw describes his job in a May 30, 1992, interview with The Seattle Times:

'Right place, right time'

I don't think I'm the most natural anchorman in the world. I think Peter [Jennings] is. I think Peter's got anchor elan. But I have enormous curiosity, I've worked hard at this business. And I've had the rare good fortune of being in the right place at the right time and not screwing up when I was there.

Connie Chung

1946–

She's the best-known Asian-American newswoman in TV history. Connie Chung joins CBS as a correspondent in 1971 and 20 years later joins Dan Rather as co-anchor of the *CBS Evening News*. One poll lists her as the nation's most popular anchor. But the pairing ends when Chung resigns. TV news, she says, "has always been a very male-dominated profession ... and the evening news has been the last bastion of that."

USA TODAY

An excerpt of Connie Chung's interview for the 1989 book, The Imperfect Mirror — Inside Stories of Television Newswomen:

'Grow old on camera'

Those of us who are in our forties are going to be able to grow old on camera. We haven't been kicked out the door yet. ... I thought that if I were ever pushed out of this business, it would be because they don't like my work anymore, not because I became gray and wrinkled.

Peter Jennings

1938–

World News Tonight anchor Peter Jennings helps lead longtime runner-up ABC to the top of the ratings in the late 1980s. Jennings gets a reputation for calm clarity amid crisis and complexity, especially in stories from the Middle East. He demonstrates this early on as the network's Beirut correspondent during the terrorist attack at the 1972 Olympics. On his job: "I think of myself as a broadcaster who has the privilege of access to the public airwaves."

USA TODAY

In a winter 1989 Gannett Center Journal *interview, Peter Jennings talks about the influence of the TV anchor:*

'How we position stories'

Someone on the [*Power in Washington*] show said, "You know what we've got to do is influence those lobbyists and those anchormen." I really have no sense of that. ... I think our real influence on the outside world is in story selection, how we behave in live events, how we position stories in the broadcast, what we put on as news.

María Elena Salinas

1954–

She's one of the most familiar faces in America's Spanish-speaking households. Starting in 1987, María Elena Salinas co-anchors the popular nightly newscast on the Univisión TV network. She starts in Los Angeles at Spanish-language radio and KMEX-Channel 34. Univisión reaches as many as 20 million U.S. viewers, 12 Latin American countries and Puerto Rico. Says Salinas: "We are the eyes and ears for Latinos in the United States, their liaison to their neighborhood and their country."

THE ASSOCIATED PRESS

Univisión's María Elena Salinas and colleague Jorge Ramos interview Mexican president Ernesto Zedillo in October 1996 about his ties with former president Carlos Salinas:

'We have information ...'

Do you remember when was the last time you spoke with him?

"December 1, 1994."

We have information that in March of '95 you met with him.

"It's absolutely false. Whoever wrote that is lying. It's absolutely false."

Do you owe your candidacy to Salinas ...?

"In the first place, I want to correct something you said: the President of Mexico does not choose his successor. ... I am President ... because more than 17 million Mexicans voted for yours truly."

Tabitha Soren

1967–

"Young people aren't ignorant, they're not unintelligent, and they're not uninterested — they're just uninspired." So says Tabitha Soren, MTV political correspondent. Soren, who starts out after college at an ABC affiliate, rocks Music Television's young viewers with her political reporting. During the 1992 campaign, MTV's young voter drive inspires 100,000 new voters to register.

USA TODAY

In a winter 1995 Media Studies Journal *article, Tabitha Soren discusses "infotainment" and traditional news:*

'An entirely new audience'

I don't think the tabloid trend and "checkbook" journalism are any good. I don't think paying someone gives the interviewee any credibility. However, if President Bush or Vice President Gore goes on Letterman, or Oprah or Donahue ... they're going to garner an entirely new audience that they wouldn't necessarily reach otherwise. And I don't think that's a bad thing.

Bernard Shaw

1940–

In 1991, Cable News Network anchor Bernard Shaw speaks from "the center of Hell" — the ninth floor of Baghdad's Al Rashid Hotel — as America bombs Iraq. Shaw offers blow-by-blows of TV's Persian Gulf War the way his boyhood hero did on the radio during World War II. "I used to stand up my dates to watch [Edward R.] Murrow specials," he says. "I want to be like that man. ... I didn't see him as white. I saw him as a journalist." In 1965, Shaw starts as a Chicago newsreader. In 1980, he gambles, anchoring fledgling CNN. In the 1990s, he plays himself in Hollywood movies.

COURTESY CNN

CNN anchor Bernard Shaw, one of the nation's best-known African-American broadcasters, talks to the Chicago Tribune *after Los Angeles riots follow the Rodney King verdict:*

'Controlled rage'

I can afford my controlled rage. People who have jobs, who are gainfully employed, and who get rewards for their efforts and contributions to society, can afford [controlled] rage. It would be insulting presumptuousness on my part to say that people in South Central Los Angeles or elsewhere who are rebelling against what they perceive as injustice should control theirs.

CHAPTER 13

Martyrs

'To preserve the freedom of the human mind ... and freedom of the press, every spirit should be ready to devote itself to martyrdom.'

— THOMAS JEFFERSON

PHOENIX, ARIZONA, 1975 —

AFTER 15 YEARS EXPOSING POLITICAL SCANDALS and organized crime, Don Bolles has had enough: "This isn't worth it to me or my family. ... I told my editors, no more. I'm no longer in investigative reporting."

Seven months later, *The Arizona Republic* reporter is dead, the victim of a car bomb that rips off both his legs after he tries to meet a source for a story about land fraud. Lying mortally injured, Bolles whispers to rescuers, "Mafia."

Within a week, dozens of journalists from across the nation form the Arizona Project to continue the reporter's work. Within a year, the project reveals a web of corruption leading to 18 indictments.

Like so many who take on the dangerous stories, Don Bolles never sets out to be a martyr. He just wants to report. He'd no doubt agree with Veronica Guerin, slain in 1996 for reporting on Ireland's most notorious thugs: "Crime is an evil subculture existing within our culture, and to me, exposing it is what journalism is about. I suppose that's why I do it. It is a story that has to be told."

Journalists dying in the line of duty. It is not quite as

easy to see or believe, somehow, as police officers dying on the street or soldiers dying in war. But too often, journalists are murdered for what they represent and what they report. Sometimes, the danger of a story leads them too close to the edge. Often, they are at the wrong place at the wrong time, downed in a plane crash, smothered by a volcano, hit by a train.

But the single greatest cause of job-related death among newspeople worldwide is political assassination. "The targets ... typically are not foreign correspondents," says the Committee to Protect Journalists. "They are local reporters covering local stories." Like Don Bolles covering organized crime in Arizona.

Or like James M. Lingan — the first recorded journalistic casualty on American soil — who in 1812 is

stomped to death by a mob for trying to publish the feisty Baltimore *Federal Republican*, which opposes the "highly impolitic and destructive" War of 1812. Lingan's name is the first of more than 1,000 on The Freedom Forum Journalists Memorial in Arlington, Va. — men and women First Lady Hillary Rodham Clinton calls "democracy's heroes." They "endure hardships, danger, give their lives," says the president and CEO of The Associated Press, Louis D. Boccardi, "so that free people may know the truth as best we can find it."

Political assassination of newspeople is an international story. But the felling of "democracy's heroes," beginning with Lingan and his ill-fated *Republican*, also has an undeniably American cast. One moment, Ernie Pyle is the most popular columnist of World War II, sending home reports from "the worm's eye view," the words of soldiers in foxholes. The next moment, he is dead, victim of a Japanese sniper's bullet. In another American place and time, Mark Kellogg, who rides to the Battle of the Little Bighorn, files his final dispatch with The Associated Press: "By the time this reaches you we will have met and fought the red devils, with what result remains to be seen. I go with Custer and will be at the death." His own death, which Pyle would have called another part of war's "emotional tapestry of one dull dead pattern."

Photographer Dickey Chapelle does it for freedom. "I know the world won't come to an end just because American press freedom shrinks. ... But I'm not going to like it. ... And I'm going to scream and splutter and hit out and, if I'm lucky enough to have the chance, expand whatever credibility I personally have saved up in the act of somehow holding some outer line some little longer." Chapelle looks for freedom in the dangerous places

Inset: Mark Kellogg carries this satchel as he rides with Custer to Little Bighorn.

where truth can be hard to find. Fidel Castro says she has "tiger blood in her veins." During the Vietnam War, she steps on a land mine.

CBS correspondent George Polk does it for the story. He covers 1948's civil war in Greece, communists fighting monarchists. His battered body, bound at the wrists and ankles, washes up on the shores of Salonika Bay. He's been shot through the back of the head at point-blank range. "Why?" former AP correspondent Terry Anderson wonders in 1996. "Why is such force mustered against reporters?" He answers his own question: "Because what journalists do is important. An active press often plays a key role in bringing freedom to a society." Anderson becomes a living martyr after nearly seven years as a hostage of a radical Islamic faction in the Middle East.

Photographer Sean Flynn does it for the thrill of the chase. Some call news "the cocaine of crafts." And Sean, says author William Prochnau, "spent most of his time playing out in real life the Hollywood derring-do of his swashbuckling father, Errol Flynn. ... [Sean] Flynn had death wish written all over him." Flynn's friend and fellow photographer Dana Stone also loves the glory of the story. "Got another *Time* cover," he says in a 1967 interview. "I think that's the eighth picture I've had in *Time* and *Newsweek* ... I guess it pays off." In 1970, Flynn and Stone

vanish at the Cambodian border.

At times the world of journalists seems so dangerous it's almost comical. Once, in Africa, a driver is hauling NBC newsman Ted Yates in a yellow, rented Mercedes across the plain near Lake Albert when "we suddenly were stopped and challenged by a large hippopotamus. ... For an hour in the murderous heat he watched us. It became an absurd nightmare. What a hell of a way, I thought, to die — scared to death by a hippo while covering an undeclared war." During the Six Day War in 1967, Yates is shot and killed in Jordan.

Rubén Salazar's Aug. 29, 1970, death becomes a cause. Salazar, the best-known Latino journalist of his generation, is an investigative reporter for the Spanish-language station KMEX-TV and columnist for the *Los Angeles Times*.

After covering a huge anti-war demonstration in Los Angeles, Salazar is sitting in a bar, relaxing with friends. A sheriff's deputy who says he thought troublemakers were inside fires a tear-gas canister into the tavern. The canister strikes Salazar full in the head.

A coroner's inquest finds the death to be accidental. But nearly 30 years later, journalists hold panel discussions with such titles as "Rubén Salazar: The Myth and the Man." From California to Texas, parks, libraries and housing projects carry his name; his life inspires

> 'A hell of a way ...
>
> to die — scared
>
> to death by a hippo.'
>
> — TED YATES

characters in novels; murals depict his resistance to an unjust society.

Unlike most of the men and women here, Salazar actually ponders the fate that awaits him: "Everything's going so well for me," he says. "Something has to go wrong. Something has to happen. You know, they need a martyr."

James M. Lingan

1752–1812

Former Revolutionary War general James M. Lingan co-owns the Baltimore *Federal Republican,* whose editorial columns oppose the "highly impolitic and destructive" War of 1812. After the newspaper's anti-war edition, an opposing mob destroys his newspaper office. Later, foes stomp Lingan in a Baltimore jail, making him the earliest known free press martyr in U.S. history.

SMITHSONIAN INSTITUTION

An excerpt of an editorial in the Baltimore Federal Republican *denouncing the War of 1812:*

'The war is unnecessary'

We mean to represent in as strong colors as we are capable, that the war is unnecessary, inexpedient, and entered into from partial, personal and, as we believe, false motives bearing upon their front marks of undisguised foreign influence which cannot be mistaken.

Elijah Parish Lovejoy

1802–1837

At first, Elijah Lovejoy supports slavery. But when he becomes a minister, he calls for the abolition of slavery in the *St. Louis Observer,* a Presbyterian weekly. Charging his paper is "calculated to incite insurrection," angry citizens toss his printing press into the Mississippi River. Lovejoy keeps writing. Within a year, two more of his presses are destroyed. On Nov. 7, 1837, while protecting a fourth press, Lovejoy is shot five times. His murderers go unpunished.

LIBRARY OF CONGRESS

Two months before he is slain, in a Sept. 8 letter to the American Anti-Slavery Society, Elijah Parish Lovejoy foresees the trouble ahead:

'Violence will be committed'

We have, on the whole, come to the conclusion, that duty requires the press to be re-established here, without delay. Some think it will be mobbed again, as soon as it arrives. In my own opinion, it will not be; but I anticipate that violence will be committed on my person. I do not, however, think it will amount to more than tar and feathers, and perhaps a riding on a rail.

Elias Boudinot

1803–1839

Born "Buck Deer," Cherokee Elias Boudinot takes the name of the Anglo man who pays for his schooling. In 1828, he starts the first Native-American newspaper, *Cherokee Phoenix* (in both English and Cherokee), to "pay a sacred regard to the truth." Boudinot favors government plans to move his tribe west. Tribal leaders won't debate it in print, so he quits and moves to Oklahoma. In 1834, the Georgia militia throws the paper's press down a well. Many die along the "Trail of Tears," as the rest of the tribe is forced west. Boudinot is building a new house when three Cherokee approach, asking for help. They get him alone and kill him.

UNIVERSITY OF OKLAHOMA PRESS

Elias Boudinot, to a Philadelphia audience in 1826:

'Sad story of extinction'

When before did a nation of Indians step forward and ask for the means of civilization. ... I view my native country, rising from the ashes of her degradations, wearing her purified and beautiful garments. ... We have seen one family after another, one tribe after another, nation after nation, pass away; until only a few solitary creatures are left to tell the sad story of extinction.

Mark Kellogg

1833–1876

Reporter Mark Kellogg of the *Bismarck Tribune* in North Dakota is the only journalist to accompany Lt. Col. George Custer at the Battle of the Little Bighorn. The famous battle of the 7th U.S. Cavalry Regiment against Sioux and Cheyenne warriors is a newsman's dream — "with what result remains to be seen." Astride a gray mule, Kellogg rides into battle carrying satchel, light clothing, tobacco, pencils and paper. He dies along with Custer and his 210 men. Only two bodies are not mutilated: Custer's and Kellogg's. The reporter's satchel survives.

COURTESY SANDY BARNARD

Mark Kellogg's final dispatch, filed to The Associated Press on June 24, 1876:

'I go with Custer'

We leave the Rosebud tomorrow and by the time this reaches you we will have met and fought the red devils, with what result remains to be seen. I go with Custer and will be at the death.

Narciso Gener Gonzales

1858–1903

A political squabble kills Columbia *State* editor N. G. Gonzales, shot by South Carolina Lt. Gov. James H. Tillman just half a block from the downtown newspaper office. Tillman, whose character is "a matter of public concern" according to the newspaper, pulls out a German Luger and shoots the unarmed Gonzales as he walks home to lunch. The editor dies four days later. The politician is acquitted of his murder.

THE STATE-RECORD COMPANY NEWSPAPER

N. G. Gonzales writes a March 24, 1902, front-page story in The State, *triggering Tillman's rage:*

'Evidence is complete'

The evidence proves that Lt. Gov. James H. Tillman deliberately and formally spread upon the Journal of the Senate of South Carolina a statement he knew to be false, such statement being made for the purpose of deceiving the Senate on an important question touching the rules of that body. The chain of evidence is complete and cannot be broken.

An accompanying editorial:
As a candidate for governor, Tillman's character as a man is therefore a matter of public concern. Still more so is his character as an officer of the state.

Byron Darnton

1897–1942

New York Times reporter Byron Darnton dies "somewhere in New Guinea" when the landing craft he's riding in is bombed from the air. As the plane flies overhead, its markings unclear, Darnton scribbles in his pocket-sized notebook: "Jap or ours?" The plane is American — but mistakenly attacks. Darnton continues taking notes as the aircraft banks, returns and drops a second bomb. The World War I veteran dies instantly.

The last story Byron Darnton files for The New York Times *begins:*

'A little article'

SOMEWHERE IN NEW GUINEA (Delayed), Oct. 7, 1942 — If the flies will please get off my arms and out of my mouth and eyes, I will write a little article comparing the job of war correspondent in this war and in the last one. In the last war, I was not a correspondent, but I saw some in France. One difference between ... the last war and this war is that this time I don't dislike correspondents. I hope the soldiers don't. I hope the soldiers don't take what is known here as a "dim view" of us.

George Polk

1913–1948

Covering the Greek Civil War for CBS Radio, George Polk insists on finding his own information rather than relying on government press handouts. Polk's Athens dispatches question Greek government motives, as well as American policy. Within a year, the reporter's bound body is found in Salonika Bay, shot once in the back of the head. Polk's murder remains unsolved. Colleagues establish one of the nation's most prestigious journalism awards in his honor.

UPI/CORBIS-BETTMANN

CBS Radio reporter Don Hollenbeck talks about the murder of George Polk:

'Murder of truth'

In these days, when more and more obstacles are put in the paths of reporters who are trying to learn the truth and to communicate that truth to readers and listeners, the murder of a good reporter is more than the death of one man; it is the murder of truth, and truth is having enough trouble surviving these days.

Dickey Chapelle
1918–1965

When she lands in Vietnam in 1962, free-lance writer-photographer Dickey Chapelle already has covered five wars. The pilot and para-chutist joins the troops at Iwo Jima, but gets tossed out of Okinawa because she's a woman. Chapelle writes sev-eral books, including *What's a Woman Doing Here?* In 1965, on assignment for the *National Observer,* she trips a jungle land mine and is killed by the story she's covering — the Vietnam War. One of the war's most dramatic pic-tures shows Dickey Chapelle receiving last rites. Marine honor guards take her body home to Milwaukee.

UPI/CORBIS-BETTMANN

In a 1962 Reader's Digest *article, Dickey Chapelle writes about the Vietnam War:*

'Hide-and-seek'

How can it be that in this nuclear age, with all the disarmament negotiations, all the arts of modern diplomacy, and all the world's will for peace, the real course of history is still being written by strong young men betting their lives at hide-and-seek on foot in the darkness?

Ted Yates

1930–1967

Veteran NBC producer Ted Yates livens up late-night TV with the combative, tough-talking *Night Beat*. Later, he has had his share of real-life combat as a correspondent in Vietnam and Laos. In 1967, Yates visits the Jordanian sector of Jerusalem for a documentary on the Six Day War when he is shot in the head and killed. Yates, says network president Reuven Frank, "brought to his skill with a camera a fearlessness bordering on folly."

NBC/GLOBE PHOTOS

60 Minutes correspondent Mike Wallace talks about his TV partnership with Ted Yates in a 1990 Los Angeles Times *interview:*

'Abrasive, irreverent questions'

Ted Yates came up with the notion of something called *Night Beat*. It was an interview show, but with a big difference. Interviews by and large then had been ritual minuets. A microphone was planted in the flowers on the table between the two people and you would ask bland questions. He [Yates] insisted that we do a good deal of research, ask abrasive, certainly irreverent, questions. We went on from 11 to 12 at night and would have two guests. If one guest was not very good, you would just go and get rid of that one and go on to the other. It struck a nerve. Suddenly ... everybody started to watch.

Rubén Salazar

1928–1970

Investigative reporter Rubén Salazar exposes drug abuse and prison atrocities. As a *Los Angeles Times* columnist, he covers the Chicano civil rights movement. "I'm a journalist who happens to be Chicano," he says. Salazar next brings hard-edged coverage to KMEX-TV, a Spanish-language station. Sitting in a bar after the Chicano Moratorium anti-war demonstration in 1970, he is hit by a tear-gas shell and dies. Authorities rule the shooting by sheriff's deputies accidental, but decades later many Latinos remain unconvinced.

THE LOS ANGELES TIMES

Sally Salazar writes for Hispanic Link News Service about her husband's death:

'They need a martyr'

Everyone knew that the day would be one of extreme tension. Emotions were building about U.S. involvement in the war. ... Rubén was news director of KMEX. He had assigned a crew to cover the event. He didn't have to go. He didn't really want to. He dragged his feet all morning. I probably could have talked him into staying home. ... Only days before, an old Associated Press friend was over for dinner and Rubén was talking about his job and his new involvement in the Mexican-American community. "Everything's going so well for me," I remember Rubén saying. "Something has to go wrong. Something has to happen." "You know," he added, "they need a martyr." For whatever reasons news people have for doing those things, Rubén went to the parade that Saturday. It's history that he never came home.

Sean Flynn
1941–1971

Free-lance photographer Sean Flynn, son of swash-buckling actor Errol Flynn, finds himself drawn to danger. Covering the Vietnam War for *Time* in 1970, he hears reports of Viet Cong activity in rural Cambodia. On the way to check them out, Flynn and a fellow newsman ride their motorcycles into an ambush and disappear. A CIA report declassified in 1974 reveals that both were captured by Khmer Rouge near the South Vietnamese border and held for a year before being clubbed to death.

THE ASSOCIATED PRESS

In 1991, photographer Tim Page recounts his visit to the village of Bei Met and, with a guide, to the burial place of his friend, Sean Flynn:

'It was spooky'

I walked behind him, feeling a sinking yet hopeful feeling — sort of like shutting a light off and turning it on at the same time. It was spooky, eerie, I was on the verge of crying, overwhelmed. I went and sat at a distance, watching them dig. For a long while, everyone left me alone, in a kind of daze. Then, one of the Cambodian guides came over, and put an arm around me. He understood.

Don Bolles

1929–1976

In June 1976, *Arizona Republic* reporter Donald F. Bolles goes to a Phoenix hotel to follow a tip about land fraud and scams at state dog-racing tracks. A car-bomb blast rips off both his legs and right arm. "Mafia," he whispers to rescuers before he dies. His murder prompts the fledgling Investigative Reporters and Editors to bring dozens of journalists to Arizona to finish the stories Don Bolles had begun. Newspapers across the country print the results: the Arizona Project identifies more than 200 people with Mafia ties; 18 are indicted. Police jail the Bolles bombers, but no mastermind does time.

THE ASSOCIATED PRESS

In a November 1975 interview, Don Bolles expresses frustration about harassment from targets of his stories, a frustration that almost ends his investigative efforts:

'No more'

The harassment ... was the turning point of my career. I thought, "This isn't worth it to me or my family" of seven children. Also, we have an incompetent county attorney here and after years of seeing our investigations die at his doorstep, I told my editors, no more. I'm no longer in investigative reporting.

Bill Stewart
1942–1979

ABC News correspondent Bill Stewart, veteran of two wars and three rebellions, knows how dangerous international hot spots can be. In Nicaragua to cover the civil war between government troops and Contra rebels, Stewart is stopped at a roadblock on a quiet Managua street, forced to his knees, then shot in the head by a government soldier. He worries about the dangers of his last assignment, telling friends before he leaves, "I'm not a hero."

CAPITAL CITIES/ABC. INC.

When the Shah of Iran falls, Bill Stewart is there. In 1979, he worries about his work:

'Bound to do it'

You kept wondering how long you could go before one of those guns went off accidentally. Now, I want to tell you, if there is anything that scares me to death, it is going out into the provinces of these countries that are in rebellion and trying to cover the story. It is a dangerous thing to do, and I was never eager to do it because I'm not a hero. But I nonetheless find myself bound to do it. When your competition is there, you have to be there too.

Kenneth Green

1941–1982

Oakland Tribune photographer Kenneth Green dreams up the unusual picture, always "something you never saw," says Tribune owner-editor Robert C. Maynard. Green's motto: "Never make anybody invisible." For a story about the effects of recession on railroads, he heads down to the tracks to shoot empty boxcars. The photographer misjudges his distance from an oncoming train. He is struck and killed.

THE OAKLAND TRIBUNE

In a June 27, 1982, "Letter from the Editor," The Oakland Tribune's Robert C. Maynard recalls a photo shoot with Kenneth Green:

'Stood out brilliantly'

A magazine back East assigned Kenny Green to make a color portrait of me with Oakland in the background. ... "We're going to make a picture of you and Oakland that has never been made before," Kenny declared. ... A few minutes later, thanks to the assistance of a friendly police officer, Kenny and I were standing in the left lane of the downtown Oakland off-ramp of Highway 24. True, Oakland stood out brilliantly in our background, but in the foreground there was a different picture: Cars whistling within five to 10 feet of us, barreling off the freeway at 50 mph or better.

Triet Le

1929–1990

Triet Le, part of a five-person staff of Vietnamese immigrants, is a columnist for the Arlington, Va.-based magazine *Van Nghe Tien Phong*. Under the pen name Tu Rua, he attacks communists with a power that makes enemies. In the 1970s and 1980s, he harps on "failures" of Vietnam's government, but also criticizes its foes. Le and his wife are gunned down outside their suburban Virginia home by suspected political enemies.

WUSA-TV/COURTESY THE JOURNAL NEWSPAPERS

In Tien Phong *in 1990, Triet Le questions whether Vietnam should honor communist leader Ho Chi Minh:*

'Thousands have died'

What good deeds have been done by Ho to deserve all this? Tens of thousands of people have died under Ho's orders. Doesn't the regime feel dirty or filthy or obscene to build something like this museum?

Nathaniel Nash

1952–1996

Nathaniel Nash is an economics writer on routine assignment covering Commerce Secretary Ron Brown's trip to the former Yugoslavia. *The New York Times* Frankfurt bureau chief dies along with Brown and 31 others when their plane goes down in bad weather outside Dubrovnik. The energetic, Harvard-educated, deeply religious Nash had written about financial news and Congress before Latin America, and finally, Europe. Colleague Thomas Friedman remembers Nash's kind heart: "In April 1982, the *Times* assigned me to cover the Lebanese civil war, and at my goodbye party Nathaniel whispered to me: 'I'm going to pray for your safety.'"

NEW YORK TIMES PICTURES

Nathaniel Nash brings a feature writer's touch to a dispatch on Porsche, Jan. 20, 1996:

'The salvation of Porsche'

ZUFFERHAUSEN, Germany — Not too long ago, the production floor of Porsche's factory was not a pretty sight. Workers would storm off in a huff. Managers would fume. Voices would rise above the hum and bang of the line. And Japanese engineers — mostly Toyota alumni — would wave their fingers, demand explanations, scold, lecture and brow beat, essentially telling some of Germany's finest auto craftsmen how poorly they were doing their jobs. What was in process was the salvation of Porsche AG, Germany's ultimate symbol of racing car performance and autobahn freedom.

Terry Anderson

1947–

Not all martyrs sacrifice their lives. Some, like Terry Anderson, give their freedom in the line of duty. In 1985, Anderson is covering terrorism in Lebanon as chief Middle East correspondent for The Associated Press. Radical Shiite Muslims kidnap the former Marine and hold him for nearly seven years. After his release, Anderson writes *Den of Lions* about his ordeal, crusading for freedom of information after U.S. officials won't let him look at files on his own captivity. Anderson goes on to teach. Reporting hard news can take a terrible toll, he says: "So much violence to take in ... no wonder I knew no more than two or three journalists still on their first marriage, and so many who were semi-alcoholic, or bitter or cynical, or just weird."

THE ASSOCIATED PRESS

In 1998, Terry Anderson tells how he nearly lost his most prized possession, a rosary he had made out of worry beads, carpet string and bits of stolen wire.

'The thing I managed to keep'

I kept that rosary for nearly six years of the six years and nine months I was captive. It was a symbol. It was, as Catholics use it, an aid to prayer, a focus ... the only thing I managed to keep with me ... they would come into the cells and abruptly say, 'stand up,' tape you up, and take you away and you would lose everything. ... But the rosary I always managed to keep because I wore it on my wrist so they couldn't surprise me. One day they did surprise me. ... It was lying on the floor next to my mattress and they came in and said, "Get up." ... They started taping us up ... this was several years into my captivity, and one of my guards — none of whom were terribly gentle men — saw the rosary lying on the floor. And he picked it up ... and he draped it around my wrist and wrapped a piece of plastic tape around it so it wouldn't come off in the move.

CHAPTER 14

Society's Critics

> 'Two cheers for Democracy; one because it admits variety and two because it permits criticism.'
>
> — E. M. FORSTER

NEW YORK, 1975 —

IN THE MOUTHS OF PREPPY MIKE DOONESBURY, SPACEY Zonker and drug-addled Uncle Duke, no topic is sacred. The *Doonesbury* comic strip roasts right-wing and left-wing zealot alike. It takes on the rich, the power-ful, the presidential, fairly relishing the woes of Richard M. Nixon, whose minions are "guilty, guilty, guilty!" before they ever enter a courtroom.

Doonesbury's young creator, Garry (G. B.) Trudeau, becomes the first comic-strip artist to win a Pulitzer Prize for editorial cartooning. Small wonder. For some time,

newspapers have been moving the strip from the funnies to the editorial page, believing that Mike, Zonker and the gang were better suited to the province of pundits and critics — the people, as H. L. Mencken put it, whose job is "to make an articulate noise in the world."

Beyond that, what elevates *Doonesbury* from comic to editorial weapon is the quality of the people it irks. George Bush wants to "kick the hell" out of artist Trudeau for portraying him as the invisible president. Song legend Frank Sinatra calls the cartoonist "about as funny as a tumor" for linking him to organized crime.

Ah, to be so gloriously despised.

Such is the job of society's professional critics. In their hands, the pen can accomplish things the sword can only dream of. Without shedding blood, they can make or break a politician, actor or writer; they can launch great causes, pillory villains, make us laugh at our lot, help vent the national spleen. The challenge for even the most even-handed is to keep the power they wield from going to their heads. Citizens of 1920s Broadway tremble at colum-nist Walter Winchell, not only because his fierce opinions can close a show, but also because he uses his column to carry out grudges and settle scores. As Winchell himself puts it: "Democracy is where everybody can kick every-body else's ass … but you can't kick Winchell's."

Are critics (as composer Stravinsky once dreamed them) "small and rodent-like with padlocked ears, as if they had stepped out of a painting by Goya"? Or are they — as Mencken says in his critical essay on critics — pos-sessed with "the simple desire to function freely and beautifully, to give outward and objective form to ideas that bubble inwardly and have a fascinating lure in them?"

If reporters serve up the news, it is the editorial writers, cartoonists and critics who chew it over and help us digest it all. And it often results in heartburn. "What power," says Chicago's working-man columnist, Mike Royko. "You could write 500 words and get people all excited." Of the great Mencken, Walter Lippmann says: "He calls you a swine and an imbecile and he increases your

will to live." Your will to live, more likely than not, to see him run out of town.

Proverbs: "As cold waters to a thirsty soul, so is good news from a far country."

Critics: Forget good news. Go for the well-deserved, well-placed blow to the gut.

"What the hell is the point of writing if you're writing banality?" says the fierce critic of film Pauline Kael. And editorial cartoonist Signe Wilkinson: "You can never please everyone, so you might as well go ahead and offend the people who are looking to be offended any-way."

But for the criticized — or, as political cartoonist Pat Oliphant calls his, the "lickspittles" and "greedmon-gers" — there is little worse.

In the 1870s, *Harper's Weekly* cartoonist Thomas Nast takes on bloated political "Boss" William Marcy Tweed, who offers the artist $500,000 to leave the coun-try "to study art." Nast stays to lampoon Tweed. The cartoons help bring the boss to his corrupt knees.

The critic, for one, finds certain satisfaction in the art of the just desert. As Royko says, "The people I call bums and crooks *are* bums and crooks."

Those being criticized, of course — usu-ally in the public arena willfully — need hides tough enough to withstand the barbs. But then, so do their critics, no doubt journalism's least loved creatures, "witty" or "brilliant" when we agree with

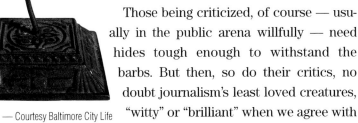

— Courtesy Baltimore City Life Museums at the Maryland Historical Society/ Max Reid photo

Inset: H. L. Mencken's copy spike, twisted in Baltimore's great fire.

them, but in bed with the rodents as soon as we don't.

In 1950, *Washington Post* music critic Paul Hume takes on the "unpleasant duty" of reporting that symphony soprano Margaret Truman "still cannot sing." The singer's father, President Harry S Truman, responds by calling Hume lower than "a guttersnipe" and threatening, should they chance to meet, to punch him in the face.

Columnist George F. Will, who isn't afraid to poke at his fellow conservatives, calls the abuse heaped on him "more entertaining than wounding," useful for teaching his own children "stoicism about slings and arrows." Literary critic Mary McCarthy measures her effectiveness by the quality of her enemies. And press critic George Seldes comments on his book title *Tell the Truth and Run:* "They said I should've called that book 'Tell the Truth and Stay.' Stay and get killed! Sometimes it's better to run and get another chance to tell the truth."

Down the ages, the critic has been attacked as the least creative of artists, dismissed, as drama's Kenneth Tynan puts it, as "a man who knows the way but can't drive the car." Or who revels in the low blow, human nature at its basest. "Panning can be fun," says film critic Kael, "but it's also show-offy and cheap." And it destroys credibility while fanning the notion of critic as also-ran.

Mencken, variously called "the sage of Baltimore" and "the man who hates everything," believes the effective critic needs the "intellectual agility and enterprise" to make the leap from the subject at hand "to the vast and mysterious complex of phenomena behind it," or risk being "no more than a fugleman or policeman to his betters."

Washington Post editorial cartoonist Herblock puts a similar sentiment another way: "First be right, then be effective."

Thomas Nast

1840–1902

In *Harper's Weekly,* cartoonist Thomas Nast hounds the New York "ring" run by corrupt politician William Marcy "Boss" Tweed. The powerful Democrat offers Nast $500,000 to quit and "study art" abroad. Nast refuses. Tweed goes to prison for stealing public funds. The political boss isn't especially angry about the stories that exposed him; he thinks most voters can't read. But Tweed fumes about Nast's "damned pictures."

In Th. Nast: His Period and His Pictures, *author Albert Bigelow Paine tells the story of how one of Boss Tweed's bankers tries to bribe Thomas Nast:*

'$500,000 in gold'

The bank official scarcely hesitated. "You can. You can get $500,000 in gold to drop this Ring business and get out of the country." Nast laughed a little. He'd played the game far enough. "Well, I don't think I'll do it," he said. "I made up my mind not long ago to put some of those fellows behind bars, and *I'm going to put them there!*" The banker rose, rather quietly. "Only be careful, Mr. Nast, that you do not first put yourself in a coffin!" he smiled. It was not until two years later that he met Nast one day on Broadway. "My God, Nast!" he said; "you did it, after all."

Francis P. Church

1839–1906

Who wrote the most famous U.S. newspaper editorial? The New York *Sun*'s Francis P. Church, when he answers the 1897 query of an eight-year-old girl: "Yes, Virginia, there is a Santa Claus. He exists as certainly as love and generosity and devotion exist." A former Civil War reporter, Church spends 32 anonymous years writing editorials and working on the *Sun* copy desk. He isn't credited as the author of "Yes, Virginia" until his death. Every Christmas, newspapers reprint Church's attack on "a skeptical age" and defense of "love and generosity and devotion."

THE CENTURY ASSOCIATION

From Francis P. Church's editorial in the Sept. 21, 1897, New York Sun:

'Is there a Santa Claus?'

We take pleasure in answering at once and thus prominently the communication below:

Dear editor: I am 8 years old. Some of my little friends say there is no Santa Claus. Papa says "If you see it in THE SUN it's so." Please tell me the truth; is there a Santa Claus?

VIRGINIA, your little friends are wrong. They have been affected by the skepticism of a skeptical age. They do not believe except they see. They think that nothing can be which is not comprehensible by their little minds. All minds, Virginia, whether they be men's or children's are little. In this great universe of ours man is a mere insect, an ant, in his intellect, as compared with the boundless world about him. ... Yes, VIRGINIA, there is a Santa Claus. He exists as certainly as love and generosity and devotion exist, and you know that they abound and give to your life its highest beauty and joy. Alas! how dreary would be the world if there were no Santa Claus. It would be as dreary as if there were no VIRGINIAS.

Dorothy Dix

1861–1951

Advice columnist Elizabeth M. Gilmer is America's shoulder to cry on. Writing as "Dorothy Dix" in more than 200 newspapers, she covers marital tiffs, removal of unsightly hair and more. Earlier, until 1917, she was a *New York Journal* "sob sister." But Dix quit the crime beat. "I was dreadfully tired of murder stories. They didn't do anyone a bit of good." By 1948, she earns $100,000 a year, tops for women in journalism.

HISTORIC NEW ORLEANS COLLECTION

Dorothy Dix writes about the status of women in 1908:

'No voice'

Taxation without representation is tyranny, whether the individual who pays the taxes wears trousers or petticoats. ... Women form one half of the population, and as long as they have no voice in the government, they are held in serfdom.

George Seldes

1890–1995

Gadfly George Seldes says he "caused an uproar" when he tried to report plain facts. As a *Chicago Tribune* reporter, his World War I coverage is censored, even stories revealing German military mistakes. In the 1940s, his *In Fact* newsletter exposes "falsehood in the daily press." He tackles issues dailies won't, like the link between smoking and cancer, and writes 21 books, his last at age 97.

George Seldes explains the press in The George Seldes Reader:

'Why can't you trust the press?'

But, why can't you trust the press? Answer: because it has become Big Business. The big city press and the big magazines have become commercialized, or big business organizations, run with no other motive than profit for owner or stockholder (although hypocritically still maintaining the old American tradition of guiding and enlightening the people).

H. L. Mencken

1880–1956

At age eight, he uses a toy press to print a card with his name. "Henry Louis Mencken" doesn't fit. From then on, it's "H. L. Mencken." By the 1920s, the cigar-chomping reporter, editor and critic makes his literary mark as "the man who hates everything." The Baltimore *Sun* fixture says journalists should "comfort the afflicted and afflict the comfortable." He co-founds *The American Mercury* magazine and writes more than 30 books, including *The American Language*. If Mencken hates the culture so, why even live in the United States? "Why," he replies, "do men go to zoos?"

REPRINTED WITH PERMISSION OF JOANNA T. STEICHEN

H.L. Mencken writes about reporters in his autobiography, Newspaper Days:

'Grand and gaudy time'

A newspaper reporter, in those remote days, had a grand and gaudy time of it, and no call to envy any man. ... I ... like every other journalist I met, listened to and smelled all sorts of magnificoes, including Presidents and Vice-Presidents, generals and admirals, bishops and archbishops, murderers and murderesses. ... I edited both newspapers and magazines, some of them successes and some of them not, and got a close, confidential view of the manner in which opinion is formulated and merchanted on this earth.

Louella Parsons

1881–1972

Hollywood columnist Louella Parsons can ruin a mogul's day — or career. Movie producers and stars court her, terrified of what she might write (or not write). By the 1930s, her gossip column reaches one in four American households. Parsons is a favorite of her powerful boss, William Randolph Hearst, because of the glowing reviews she gives Marion Davies, Hearst's starlet mistress.

UPI/CORBIS-BETTMANN

The Jan. 15, 1954, issue of the Los Angeles Examiner *quotes Louella Parsons on the marriage of Marilyn Monroe and Joe DiMaggio:*

'This I had straight'

I predicted this marriage would take place this month because our No. 1 box office girl and her Joe went house-hunting in Burlingame, the fashionable suburb of San Francisco. This I had straight and not only printed it in my column, but told it on the radio. Marilyn ... had her telephone disconnected so that reporters could not reach her.

Heywood Broun

1888–1939

In 1933, highly paid *New York World-Telegram* columnist Heywood Broun is outraged that most newsroom wages (as low as $10 week) are low and working conditions bad. He says he'll start a union. And he does. The American Newspaper Guild begins in Cleveland. In its first five years, the Guild holds 20 strikes. By the 1990s, The Newspaper Guild has 35,000 members, many earning at least $725 a week, and it merges with the even larger Communication Workers of America.

THE ASSOCIATED PRESS

Heywood Broun's Aug. 7, 1933, syndicated World-Telegram *column on starting a union:*

'I could die happy'

The fact that newspaper editors and owners are genial folk should hardly stand in the way of the organization of a newspaper writers union. There should be one. Beginning at nine o'clock in the morning of October 1st, I am going to do the best I can helping to get one up. I think I could die happy on the opening day of the general strike if I had the privilege of watching Walter Lippmann heave a brick through the *Tribune* window at a nonunion operative who had been called in to write the current "Today and Tomorrow" column on the gold standard.

Walter Lippmann

1889–1974

Political columnist Walter Lippmann helps shape American thought for half a century, co-founding *The New Republic* and writing, in 1922, the classic book *Public Opinion.* Striving to be an insider, he serves as assistant secretary of war. Lippmann goes on to write a hugely influential *New York Herald Tribune* column. Decades before the 1947 Hutchins Commission says newspapers fail to put events "in a context that gives them meaning," Lippmann predicts the rise of public relations because "reporters cannot give shape to facts." He says democracy is in danger because an American public, hobbled by "stereotypes," can't digest the complexity of politics.

LIBRARY OF CONGRESS

Walter Lippmann tells what news is in Public Opinion:

'The first sprout'

The news does not tell you how the seed is germinating in the ground, but it may tell you when the first sprout breaks through the surface. It may even tell you what somebody says is happening to the seed under ground. It may tell you that the sprout did not come up at the time it was expected. The more points, then, at which any happening can be fixed, objectified, measured, named, the more points there are at which news can occur.

Dorothy Parker

1893–1967

In 1925, literary critic Dorothy Parker becomes one of *The New Yorker*'s first regular contributors. Quick, searing wit makes her "Constant Reader" column a rave feature. "I had an office so tiny," she recalls, "that an inch smaller and it would have been adultery." Parker is a regular at the celebrated, hard-drinking wits' forum known as the Algonquin Round Table. Typical Parker, on how to use "horticulture" in a sentence: "You can lead a horticulture but you can't make her think."

UPI/CORBIS-BETTMANN

Dorothy Parker displays typical wit in her 1926 poem:

'Unfortunate Coincidence'

By the time you swear you're his,
Shivering and sighing,
And he vows his passion is
Infinite, undying —
Lady, make a note of this:
One of you is lying.

A. J. Liebling

1904–1963

New Yorker writer Abbott Joseph Liebling paints earthy, erudite word-pictures of city life, boxing, the London blitz and D-Day. He turns critic in his *Wayward Press* columns. He churns out quotable quotes: "Freedom of the press is guaranteed only to those who own one." Or "Money is not made by competition among newspapers, but by avoiding it." Liebling leads a generation of press critics.

UPI/CORBIS-BETTMANN

A.J. Liebling talks about how money is really made in the insect-eat-insect world of journalism, from the 1961 preface to a collection of his press pieces:

'Theoretically ...'

The corrective to the deterioration of a newspaper is provided, in 19th-century theory, by competition. ... Theoretically, a newspaper that does not give news, or is corrupt, or fails to stand up for the underdog, attracts the attention of a virtuous newspaper looking for a home, just as the tarantula ... attracts the blue hornet. Good and bad paper will wrestle. ... Virtue will triumph, and the good paper will place its sting in the bad paper's belly and yell, "Sic semper Newhouse management!" ... Then it will eat the advertising content of the bad paper's breadbasket. This no longer occurs. Money is not made by competition among newspapers, but by avoiding it.

Mary McCarthy

1912–1989

Novelist and critic Mary McCarthy spends 40 years in the top echelon of American letters. Her book reviews appear in *The New Republic* and *The Nation*. Her political essays on Vietnam result in two books on the war. As well as bringing her numerous awards, her frank style draws vocal critics, including writer Lillian Hellman, who sues McCarthy for libel. "Everything she writes is a lie," McCarthy says of Hellman in a famous TV interview, "including 'and' and 'the.' "

UPI/CORBIS-BETTMANN

In 1967, Mary McCarthy writes about the Vietnam War and its effect on Americans:

'War is hell'

If one describes landscapes once filled with life now pitted and scarred from bombing and shelling, "free fire zones" in which anything moving constitutes a target, one is told that war is hell, that terrible things inevitably happen. The United States, one is assured, regrets this deeply.

Paul Hume

1915–

When Margaret Truman makes her 1949 singing debut with the National Symphony Orchestra, *Washington Post* music critic Paul Hume is lukewarm. With practice, he writes, her singing might improve. A year later, Hume says the singer, daughter of President Harry S Truman, is still "flat a good deal of the time." The president fights back in a famous letter calling Hume an "eight ulcer man on four ulcer pay" and threatening to punch him in the nose. The *Post* doesn't publish the letter, but it leaks out anyway. Hume continues as a *Post* critic, staying at the newspaper until 1982 — 36 years.

Paul Hume's Dec. 6, 1950, Washington Post *review of Margaret Truman's recital:*

'Still cannot sing'

Margaret Truman, soprano, sang in Constitution Hall last night ... she is flat a good deal of the time — more last night than at any time we have heard her in past years. ... Miss Truman has not improved in the years we have heard her. ... She still cannot sing with anything approaching professional finish. ... It is an extremely unpleasant duty to record such unhappy facts about so honestly appealing a person.

President Truman's response:

Mr. Hume: I've just read your lousy review of Margaret's concert. I've come to the conclusion that you are an 'eight ulcer man on four ulcer pay.' It seems to me that you are a frustrated old man who wishes he could have been successful. ... Some day I hope to meet you. When that happens you'll need a new nose, a lot of beef steak for black eyes, and perhaps a supporter below!"

Herblock

1909–

In 1946, Herbert Lawrence Block — "Herblock" — joins *The Washington Post*. The three-time Pulitzer Prize winner's editorial cartoons consistently criticize political, economic and social injustice. His relentless attacks on Sen. Joseph McCarthy during the 1950s coin the term "McCarthyism." Herblock's philosophy: "First be right, then be effective, then be a good artist."

NATIONAL ARCHIVES

Herblock reveals the inspiration for a Richard Nixon caricature in his 1993 memoir, A Cartoonist's Life:

'Traveling the country by sewer'

In 1954, when, as vice president, he conducted a mud-slinging, Red-smearing campaign against some of the most respected senators up for re-election, it occurred to me that he was traveling the country by sewer, and I pictured him climbing out of one, traveling bag in hand. It fit.

Pat Oliphant
1935–

Syndicated political cartoonist Patrick Oliphant uses a distinctly biting wit to attack presidents. The Australian-born artist pioneers the acerbic alter-ego voice in modern editorial page cartooning with his character *Punk the Penguin.* Oliphant simply refuses to socialize with politicians. "Liking them does me no good at all," he says. "They are the enemy."

UPI/CORBIS-BETTMANN

Pat Oliphant, in 1995, explains the inspiration for his cartoons:

'Charlatans of all shades'

I owe America so much for providing such a beautiful and varied canvas as a backdrop and then peopling the foreground with a rich, almost overabundance of charlatans of all shades — wonderful Barnum politicians of varying degrees of shamelessness, cabinet opportunists, self-aggrandizing public servants, shiftless bureaucrats, and assorted lickspittles, greed-mongers, and common thieves.

Walter Kerr

1913–1996

Drama critic for *The New York Times,* Walter Kerr is known as "supercritic" by fans and foes alike. "At its best," Kerr says of theater, "it brings out the blood brotherhood of total strangers." His reviews make or break careers and productions. In 1990, Kerr, author of 10 books and winner of the 1978 Pulitzer Prize for criticism, becomes one of only two critics to have a Broadway theater renamed for him.

NEW YORK WORLD TELEGRAPH & SUN COLLECTION, LIBRARY OF CONGRESS

From Walter Kerr's 1970 review of Stephen Sondheim's Company:

'Sorry-grateful'

Original and uncompromising. It is brilliantly designed, beautifully staged, sizzlingly performed, inventively scored, and it gets right down to brass tacks and brass knuckles without a moment's hesitation, staring contemporary society straight in the eye before spitting in it. Now ask me if I liked the show. I didn't like the show. I admired it personally. I'm sorry-grateful.

Pauline Kael

1919–

UPI/CORBIS-BETTMANN

Pauline Kael writes about the movie Bringing Up Baby:

'Beautiful set of bones'

Katharine Hepburn's first comedy, made in 1938, rescued her from the tremulous anguish in crinoline which had made her one of Hollywood's surest guarantees of financial disaster. Lunatic comedy of the 30s generally started with an heiress; this one starts with an heiress (Hepburn) who has a dog and a leopard, Baby; Cary Grant is a paleontologist who has just acquired the bone he needs to complete his dinosaur skeleton. ... Grant ... winds up with Hepburn and no paleontologist ever got hold of a more beautiful set of bones.

Mike Royko

1932–1997

Chicago native Mike Royko, the hard-living son of a saloon-keeper, gives voice to the city's blue-collar, working-class people. "I love neighborhood characters," he says. In 1972, Royko's *Chicago Daily News* column wins a Pulitzer Prize. But the newspaper dies. So he switches to the *Chicago Tribune*. Through it all, Royko remains a throwback to the storied days of "Front Page" journalism.

THE ASSOCIATED PRESS

From Mike Royko's Pulitzer Prize–winning column on City Hall in the Nov. 17, 1971, Chicago Daily News:

'A miserable dump'

For today's cigar-chomping civics lesson, let's look at two buildings in this city. One of them belongs to Ted Korshak, a divorce lawyer ... and it is a miserable dump. ... And what does the city do about such a building? In this case, not much. ... Why is Korshak treated so nicely? ... Maybe it's because he's the cousin of Marshall Korshak, the City Hall powerhouse.

George F. Will

1941–

Conservative columnist George F. Will can irritate even conservative politicians. Will explains: "I trace the pedigree of my philosophy to [Edmund] Burke ... and others who were more skeptical, even pessimistic, about the modern world than most people who call themselves conservative." The learned syndicated columnist starts at *The Washington Post* in 1974, bringing his logic and engaging wit to books and TV commentary.

SIGRID ESTRADA

George Will writes in a June 17, 1976, Pulitzer Prize–winning column in The Washington Post:

'Common denominator'

A nation that feels a democratic imperative to celebrate the lowest common denominator sooner or later will get the lowest common denominator everywhere, including its legislatures. The empty-headed celebration of the common man will produce many "leaders" who are, to be polite, common. ... But there was an era ... when the premise of American government was that uncommon men should rule.

Garry Trudeau

1948–

Doonesbury cartoonist Garry Trudeau so effectively skewers tobacco czars, anti-abortionists and politicos that many newspapers move the strip to their opinion pages. In 1975, when *Doonesbury* is barely five years old and Trudeau still in his 20s, he wins a Pulitzer Prize for editorial cartooning. "Criticizing a political satirist for being unfair," Trudeau says, "is like criticizing a 260-pound nose guard for being too physical." He'll draw the strip "as long as people want to read it."

THE ASSOCIATED PRESS

Garry Trudeau tells The Washington Post *what it's like to be a cartoonist:*

'Perfect profession'

It's the perfect profession for somebody with quintessential '60s sensibilities. ... Because, in effect, I was being permitted to do the same things I was doing when I was in college — which was to act on my social concerns and to share my view of the absurdity of society.

Roger Ebert
1942–

Gene Siskel
1946–1999

Siskel and Ebert — the *Chicago Tribune*'s Gene Siskel (right) and the *Chicago Sun-Times'* Roger Ebert — join television rather than try to beat it. In 1978, the two movie critics take their debate from newspapers to public TV — and win an Emmy. In 1982, they go commercial with the show *Siskel & Ebert At The Movies*. Their thumbs-up, thumbs-down ratings are widely repeated.

THE ASSOCIATED PRESS

In a Jan. 3, 1993, interview with the Los Angeles Times, *Gene Siskel talks about on-the-air antagonism with partner Roger Ebert:*

'Play fair'

We hear, "We love it when you disagree because so much of TV is scripted and phony." On the other hand, we know when it gets vicious it's uncomfortable for the audience. So there are some rules. One is we're going to play fair with the arguments.

Signe Wilkinson

1952–

In 1992, *Philadelphia Daily News* artist Signe Wilkinson breaks the political cartoon gender barrier: Her clear, incisive style makes her the first woman to win the Pulitzer Prize for editorial cartooning. Wilkinson says cartoons "can be a quick, visible reminder that no matter how complicated the questions get, you can put the bottom line in black and white."

COURTESY SIGNE WILKINSON

Signe Wilkinson, in a Sept. 12, 1992, Editor & Publisher interview, talks about women and cartooning:

'Like sandhill cranes'

There is about the same proportion of women in editorial cartooning as there is in the U.S. Senate. It's sort of like a population of sandhill cranes that can be wiped out by one good hurricane.

CHAPTER 15

Sports People

'The drama of sport is a big part of the drama of life, and the scope of this drama is endless.'

— GRANTLAND RICE

LAKE PLACID, N.Y., 1980 —

"*DO YOU BELIEVE IN MIRACLES?*" THEY HAPPEN before our eyes on ABC-TV. The underdog U.S. hockey team pulls off one of the great upsets in Olympic history, downing the heavily favored Soviets, 4-3. The sports victory is sweet — a miracle, says ABC's Al Michaels. But sweeter still is the jingoistic symbolism of the event: America trouncing the Soviet Union, whose dominance in Olympic ice hockey stretches back to the early 1960s, to the most frigid days of the Cold War. Against the deafening chorus of "*USA! USA!,*" the press plays the hockey story as national triumph, not just the drama of one team squeezing another off the ice.

"It became apparent with the Olympics ... that if you had an American against a Russian, it didn't matter what they were doing," says sports innovator Roone Arledge. "They could have been kayaking and people would watch."

Sports spectacle as international morality play; sport as metaphor for life. Or above all, sports as great read. In the 1920s, the *New York Herald Tribune*'s Grantland Rice writes sports as dramatic poetry. Of our inevitable meeting with the One Great Scorer: "He writes — not that you won or lost — but how you played the Game." In the 1960s, ABC-TV's Arledge transforms the drama into spectacle. "We will have cameras mounted on jeeps, on mike booms, in risers of helicopters ... in short — we are going to add show business to sports!" By the 1980s, Arledge's vision has become the modern institution of television sports.

But it begins earlier. "You're confident," ABC's Howard Cosell prods Muhammad Ali in 1967, just before The Champ KOs Zora Folley.

Ali: "I'm confident I can whup all of them! This ain't nothing new. What are you trying to make it look like something new for? I'm always confident."

"You're being extremely truculent."

"Whatever truculent means, if that's good, I'm that!"

Back and forth fly the barbs in what Ali himself calls "the number-one act in sports" — the brash black boxer and the equally brash white Jewish announcer, live on TV before the match begins.

Does sports journalism cross over the line to just plain fun? Should it? Let's ask ex-lawyer Cosell, whose nasal broadsword — "I tell it like it is!" — gets him named 1970 *TV Guide*'s most popular sportscaster and, the same year, least popular. "Let's face it," says Cosell of sports journalism: "This is the toy department of life." Adds Robert Lipsyte, *New York Times* sports columnist and author: "Sports journalism has always lagged behind what 'capital J' journalism thinks it's about. Sports journalism has had a very difficult time deciding whether you're cov-

ering news or whether you are extending the pleasure of the entertainment for your readers. Are you a movie reviewer? Or are you a street reporter?"

How high is the place in the American pantheon occupied by the Gods of Sport, and perhaps by their scribes, too? High indeed, if measured in the deluge of commentary, stories and raw data, the billions wagered in the office pools or in advertising dollars. Higher still, according to Red Smith, the legendary scribe who finally gets his Pulitzer Prize at *The New York Times* in 1976: "It's the real world. The people we're writing about in professional sports, they're suffering and living and dying and loving and trying to make their way through life just as the bricklayers and politicians are. Games are a part of every culture we know anything about. And often taken seriously."

Rewind back to 1829, when Rev. W. B. Daniel launches Vol. 1, No. 1 of *American Turf Register and Sporting Magazine*, calling sports "one of the best preservatives of health, and no inconsiderable guard against immoral relaxation." But sports doesn't cure all ills. "Entertaining the people back home isn't part of the Big Job," says an editor with *Stars and Stripes* during World War I — Grantland Rice — who cancels the sports page "until an Allied victory brings back peace."

Sports, a metaphor for life? Yeah, in the earthy tone of Ring Lardner, who writes the way the players talk, chronicling the "bums" and "big shots" present at the creation of baseball, the Great National Pastime. Lardner gets his

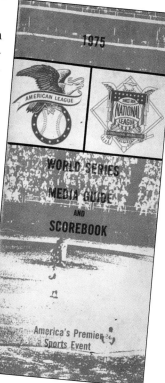

— The Red Smith Collection, University Libraries of Notre Dame/Ben Lourie photo

Above: Red Smith tracks every hit, out and run in this 1975 World Series scorebook.

stuff "spending about ninety nights per annum in lower berths" and in "Pullman car poker games among players and coaches, in dugouts, and in locker rooms." Like a street reporter.

Sports as a moral messenger? America's first baseball editor, Henry Chadwick, inventor of the box score, says his tiny-type statistics tell the tale of the tortoise and the hare. "By these matter-of-fact figures," he writes, "we are frequently surprised to find that the modest but efficient worker, who has played earnestly but steadily through the season, apparently unnoticed, has come in, at the close of the race, the real victor."

Sports as star-maker? Remember the drawl of Mel Allen, voice of the New York Yankees, so well-loved in life that in death, on a rainy day, he draws them all — Joe DiMaggio, Yogi Berra, Phil Rizzuto — all to his funeral, to say, as Mike Lupica, in the *New York Daily News* puts it, "a last good-bye to the man who always began broadcasts with 'Hello There, Everybody.' "

Broadcasting, Red Barber tells us, "is satisfying to the human ego. ... You are free at the microphone to just cover the whole playing area, cover the grandstands. You paint the picture ... the radio announcer is the supreme — the complete artist." Sports as life itself? In Brooklyn Dodger

> '**Sports is just corporate America in cleats. It should be listed on the Big Board.**'
>
> — JIM MURRAY

lore, Barber's soft-voiced appeal raises attendance of female fans from a handful to 15,000 per game. On National Public Radio, whenever Red speaks with *Morning Edition*'s Bob Edwards, it's hard to decide if he is talking sports or "waxing eloquent about life."

Sports as game? Soon after joining ABC, Roone Arledge sends a memo to his boss about college football: "We will utilize every production technique that has been learned in producing variety shows, in covering political conventions, in shooting travel and adventure series." Could *Monday Night Football* be far away?

Sports as news? In 1972, ABC-TV's Jim McKay covers the Munich Olympic games, anchoring live coverage of terrorists who invade the Israeli compound. "You've come to report some joy and excitement and fun and suddenly you have to report something very serious and sad," he says. "Simply put: You have to remain a reporter. You have to make sure what you say is accurate, and it's a little more important than whether the 100 meters was in 10.4 instead of 10.3."

Contract disputes, jail terms, crime, multimillion-dollar salaries, teams-on-wheels ... sports as business? "Sports," says Pulitzer Prize–winning columnist Jim Murray, "is just corporate America in cleats. It should be listed on the Big Board." But to write about it, Murray says, scribes must remember that "people are interested in people. People are not interested in things. The essence of journalism is high-level gossip."

Sports as literature? "It should be the best writing," says Frank Deford. "You're writing about young, vibrant people; there are wins and losses. In other words, it's great drama. ... Sportswriting has had to go beyond the game. We've had to be less and less reporters and more and more commentators, because you see the game on the screen."

As a reflection of society? Says Melissa Ludtke, *Sports Illustrated* reporter barred from men's locker rooms until she sued: "Without equal access to players, women clearly could not match their male colleagues." And Sam Lacy, of the *Baltimore Afro-American*, who before Jackie Robinson integrated baseball, sees black players just as good as white players, "and I couldn't understand why there was this barrier."

Sports as nostalgia? "To me," says NBC's Bob Costas, "a game wasn't a game unless an announcer was describing it. I grew up listening to people like Mel Allen, Red Barber, Lindsay Nelson and Vin Scully. ... It was sports, but it was also storytelling, history and romance. There was mystique to radio broadcasting. I wanted to be one of those voices in the night."

As spontaneous coarseness and beauty? "It's just one of those things that you just play and let happen," says coach-turned-commentator John Madden. "I think if you do plan it, it doesn't work. ... What I do is react. I don't plan."

As all of the above? "Sports," says Robert Lipsyte, "is in transition from being a moral crucible for America to being just another theme park, just another entertainment, which complicates the reporter's life even more. We are now guides in Disneyland when once we thought we were somewhere between being real reporters and moral arbiters."

Henry Chadwick

1824–1908

In 1856, British-born Henry Chadwick becomes America's first baseball editor. The game, he says, reflects national life: "In baseball, all is lightning." Chadwick writes the first rule book, persuades New York dailies to run results and popularizes the box score. On June 14, 1859, he changes baseball forever: Writing for the *New York Clipper* and chairing the National Association of Base Ball Players, he rules that a tie game must be settled in extra innings. Chadwick is the only writer enshrined in the main wing of the National Baseball Hall of Fame.

Henry Chadwick believes baseball resembles the British "rounders," fun for the whole family to enjoy. He crusades to clean up gambling, drinking and rowdyism at ballparks. His philosophy:

'A remedy'

Baseball is a remedy for the many evils resulting from the immoral associations that boys and young men of our cities are apt to become connected with.

Hugh Fullerton

1873–1945

A Chicago baseball writer noted for his accurate sports predictions, Hugh Fullerton figures the White Sox to be an easy winner in the 1919 World Series against Cincinnati. When the Sox lose, his groundbreaking investigative reporting helps uncover the Black Sox scandal. Eight White Sox players, including "Shoeless Joe" Jackson, are expelled from the sport for taking bribes.

UPI/CORBIS-BETTMANN

The Chicago Daily News *covers the Black Sox scandal on Sept. 28, 1920:*

Conspiracy to throw the World Series

[Eddie] Cicotte, it is learned, confessed that he received $10,000, and said that [Joe] Jackson asked for $20,000, but received only $5,000. "I refused to pitch a ball until I got the money," Cicotte said. "It was placed under my pillow in the hotel that night before the first game of the series. Every one was paid individually, and the same scheme was used to deliver it."

Harold Arlin

c. 1896–1986

Harold Arlin is one of the first full-time radio announcers, perhaps the first to broadcast a baseball game, for Pittsburgh radio station KDKA. "Our guys ... didn't even think that baseball would last on the radio," he says of the 1921 broadcast. "I did it sort of as a one-shot project." Five years later, Arlin resumes his engineering job with Westinghouse.

UPI/CORBIS-BETTMANN

In an interview shortly before his death, Harold Arlin recalls his 1921 baseball broadcast:

'We didn't know ...'

Sometimes the transmitter worked and sometimes it didn't. Sometimes the crowd noise would drown us out and sometimes it wouldn't. Quite frankly, we didn't know what the reaction would be, whether we'd be talking into a total vacuum or whether somebody would actually hear us.

Grantland Rice

1880–1954

He's called the "dean of American sportswriters," on top during the Golden Age of American sport — an age made largely by his vision. His florid, upbeat accounts of Babe Ruth, Bobby Jones and Jack Dempsey reach millions. In 1924, in the *New York Herald Tribune,* Grantland Rice turns Notre Dame's winning football backfield into the Four Horsemen of the Apocalypse. Writes Rice: "When the One Great Scorer comes to mark against your name, He writes — not that you won or lost — but how you played the Game."

The first paragraph of Grantland Rice's classic story, in the Oct. 19, 1924, issue of the New York Herald Tribune:

'The Four Horsemen'

Outlined against a blue-gray October sky, the Four Horsemen rode again. In dramatic lore they were known as Famine, Pestilence, Destruction and Death. These are only aliases. Their real names are Stuhldreher, Miller, Crowley and Layden. They formed the crest of the South Bend cyclone before which another fighting Army football team was swept over the precipice at the Polo Grounds yesterday. ...

Same story, as reported by *The New York Times:*

Moving with speed, power and precision, Knute Rockne's Notre Dame football machine, 1924 model, defeated the Army, 13-7, before 60,000 at the Polo Grounds yesterday.

Ring Lardner

1885–1933

Sportswriter Ringgold "Ring" Lardner dazzles the nation with his offbeat, wise-cracking writing style. His Chicago newspaper columns — first in the *Examiner* and later, the *Tribune* — help shape the sports-hero mania of the era. "Well friends," he writes, "today is another day and may the best team win." He loves to parody popular songs. On the Black Sox scandal: "I'm forever blowing ball games/Pretty ball games in the air." After leaving his mark on sports journalism, the baseball-crazy Lardner moves on to fiction.

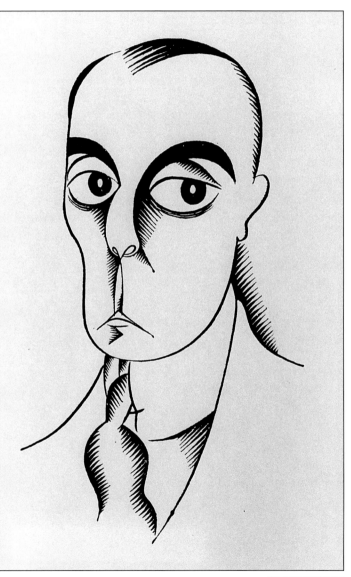

A verbatim excerpt from a Ring Lardner column, A World's Serious:

'Yank ball'

Well friends, I prophesied in these columns earlier in the week that Bob Shawkey would be a whole lot better this fall than he was last fall and that prophecy certainly come true, but the boy has still got the habit of pitching bad in the first innings and if I was running the Yank ball club here is what I would do. When it was Bob's turn to pitch, why just before the game started I would call Bob to one side and I would say, "Well Bob, it's the second inning all ready." If he believed it, why they would be nothing to prevent him from stepping right in and pitching his best from the start.

Sam Lacy

1903–

Baltimore Afro-American sports editor for half a century, Sam Lacy is one of the first sportswriters calling for an end to the color ban in Major League Baseball. Long before 1947, when Jackie Robinson breaks the color barrier, Lacy, a one-time Negro League ballplayer, begins campaigning for integration. How can baseball be the national pastime, he wonders, when the whole nation isn't part of it? On the road, Lacy and Robinson — the only two people of color traveling regularly with the Brooklyn Dodgers — room together in black hotels in the segregated South. "I was trying to get something accomplished," says Lacy. "My own comfort and my own sense of embarrassment — I just forgot that."

COURTESY SAM LACY

In a 1945 Baltimore Afro-American *column, Sam Lacy makes the case for integrating baseball:*

'Because he is colored'

Baseball has given employment to known kleptomaniacs and a generous scattering of saints and sinners. A man who is totally lacking in character has turned out to be a star in baseball. A man whose skin is white or red or yellow has been acceptable. But a man whose character may be of the highest and whose ability may be Ruthian has been barred completely from the sport because he is colored.

Mel Allen

1913–1996

He's the legendary voice of the New York Yankees. Mel Allen dubs Joe DiMaggio "Joltin' Joe." He's the first to say a home run is "Going ... going ... gone!" The Hall of Famer starts with Yankees radio in 1939 and follows the team into the TV era. *Variety* calls his distinctive voice one of the 25 most recognizable in the world, along with Winston Churchill's.

UPI/CORBIS-BETTMANN

In an April 10, 1988, interview with Newsday, Mel Allen talks about being on hand for Joe DiMaggio's 56-game hitting streak:

'In the right place'

You realize how lucky you were to be in the right place at the right time when amazing things were happening.

Red Barber

1908–1992

Sports radio trailblazer Walter "Red" Barber announces the first professional baseball game broadcast on TV, a 1939 Cincinnati Reds–Brooklyn Dodgers doubleheader. Barber-isms like "sittin' in the catbird seat" and "Oh, doctor!" make him an instant celebrity. In 1966, the New York Yankees fire Barber for announcing a record-low turnout at Yankee Stadium.

UPI/CORBIS-BETTMANN

Red Barber recalls the 1947 World Series and the beginning of Barber-isms:

'Oh, doctor!'

DiMaggio hit what looked like a home run and Gionfriddo caught it. ... I said, 'Oh, doctor!' And people have remembered that. And I hadn't planned it. It just came out. That's what you do in ad-lib broadcasting. When you realize that, things just suddenly come out of your subconscious ... you're talking in front of an open microphone, it sometimes frightens you.

Roone Arledge

1931–

ABC's Roone Arledge, innovator of TV sports coverage and creator of *Monday Night Football*, pioneers on-screen graphics, hand-held cameras, field microphones, taped replays and overhead stadium shots. In 1972, ABC's live coverage of the 1972 Summer Olympics in Munich — when 11 Israeli athletes are killed — sets a new standard. In 1977, Arledge takes over ABC News. He's on hand as sports coverage begins to become a multibillion-dollar business.

THE ASSOCIATED PRESS

An excerpt of Roone Arledge's 1960 memo outlining his vision for sports on ABC:

'Show business'

Heretofore, television has done a remarkable job of bringing the game to the viewer — now we are going to take the viewer to the game! We will utilize every production technique that has ever been learned in producing variety shows, in covering political conventions ... cameras mounted in jeeps ... we are going to add show business to sports!

Howard Cosell

1918–1995

Love him or hate him, lawyer-turned-broadcaster Howard Cosell dominates sports broadcasting from the 1960s through the 1980s. His formula? "Telling it like it is." An original *Monday Night Football* announcer, Cosell is called arrogant, pompous, obnoxious, vain, cruel, verbose, a showoff. Is he? "Of course I am." One *TV Guide* poll calls him the most hated sportscaster in America. The same poll calls him the most beloved.

THE ASSOCIATED PRESS

In his 1985 memoir, I Never Played the Game, *Howard Cosell explains how he helps* Monday Night Football *reach a viewership of more than 25 million:*

'Primarily an entertainment'

By standing parallel to the game and owing nothing to it, by demystifying it, by bullying it and not being bullied by it — by regarding the game as primarily an entertainment ... I was able to turn "Monday Night Football" into an Event — and I do mean to use the capital E.

Jim McKay

1921-

ABC sports reporter Jim McKay sits center stage in a world drama when 11 Israeli athletes are taken hostage at the 1972 Summer Olympics in Munich. McKay anchors 18 hours of field coverage from reporters Howard Cosell and Peter Jennings. When the hostages are killed by Palestinian extremists, McKay's grim words alert the waiting world: "They're all gone."

THE ASSOCIATED PRESS

In a Feb. 15, 1980, interview with The Christian Science Monitor, *Jim McKay describes the challenge of covering the Olympics:*

'Tragedy changed everything'

I try to anticipate what the personality of a particular games will be, and then convey that to the audience. ... In Mexico City the question was whether they knew how to run an Olympics. ... In Munich they were supposed to be the serene games. They started that way, too, but then the tragedy changed everything.

Harry Caray

1917–1998

Play-by-play announcer Harry Caray broadcasts baseball with unbridled zest, setting the standard for celebrity sports announcers. A fan since childhood, Caray thinks early radio broadcast games "sounded routine, almost boring." The Chicago Cubs announcer's goal: to change that. His famous verbal paroxysms — "Holy Cow!" and "Cubs win! Cubs win!" — inspire other sportscasters to develop signature styles.

USA TODAY

An excerpt of Harry Caray's 1987 interview with the Sporting News:

'Exciting ... at the ballpark'

One of the first things I noticed about baseball was how exciting it was at the ballpark — the scene, the aroma, the feeling. And I noticed how much different it came across on the radio, how the games sounded routine, almost boring. ...That's what triggered me, I guess, when I figured it wasn't the games, it was the announcers.

Red Smith

1905–1982

To Walter "Red" Smith, sports is life. "Of all the monuments left of the Greco-Roman culture," he says, "the biggest is the ballpark." Smith writes for five decades, turning sports into poetry for the 15 million readers of his syndicated *New York Times* column. He can write anything, even a football practice from the perspective of a glowworm. His style is simple, his standard high. "I was very lousy yesterday," he once admits. "I had nothing to say, and, by God, I said it."

UPI/CORBIS-BETTMANN

Red Smith's description of a scene from a Yankee-Dodger World Series game, from one of the 45 World Series he covers:

'He had the ball'

In the eighth, Hermanski smashed a drive to the scoreboard. Heinrich backed against the board and leaped either four or fourteen feet into the air. He stayed aloft so long he looked like an empty uniform hanging in its locker. When he came down, he had the ball.

Jim Murray

1919–1998

In 1953, Jim Murray is a founding writer for *Sports Illustrated* magazine. Eight years later he moves to daily journalism and becomes a pioneer in the use of humor in sportswriting. "I always conceived my function," he says, "to be to entertain the reader." Murray's stand-up comic style in his *Los Angeles Times* columns inspires a Pulitzer Prize and a new generation of sports columnists.

THE LOS ANGELES TIMES

In a 1963 column in the Los Angeles Times, *Jim Murray writes about the high-scoring nature of the American Football League:*

'Packed up my adding machine'

They were playing the American Football League play-off game in San Diego, so I packed up my adding machine, abacus and ran over the multiplication tables again in my mind. ... A vendor got in front of me making change for a quarter and I missed three touchdowns and a field goal attempt. ... The game wasn't much of a test except arithmetic.

Melissa Ludtke

1951–

Sports Illustrated writer Melissa Ludtke is barred from the New York Yankees locker room during the 1977 World Series. She misses key quotes. Her story is late. Ludtke sues for equal access, and a 1978 ruling declares it's unconstitutional to bar a woman reporter from a male athlete's locker room. Ludtke moves to CBS News, then *Time*, then writes a book about single motherhood. Her advice for women sportswriters: "There's a certain sense of humor that goes along with sports. You really learn ... to take your lumps."

DON HOGAN CHARLES/NEW YORK TIMES PICTURES

Melissa Ludtke writes in the Los Angeles Times *on Oct. 14, 1990, about equal access for female sportswriters:*

Women in the locker room

Without equal access to players, women clearly could not match their male colleagues in day-to-day coverage. Nor could I, a magazine reporter, contribute the background information essential to making our weekly coverage comprehensive. Ability wasn't the issue. Without a chance to talk with sources, even the most able reporter can't do a good job. For gender to be a primary factor in determining success in securing sources was discriminatory and illegal. And unnecessary. Players in other sports were proving that. Those who wanted to undress wore bathrobes or draped themselves in towels to protect their privacy during the short time that reporters — men and women — were in the locker room.

Frank Deford

1938–

A *Sports Illustrated* fixture for 25 years, Frank Deford writes stories on top athletes and sports personalities, earning a place among the country's best-known sports writers. In 1989, Deford helps launch the all-sports daily newspaper, *The National,* taking many of the country's most talented writers with him. When the experiment in sports journalism folds after 18 months, Deford returns to the "great drama" of sports-writing.

COURTESY FRANK DEFORD

Frank Deford's 1981 Sports Illustrated *profile of Indiana basketball coach Bobby Knight:*

'All the world must be in'

In this era of athletic corruption Knight stands foursquare for the values of higher education that so many coaches and boot-lickers in the NCAA only pay lip service to. His loyalty is as unquestioned as his integrity. He is the best and brightest ... and the most honorable, too. He has it all, every bit of it. Just lying there on the table. He has only to lean down, pick it up and let the chip fall off. But he can't. For Knight to succeed at basketball — not only to win, you understand, but to succeed because "That's much harder," he says — all the world must be in the game. All the people are players, for or against, to be scouted, tested, broken down, built back up if they matter. Life isn't lived; it's played.

Claire Smith

1953–

Baseball writer Claire Smith is barred from the San Diego Padres locker room during the 1984 National League Championship Series. Her paper, *The Hartford Courant,* protests and wins her entry. The baseball commissioner declares that should the Padres win the championship series and eventually the World Series, the clubhouses "will be open to both male and female reporters." Ten years later, Smith, who moves to *The New York Times,* is the first woman elected president of the New York chapter of the Baseball Writers Association of America.

COURTESY CLAIRE SMITH

In an Oct. 10, 1984, interview with The New York Times, *Claire Smith describes the San Diego Padres clubhouse incident:*

'Are you all right?'

I was aware of some commotion, but I'd rather remember how Bobby Brown of the Padres came over and asked, "Are you all right?" and Goose Gossage, whom I knew from the Yankees, came over on Wednesday and said, "Hey, you're in there today, count on it," and Steve Garvey left the clubhouse to help me.

John Madden

1936–

One-time Oakland Raiders coach John Madden turns NFL analyst and ends up dominating the field of TV football commentary. When Fox Broadcasting outbids CBS Sports in 1993 for rights to NFL games, Madden jumps to Fox, which, critics say, gives the fledgling network instant credibility. Says Madden, who peppers descriptions of gridiron collisions with words like *doink* and *boom:* "Nothing jazzes me up like football."

CBS PHOTO ARCHIVE

John Madden talks about being a commentator in the Aug. 20, 1991, New York Times:

It's 'all reaction'

I'm very hard on myself, credibilitywise. I read all the papers the day after a game, at least 10 of them, to see if I had everything they had. If a guy writes that a team switched from a three-man front to a four-man front and I never mentioned it, I get really upset with myself. I work hard at this. I screen films. I watch tapes. I watch practices. I talk to players and coaches. But what I do in the booth is all reaction. I don't write anything down. If what I know doesn't stick, that's it. If something happens — boom! — you've got to react. No time to look for your anecdotes.

Bob Costas

1952–

In 1980, Bob Costas joins NBC and realizes a childhood dream: to announce baseball games. "I wanted to be one of those voices in the night," says the Emmy Award-winner with the encyclopedic memory for sports statistics. Costas covers the NFL, the NBA, the Olympic Games and, in 1988, hosts a late-night talk show. But his first love is baseball. "Baseball isn't brain surgery," he says. "I just make sure I'm not frivolous at the expense of the game."

WALTER WEISSMAN, GLOBE PHOTOS

Bob Costas talks about his most embarrassing moment as a broadcaster:

'Champagne-filled eyes'

First time the Bulls won the championship, June of 1991, we are in the visiting locker room in Los Angeles ... we can't seem to find Michael Jordan. Finally, we fight through the crowd and we find Michael sitting down on the floor cradling the championship trophy. On one side of him is his father and I see, out of the corner of my champagne-filled eyes ... a female figure off to the other side. As I am pushed towards him, I am on the air live, and I say, "Here's Michael Jordan with his father and mother." Then the camera widens out and clearly there is a young woman next to him ... his wife, Juanita. Michael says, "No, that would be my wife." Misidentifying the wife of America's No. 1 sports star as his mother, on live national TV, is not the crowning achievement of one's career.

Global Villagers

IN THE 1960S, CANADIAN ACADEMIC MARSHALL McLuhan predicts radio, television and computers will turn the whole world into one Global Village. "Once any new technology penetrates a society, it saturates every institution of that society," he says. "New technology is ... a revolutionizing agent."

McLuhan proves to be a prophet. A digital revolution — McLuhan's Global Village — is here. Because pictures and sounds and words can be transformed into "0s" and "1s," into bits and bytes, we can see the other person speaking at the end of the telephone line — or in front of a computer screen — thousands of miles away. We can download vast storehouses of knowledge into our homes in a matter of minutes. With a few clicks of the ubiquitous mouse, we can mine the most arcane facts — from the most distant sources. And fetch up-to-the-second stock prices or sports scores, the latest headlines and the freshest opinions from the great newspapers and the leading journals. We can view satellite images of the weather system over our heads, or receive pictures and audio from almost any event from almost any place on the globe — or even signals sent back from distant planets.

This is the revolution, and the pioneers of the Global Village are building a digital city, a digital world, bit by byte by bit.

But flash back a moment to the distant 1980s. The first Global Village pioneer is an unlikely one, indeed: a college dropout and world champion sailor who inherits his father's billboard business — Ted Turner.

Turner has no experience in news, but he has a vision. He sees a global, 24-hour television network, reaching out to information-hungry consumers. First he thinks of a sports network, but ABC and ESPN have bought most of the rights. He thinks of weather, but Landmark already has The Weather Channel. So news is it.

Turner builds on a classic idea from the movies — Build It And They Will Come. His twist: Broadcast It And They Will Watch. In 1980, it begins as one channel. By 1998, CNN is nine separate news services seen in 210 countries by billions of people, and it has many new competitors.

In 1991, CNN's power and global reach are proven during the Persian Gulf War. Close to one billion people watch CNN to see the first strikes of Desert Storm. *Time* magazine names Turner its "Man of the Year," the first newsperson to win the 64-year-old distinction. Turner,

— Toshiba

Time says, had helped the world become "a truly global village . . . the very definition of news has been rewritten — from something that has happened to something that is happening."

The print pioneer of the 1980s is Al Neuharth. This restless, far-seeing former reporter travels the country adding to the Gannett newspaper empire. As he jets from city to city, from Gannett newsroom to newsroom, he realizes the company has a nationwide news and printing network in place. All it needs is a national daily to distribute the information. And so the idea of *USA TODAY*, the nation's first general-interest national newspaper, is born.

He designs the newspaper's racks to look like TV sets, to grab a television generation of infrequent readers. He steals the weather map from television and the crisp writing from magazines. With its bright color reproduction and fine graphics, *USA TODAY* launches a revolution in newspaper design and production.

Newspaper traditionalists say *USA TODAY* is fast-food journalism. They dub it "McPaper." But people read it — by the millions. In just more than 10 years, it becomes the No. 1 circulation newspaper in the country

Inset: For many, getting news on the personal computer is a daily activity.

and proves that innovation in print is still alive. Neuharth says newspapers need not fear new technology: "The most important thing I can tell you about the newspaper of tomorrow," he writes, "is that there will be one."

The public affairs pioneer is Brian Lamb, an Indiana native, Navy veteran and former Senate staffer fascinated by the political process. He remembers watching for hours as the Senate debates bills, marks them up, passes them and then modifies them in conference — usually with little or no broadcast coverage. Lamb imagines a cable television network that shows our elected representatives in action every minute they are in session. In 1979, C-SPAN, the 24-hour Cable Satellite Public Affairs Network, is born.

"We are better off," Lamb says, "showing people everything in our public meetings instead of managing what people see."

In just a few years, Lamb's dream becomes "America's Town Hall." Lamb is scrupulously neutral, even to the point of admonishing C-SPAN's employees to "keep our personal views away from hallway conversations." C-SPAN, he vows, will let "the American people see the political system as it is, without comment or analysis." C-SPAN quickly becomes an alternative for news consumers who scorn the 15-second sound bite, and crave the whole event. It gives Americans a close-up view of our political system.

Perhaps the most influential global village pioneer is still making his mark: Bill Gates, the Harvard dropout who hatched Microsoft in his dorm room. Microsoft is the world's software and productivity powerhouse, and it is going into the media business.

One of the first steps comes in 1995, when Gates starts MSNBC, an ingenious amalgam of a television news network and an online news service, melding traditional television with facts in a flash and online chats. What's next? Microsoft's *Sidewalk* guides, which steal a tried and tested idea from newspapers and put restaurant reviews, entertainment ideas and hip news and views online. In 1998, *Sidewalk* guides are sprouting in cities across the nation.

Clearly, Gates and Microsoft have dipped their toes in the news media's lake, and it probably won't be long before they jump in. Gates says interactive news means "consumers will get the degree of detail and background they want, and they'll get it when they want it."

What's the future of news? Here are the trends:

News will be more portable, as wireless handheld devices link people to the Internet, anytime, anywhere.

News will be more interactive, as the new digital mar-

> 'We are better off showing people everything ... instead of managing what people see.'
>
> — BRIAN LAMB

ketplace gives consumers more chances to talk back or post their own web pages.

News will be ubiquitous and universal, as the global village becomes the wired world.

News will be instant. There will be no waiting — for the next newscast or the next edition. As Jai Singh, the editor of CNET, a news-oriented web site, says: "The minute we hear about it, we write about it."

In this changing and confusing news world, says electronic news pioneer Roger Fidler, the public will have access to more information than ever, but they will need the help of "people they can trust to help them validate and make sense out of it."

So in the end, the role and responsibility of the gatekeeper — the reliable editor who makes sense out of all of the chaos, who saves truth and discards rumor — may be more valued than ever.

Marshall McLuhan

1911–1980

He's called "the prophet of the television generation." H. Marshall McLuhan is a Canadian media theorist whose dense book *Understanding Media* makes him a 1960s cultural icon. His most popular theory — "the medium is the message" — predicts the coming of a "global village" years before satellite TV, cable and the World Wide Web. McLuhan doesn't live to see the day that "hot" media (such as movies) and "cool" media (telephone calls) would all be able to flow through the same laptop computer, but he anticipates it: "For the consumer becomes producer in the automation circuit,quite as much as the reader of the (modern newspaper) makes his own news, or just is his own news."

THE ASSOCIATED PRESS

Marshall McLuhan uses a pun on his most famous comment on the media:

'Medium is the massage'

All media work us over completely. They are so persuasive in their personal, political, economic, aesthetic, psychological, moral, ethical and social consequence that they leave no part of us untouched, unaffected, unaltered. The medium is the massage. Any understanding of social and cultural change is impossible with out a knowledge of the way media work as environments.

Rupert Murdoch

1931–

Few Global Villagers are as global as media mogul Rupert Murdoch. He thinks newspapers will be "around a long time." So he buys them. His empire expands from Australia to include England's biggest paper, the tabloid *Sun,* and its most prestigious, *The Times.* Murdoch's News Corp. brings satellite TV to Europe and Asia. In the United States, he owns the Fox network and the *New York Post.*

USA TODAY

Rupert Murdoch answers charges of sensationalism in a 1989 interview with the Gannett Center Journal:

'Headless body ... topless bar'

You cannot cloud fact and must not. ...The famous [*New York Post*] headline ... said, 'Headless Body in Topless Bar.' Now, people have laughed about that or sneered at us or been shocked. The fact is it was perfectly true. There was a murder and the victim was decapitated and it was in some sleazy bar in New York City.

Nicholas Negroponte

1943–

New-media philosopher Nicholas Negroponte has been looking into the future since the early 1970s. Founding director of MIT's futuristic Media Lab — and a *Wired* magazine columnist — he exhorts individuals, companies and nations to "be digital" for our collective well-being and survival. "Computing is not about computers anymore," he says. "It is about living." His book, *Being Digital,* is considered a manifesto for a new information age.

J. D. SLOAN

Nicholas Negroponte talks about the structure of cyberspace in a Wired *magazine column, October 1997:*

'More biological'

Cyberspace is a lattice. If a part doesn't work, you go around it. The look and feel is suddenly much more biological, taking its character more from flora and fauna. ... Picture the loose-V formation of ducks flying south. ... People worry about control of the world's media being concentrated in so few hands. But those who are concerned forget that, at the same time, there are more and more mom-and-pop information services doing just fine, thank you.

Brian Lamb

1941–

In 1979, Brian Lamb founds C-SPAN, Cable Satellite Public Affairs Network. The cable station airs live House and Senate sessions and other public events. Flagging network interest in politics leaves C-SPAN poised to corner the market. The channel expands to two, then three, then into radio. "We are better off in this country," Lamb says, "showing people everything in our public meetings instead of managing what people see."

SCOTT MACLAY/THE FREEDOM FORUM

An excerpt from the introduction of Brian Lamb's 1988 book, C-SPAN — America's Town Hall:

'Our viewers'

At every turn, C-SPAN programming defies conventional television wisdom. ... Nonetheless, it is unlikely that C-SPAN programming will ever appeal to mass audiences. ... What has made C-SPAN significant, however, is "who" watches. Our viewers are public officials, the press, educators, and voters. ... C-SPAN viewers are the kind of individuals who affect our nation's political process.

Ted Turner

1938–

Ted Turner sees the future. He uses satellites to turn Atlanta station WTBS into a national "superstation." In 1980, Turner founds his 24-hour Cable News Network. By the early 1990s, CNN is the place where much of the United States — and the world — turns to watch news as it happens. Turner becomes the first newsperson selected as *Time* magazine's "Man of the Year."

SYGMA

Ted Turner's ode to his creation at the June 1, 1980, christening of Cable News Network:

'To act'

To act upon one's convictions while others wait. To create a positive force in the world where cynics abound. To provide information to people where it wasn't available before. ... For the American people, whose thirst for understanding and a better life has made this venture possible ... I dedicate the News Channel for America — the Cable News Network.

Michael Bloomberg

1942–

Michael Bloomberg becomes a billionaire by selling people news about money. Fired in 1981 as a Salomon Brothers trader, he launches the computerized Bloomberg Business News Service. He provides news-on-demand, his computer terminals glowing with up-to-the-moment news and detailed analyses of markets and thousands of companies. Bloomberg moves into magazines, radio and TV. He makes money "by gathering information once and selling it two or three times."

MCGOON/GAMMA LIAISON

Michael Bloomberg, in a speech covered by the St. Louis Post-Dispatch, *Nov. 9, 1997:*

'Move the product'

Every day I keep telling our people, "Every day we've got to go out and move the product. If you want to stay in business, if you want to be able to feed your family, you've got to write another story, be more accurate than everybody else." ... Chances are, somebody is going to come along and kill us. I don't see them out there, but I'm happy to come out here on a plane to St. Louis to keep building the brand name.

Allen H. Neuharth

1924–

In 1952, Allen H. Neuharth starts a weekly, *SoDak Sports*. It fails. He leaves South Dakota, becomes a reporter, then an editor in Miami and Detroit. He joins Gannett in Rochester, N.Y. In 1966, he starts *TODAY* on Florida's Space Coast. It flies. As president, chairman and CEO (1970-89), he builds Gannett into the largest U.S. newspaper group. In 1982, he launches *USA TODAY*, which becomes the nation's largest daily.

GANNETT COMPANY ARCHIVE

Allen H. Neuharth describes his dream for USA TODAY *in his best-selling 1989 memoir,* Confessions of an S.O.B.:

'Reinvent the newspaper'

There were two prime goals:

A national newspaper ... [that] would grab millions of readers, including many of the television generation who were then nonreaders.

A newspaper so different ... that it would pull the rest of the industry into the twenty-first century, albeit kicking and screaming. ...

"We'll reinvent the newspaper," I said with my usual modesty.

Roger Fidler

1943–

In 1981, new-media innovator Roger Fidler sees an electronic, tablet-sized newspaper. Laptop and then notebook computers move the world closer to his flat-panel dream. New technologies won't make or break media companies, he says, but "merely facilitate change and create opportunities." Former director of Knight-Ridder's Information Design Lab, Fidler sees the merger of pictures, sound and the word in digital media as part of a "third great mediamorphosis" transforming human communication. The first two: spoken and written language.

GARY HARWOOD, KENT STATE UNIVERSITY NEWS SERVICE

Roger Fidler sees the potential for the digital tablet publication, in his book Mediamorphosis — Understanding New Media, *1997:*

'New Renaissance'

Instead of completely discarding more than 500 years of accumulated printing and publishing knowledge, digital print media developed for portable tablets could lead to a new Renaissance in typographic and visual communication. In this next stage of the third great mediamorphosis, newspapers, magazines and books will routinely merge the written word and still images with full-motion video and sound in engaging and aesthetically pleasing formats.

Steve Case

1958–

In 1985, marketing wizard Steve Case develops an on-line service for Commodore computer owners. Six years later, it becomes America Online. Soon, AOL has millions of paying subscribers, more than the five largest U.S. newspapers combined. Online services can deliver thousands of times more information than traditional media. Their live "chat" functions are changing e-mail and the way the world communicates. Way back in the 1980s, Case says, "I thought it was magical … . This is going to be big."

USA TODAY

Steve Case writes about the future of computer-based communication in the March 6, 1994, San Francisco Examiner:

'Interactive medium'

It usually takes many years to build a super-highway; this one will be no different. It will be a process, not an event. It will consist of many small advancements, mostly made in the trenches. … The challenge is to … remain focused on the ultimate goal: the emergence of a new interactive medium that can enhance our lives.

Tim Berners-Lee

1955–

In 1989, MIT computer scientist Tim Berners-Lee creates the World Wide Web when he proposes a "global hypertext project." Like Johann Gutenberg centuries earlier, British-born Berners-Lee never makes money from his invention. The Web connects computers worldwide, allowing the sharing of everything from news to public relations to pornography. "The Web is like paper," says Berners-Lee. "It doesn't constrain what you use it for; you have to be able to use it for all the information flow of normal life."

DONNA COVENEY/MIT

Tim Berners-Lee reflects on a near-future scenario for his creation, a computer world in which every web site has its own address, on his company's w3 Web site, 1996:

'Digital choice'

The kitchen screen's preset buttons are set to your favourite places: the weather map, the school Parent Reminder page, an oldies station and the family's mailboxes. One is set to the web site of a small Italian town twinned with yours, where you were learning some language and art from some net friends in a rotary club there. ... Suddenly ... in skates your eldest ... [who] ... has just reached the age of digital choice. Your rights to select materials suitable for his viewing have ended.

Mitch Kapor

1950–

Techno-philosopher Mitch Kapor, Lotus 1-2-3 software pioneer, starts the Electronic Frontier Foundation in 1990, to defend civil liberties of citizens in cyberspace. A onetime disc jockey and meditation teacher, Kapor, a "recovering techno-romantic," touts Jeffersonian ideals for the Web. He calls information access a "natural right," the key to self-reliance, as Jefferson said of land. Give people a "suitably rich information environment," he says, and "you're empowering them economically."

© LOUIS FABIAN BACHRACH/ COURTESY KAPOR ENTERPRISES

Mitch Kapor makes a case for a "Jeffersonian information policy," in Wired Online, *1993:*

'Jeffersonian vision'

Life in cyberspace is often conducted in primitive, frontier conditions, but it is a life which, at its best, is more egalitarian than elitist, and more decentralized than hierarchical. ... In fact, life in cyberspace seems to be shaping up exactly like Thomas Jefferson would have wanted ... [and] if the communications industry is responsive to key ideas about openness [in technical architecture, industry structure and access to networks], then the chances of a Jeffersonian vision winning are even greater.

Steven Brill

1950–

"We'll do the Paul Newman salad dressing case before we do a case you and I never heard of," says lawyer-turned-magazine publisher Steven Brill. In 1991, he founds the 24-hour *Court TV.* Brill's bet: That Americans want to learn about their judicial system. The network becomes an American staple during the sensational O. J. Simpson trial. Rich from *Court TV* proceeds, Brill sets his sights on explaining — and exposing — the world of the media, starting with the magazine *Brill's Content.*

COURTESY COURT TV

In a Sept. 25, 1994, interview with the Baltimore *Sun, Steven Brill describes the appeal of Court TV:*

'People in peril'

A trial is a story, and that's part of the fascination. It's about people who are in peril. Someone in that courtroom is either in danger of losing his or her life or losing a lot of money. And they're trying to fight off that peril. And there's a result. Do they win? Or do they lose?

Marc Andreessen

1972–

Marc Andreessen is a University of Illinois undergrad making $6.85 an hour when he develops the first popular Web browser, Mosaic, a 1993 program that lets people explore the World Wide Web. Student Andreessen turns millionaire Netscape Communications founder and his program becomes Netscape Navigator, the world's most widely used browser — an invention some say has made us all journalists. The Web wunderkind on the pace of digital technology: "If we slow down, somebody's going to eat our lunch." In 1998, facing a threat from Microsoft, Netscape signs on with America Online in a deal that would leave Andreessen AOL's first Chief Technology Officer.

THE ASSOCIATED PRESS

Marc Andreessen touts the near-future of the Web for businesses, in the Nov. 18, 1996, InformationWeek:

'Network-centric'

Today's paradigm of browsing the Web will be replaced or complemented with customized information that's broadcast to users over the network, either from an internal corporate server or a content provider out on the Web. The information will be richer and more flexible. ... As people spend more time in network-centric environments, the era of desktop starts to fade. In its place are ubiquitous network clients, bringing information, functionality, and people together.

Chris Jennewein

1954–

"If you're two weeks ahead, you're in the forefront," says Chris Jennewein, old-style news reporter turned new-media executive for a new-media age. After developing *The Atlanta Journal Constitution*'s profitable audiotext service, he midwifes Knight-Ridder's online newspaper *Mercury Center* in 1993. Then comes News Search (electronic research), News-Hound (an online clipping service) and *Merc Center* on the Web. "Everything was happening so fast," he says, "it's hard to say who was the first at what."

KNIGHT-RIDDER NEW MEDIA

In a 1989 Gannett Media Studies Center speech on high-tech news, Chris Jennewein advocates pushing the edge:

'React faster'

In newspapers, which are typically slow-moving institutions, communications tend to travel up to the top of the hierarchy and back down .... With new information services you've got to react faster. You've got to ... [have] someone at the top who trusts you to do the right thing. And there's also got to be a willingness to experiment. Many newspapers have prided themselves on being highly accurate every day or at least trying to be perfect in appearance and tone. In introducing new services there are going to be some mistakes. ... You have to be willing to be embarrassed from time to time.

Louis Rosetto
1949–

Jane Metcalfe
1961–

Major media companies reject the digital-age magazine idea of Louis Rosetto and Jane Metcalfe. So the husband-and-wife editors get backing elsewhere. In 1993, they launch *Wired* magazine. In 15 months, circulation hits 175,000. *Wired* is a new-age publishing phenomenon. Its Internet spinoff, *HotWired*, comes next. Says Metcalfe: "*Wired* is about the digital revolution. *HotWired* is the digital revolution." But the online division saps cash, and in 1998 Rosetto and Metcalfe sell to Condé Nast. The Internet community, she says, is "no longer a cult, it's a culture."

USA TODAY

CHESTER HIGGINS, JR./NEW YORK TIMES PICTURES

Jane Metcalfe explains Wired *and the future of media to the author of the book* Digerati:

'Compete with MTV'

When Louis and I launched *Wired* ... the only people who were talking about the Digital Revolution ... were Bill Clinton and Al Gore. *Wired* came out with flashy colors and a new way of writing about what was happening around us. It represented a generation change. ... The Web is likely to become a lot more like television than like books. ... As new technologies come online — streaming audio, streaming video — big media companies will move in. ... The Web started out as a text-based intellectual space. Now it's going to have to compete with MTV. Print is still a remarkably colorful medium for delivering ideas and analysis. While images are powerful for conveying certain ideas, words allow you to go much deeper and much further.

Frank Daniels III

1956–

As *Raleigh News & Observer* executive editor, Frank Daniels III founds the company's online-publishing arm, *NandO.net,* in 1994. *NandO* (named after the *Raleigh N & O*) pioneers new media. Publishing scion Daniels leaves *NandO* in 1996 for software ventures, a seasoned old-timer. If we do electronics well, he says, newspapers in 10 years "will be different, but very well read." If not, "we may not be publishing a newspaper at all."

PHOTO BY ROGER WINSTEAD

Frank Daniels III talks about the world of NandO *in the Newspaper Association of America's new-media newsletter,* T-Leaves, *October 1994:*

'Our Community'

The Internet is like the real world — unorganized, unruly and filled with more happenings than any one person can possibly track ... and its citizens are literate. An opportunity for editors! But for us, the real attractiveness of the Internet is its sense of community. We found the same sense of community among the "Mom and Pop" bulletin board systems. So, we married the two. ... When you sign onto NandO, you are greeted with a "Welcome to Our Community" sign, and our users create that sense of community.

Jai Singh

1957–

In 1996, Jai Singh becomes executive editor of San Francisco-based *News.com,* the first online service devoted entirely to technology news. His goal: "Set the standard for electronic journalism." With a full-time staff of 30, *News.com* files its own paperless reports around the clock. "If there's even a hint of ethical compromise," Singh says, "we don't have a business."

COURTESY CNET

An excerpt of a Jan. 28, 1998, report from News.com:

'Slow growth rate'

Intel's (INTC) chief financial officer today confirmed once again that the chip giant is experiencing a slow growth rate. Andy Bryant said Intel's gross margins will be down a few points from the 58.6 percent projected for components in 1998. He reiterated that Intel's first quarter would see flat revenue growth and lower profit margins — in the 55 percent range — and laid out a roadmap for the company in 1998.

Bill Gates

1955–

AFP/CORBIS-BETTMANN

An excerpt from Bill Gates' 1995 memoir, The Road Ahead:

'Web-based journalism'

Journalism tends to be inefficient today. ... As Web-based journalism evolves, reporters will deliver information about new developments and maintain extensive background information for consumers who want to explore the context of the day's breaking story. ... Because news will be delivered interactively, consumers will get the degree of detail and background they want, and they'll get it when they want it.

Afterword

I F YOU ENJOYED THE WALK THROUGH HISTORY here, you might want to try it at the Newseum. The newspeople in this book are among the more than 500 featured on the news museum's News History Wall.

Open since April 18, 1997, the Newseum — the world's first and only interactive museum of news — tries to help the media and the public better understand each other.

To survey American attitudes about the media, the Newseum commissioned the Roper Center for Public Opinion Research.

The result was "News Junkies, News Critics," a study showing that we, as a people, realize we need and depend on news. But with our great need comes great expectations. We fear pollution of our daily news stream by bias and special interests.

Americans believe the general quality of news is improving. Still, most people say they do not trust journalists. Nearly two-thirds of those surveyed said that news is too sensational, and that reporters often are influenced by a variety of powerful interests — elected officials, big business, advertisers, corporate media owners or, most of all, the media's desire to make profits.

At the Newseum, daily discussions and debates hash out these issues. In the end, the journalists emerge with an improved view of the public's expectations. And Newseum visitors say they have a better understanding — and appreciation — for the First Amendment and the role of the media in our society.

The Newseum served a million visitors in its first two years, and reached many more people again through publications, broadcasts, education programs and at www.newseum.org, its web site on the World Wide Web.

Part of the Newseum's success comes from the care with which its exhibits were put together. The choice of newspeople was reviewed by Newseum staff and its interdisciplinary content committee, as well as by its advisers and two dozen of the nation's top journalism historians, most of them volunteers.

The biggest problem — as in any work of journalism — is not what you put in but what you leave out. Generally, this book focuses on American journalists, probably favoring journalists who are more recognizable. As any editor knows, names make news.

To see even more, visit the News History Gallery at the Newseum, in Arlington, Va. There, perhaps as here, understanding the traditions of newspeople past and present will help us make a better transition to tomorrow.

— **Charles L. Overby**
Chairman and Chief Executive Officer,
The Freedom Forum

Acknowledgments

THOUSANDS OF PEOPLE, A WORLDWIDE FOUNDATION and a new museum all helped make this book happen. We are grateful to newspeople everywhere, who have lived the lives represented here, and to every member of the extended family that makes up The Freedom Forum, the foundation that supports free press, free speech and free spirit worldwide, and its largest operating program, the Newseum, the first major museum dedicated exclusively to news. A list of the Newseum's content contributors could be the subject of an entire book — indeed it *is*, a book-sized listing of nearly 2,000 individuals and institutions, on display in the Newseum.

In 1991, a new foundation, The Freedom Forum, was born from the Gannett Foundation. From the beginning, the foundation wanted to build a news museum. The idea came from Freedom Forum Vice President Gerald M. Sass, a longtime supporter of journalism education and diversity. The idea was championed by Allen H. Neuharth, founder of The Freedom Forum, founder of *USA TODAY* and former chairman and chief executive officer of Gannett Co., Inc. The foundation, the Newseum and, of course, this book would not have been possible without him.

In 1992, an in-house team headed by Jerry W. Friedheim, former president of the American Newspaper Publisher's Association, started to work on the Newseum, along with associate Maurice Fliess. Many of their early concepts — including the name Newseum, from Friedheim — survived years of revision. All of their work, and all later efforts, were carefully overseen by Pulitzer Prize-winning editor and current Freedom Forum chairman and chief executive officer Charles L. Overby.

In 1993, Ralph Appelbaum Associates, Inc., the museum industry's leading design firm, began work on the Newseum. Besides resident genius Appelbaum, the Newseum was fortunate to have gifted designer Christopher Miceli, copyediting from Sylvia Juran and guidance of project managers Deborah Wolff and Ann Farrington.

In 1994, journalism historian Mitchell Stephens of New York University worked with me to complete a review of several hundred existing scholarly works, and construct a 10,000-item timeline covering the history of news all the way back to 100,000 B.C., when language may have begun.

Many of the nation's top journalism historians reviewed our Content Book, suggesting additions or deletions. Newseum staff, aided by Beverly Kees, former executive editor of the *Fresno Bee*, expanded the content database. Brainstorming meetings were held around the nation — many with Al Neuharth himself in the back of a special Amtrak car — and Newseum staff received advice from scores of news professionals.

Chris Wells, Freedom Forum vice president in charge of the foundation's international division, supervised a revamp of the Newseum's plans to nearly double its size and scope, expanding especially the News History Gallery.

In 1995, *USA TODAY* editor Peter S. Prichard joined the Newseum as executive director, supervising its construction and making all the final decisions. Former American Society of Newspaper Editors President Loren Ghiglione joined the project not long after. For the next 28 months, a large, wide-ranging content committee of leading educators, museum gurus and newspeople painstakingly reviewed and fleshed out the Newseum's exhibits, segment by segment. I coordinated their efforts. Curator of Exhibits Cara Sutherland joined the Newseum from The Museum of Our National Heritage to help us illustrate the story of news with rare artifacts, from Sumerian tablets to Bob Woodward's Watergate notes.

Before the Newseum opened in April 1997, we had either met with or at least been in contact with the leaders of virtually every major news organization in the United States, and many abroad. These included broadcast outlets who donated more than 450 live news feeds, arranged by Freedom Forum Vice President of Broadcasting Jack Hurley and the Newseum's current Deputy Director, Max Page. Current Newseum Executive Director Joe Urschel has expanded the Newseum's scope even further. Under his leadership, the Newseum's Education Center opened in October 1997, with Education Director Judy Hines.

In all, there are more than 500,000 words in various Newseum exhibits — not counting the books, pamphlets, guides, teacher kits, web site reports, as well as the special store products produced under the supervision of the Freedom Forum's vice president of marketing and communications, Beth Tuttle. When you count those, and add the Newseum's 25 original videos or films and more than 100 computer touch-screen exhibits, you can see how impossible it really is to name all concerned.

At the same time, some people have played such a major role in this book they can't be ignored. Joel Bloom, past president of the American Association of Museums, encouraged us to write tight, bright museum labels — "so good they can be published right off the wall." Story consultant and writing coach Mary Ann Hogan, whose writing system was used to produce the Newseum's text, contributed several chapter essays and many of the biographies. Newseum senior writer Sharon Shahid, who coordinated the Newseum's popular Newspeople Database, drafted chapter essays as well, and the remainder of the biographies. Contributing writers (a side benefit of working at a foundation where the executives can write) include Peter S. Prichard, Joe Urschel and Jerry W. Friedheim. They are joined by Paul McMasters, Freedom Forum First Amendment ombudsman; Adam Clayton Powell III, vice president, technology; Rod Sandeen, vice president, administration, and Gene Policinski, manager, special projects. Timothy Kenny, Newseum senior project manager, contributed the chapter on martyrs. Also contibuting chapter essays were J. Taylor Buckley of *USA TODAY* and Katie

Davis, the NPR writer who created the Newseum's excellent audio tour.

Our researchers included Newseum and Freedom Forum staff members Jerrie Bethel, Priscilla Trujillo, Rick Mastroianni, Yvonne Egertson, Nancy Stewart, Marion Rodgers, Caitlin Shear, Arlyn Danielson, Elizabeth Laitman, Todd Kinser and Phyllis Lyons. Special thanks also are due Linda Wallace and Kevin Washington who kept the managing editor organized, Newseum rights and permissions coordinator Karen Wyatt, who along with researcher Jeff Schlosberg found many of the photographs used here, and Freedom Forum senior graphics director Patty Casey, who, with designer Beth Schlenoff, design assistant Meredith Peck and proofreaders Brenda Reed, Jacqueline Blais and Ann Rauscher made this book look so good.

I edited the book, with help from Sylvia Juran, Don Ross, Maurice Fliess, Rod Sandeen, Joe Urschel, Peter S. Prichard and Charles L. Overby. In addition to Mitchell Stephens from New York University and Loren Ghiglione, now at the University of Southern California, many of the biographies appearing here were reviewed by journalism historians Mary Ann Watson of Eastern Michigan University, Thomas C. Leonard of the University of California-Berkeley, and Nancy L. Roberts of the University of Minnesota. Among our many scholar/volunteers were Maurine H. Beasley, University of Maryland; Rodger Streitmatter, American University; W. David Sloan, University of Alabama; David P. Nord, Indiana University; Jeffery A. Smith, University of Iowa; Wallace B. Eberhard and Louise M. Benjamin, University of Georgia; Barbara Cloud, University of Nevada-Las Vegas; Jean Folkerts, George Washington University; Jannette L.

Dates and Clint C. Wilson II, Howard University; Dwight L. Teeter, Jr., University of Tennessee; Hiley Ward, Temple University; Lauren Kessler, University of Oregon; Robert L. Stevenson, University of North Carolina; Native American press scholar Mark N. Trahant; Michael S. Schudson, University of California-San Diego; David Mindich, Saint Michael's College; the late Michael Emery, California State University-Northridge, and Freedom Forum Vice President and Pacific Coast Center Executive Director Félix Gutiérrez.

Many thanks to Newseum's advisory board, including Cynthia Baker, Barbara Cochran, Jerry W. Friedheim, Michael Gartner, I. Michael Heyman, W. Thomas Johnson, Warren Lerude, Carl T. Rowan, Carole Simpson, Jim Squires, DeWayne Wickham and Thomas Winship. And to our trustees, including Louis D. Boccardi, Gen. Harry W. Brooks, Jr., John E. Heselden, Madelyn P. Jennings, Robert MacNeil, Jan Neuharth, Charles L. Overby, Peter S. Prichard, John C. Quinn, Timothy J. Russert, Josefina A. Salas-Porras, Michael I. Sovern, Ronald Townsend, Judy C. Woodruff and ex-officio member John Seigenthaler.

Thanks as well to the staff at Times Books, who carefully and professionally reviewed and prepared the manuscript, and to our editor at Random House, Jonathan Karp, who kept us pointed in the right direction.

And finally, continued thanks to the nation's journalism historians, who quietly toil in their field, probing and preserving the story of news.

— **Eric Newton**
Managing Editor, the Newseum

Selected Bibliography

Anderson, Sherwood. *The Buck Fever Papers.* Welford Dunaway Taylor, ed. Charlottesville, Va.: University Press of Virginia, 1971.

Anderson, Terry A. *Den of Lions: Memoirs of Seven Years.* New York: Crown, 1993.

Anonymous. *Primary Colors: A Novel of Politics.* New York: Random House, 1996.

Arlen, Michael J. *Living-Room War.* New York: Viking Press, 1969.

Arnett, Peter. *Live From the Battlefield: From Vietnam to Baghdad 35 Years in the World's War Zones.* New York: Simon & Schuster, 1994.

Ashley, Perry J., ed. *Dictionary of Literary Biography: American Newspaper Journalists, 1690-1872.* vol. 43. Detroit, Mich.: Gale Research Co., 1985.

Barlett, Donald L., and James B. Steele. *America: Who Stole the Dream?* Kansas City, Mo.: Andrews and McMeel, 1996.

Barnouw, Erik. *A History of Broadcasting in the United States.* 3 vols. New York: Oxford University Press, 1966–1970.

Barnard, Sandy. *I Go With Custer: The Life and Death of Reporter Mark Kellogg.* Bismarck, N. Dak.: Bismarck Tribune, 1996.

Bates, Stephen. *If No News, Send Rumors.* New York: St. Martin's Press, 1989.

Beasley, Maurine H., ed. *The White House Press Conferences of Eleanor Roosevelt.* New York: Garland, 1983.

Beasley, Maurine H. and Sheila J. Gibbons. *Taking Their Place: A Documentary History of Women and Journalism.* Washington, D.C.: The American University Press, 1993.

Beasley, Maurine H., and Richard Lowitt, eds. *One Third of a Nation: Lorena Hickok Reports on the Great Depression* Urbana, Ill.: University of Illinois Press, 1981.

Berger, Meyer. *The Story of the New York Times.* New York: Simon & Schuster, 1951.

Berkow, Ira. *Red: A Biography of Red Smith.* New York: Times Books, 1986.

Berry, Faith. *Langston Hughes: Before and Beyond Harlem.* New York: Wings Books, 1995.

Bliss, Edward Jr. *Now the News: The Story of Broadcast Journalism.* New York: Columbia University Press, 1991.

Block, Herbert. *Herblock: A Cartoonist's Life.* New York: Macmillan, 1993.

Bloomberg, Michael. *Bloomberg by Bloomberg.* New York: John Wiley & Sons, 1997.

Brady, Kathleen. *Ida Tarbell: Portrait of a Muckraker.* Pittsburgh, Pa.: University of Pittsburgh Press, 1984.

Brinkley, David. *David Brinkley: 11 Presidents, 4 Wars, 22 Political Conventions, 1 Moon Landing, 3 Assassinations, 2,000 Weeks of News and Other Stuff on Television and 18 Years of Growing Up in North Carolina.* New York: Alfred A. Knopf, 1995.

Brockman, John. *Digerati: Encounters with the Cyber Elite.* San Francisco: Publishers Group West, 1996.

Brooks, Charles, ed. *Best Editorial Cartoons of the Year, 1996 Edition.* Gretna, La.: Pelican Publishing Co., 1974.

Brown, Les. *Encyclopedia of Television.* Detroit, Mich.: Gale Research, 1992.

Buchanan, Edna. *The Corpse Had a Familiar Face.* New York: Random House, 1987.

Buckland, Gail. *First Photographs: People, Places, and Phenomena as Captured for the First Time by the Camera.* New York: Macmillan, 1980.

Burns, Tom. *The BBC: Public Institution and Private World.* London: Macmillan, 1977.

Callahan, Sean, ed. *The Photographs of Margaret Bourke-White.* Greenwich, Conn.: New York Graphic Society, 1972.

Chesler, Ellen. *Woman of Valor: Margaret Sanger and the Birth Control Movement in America.* New York: Anchor Books, 1993.

Cloud, Stanley, and Lynne Olson. *The Murrow Boys: Pioneers on the Front Lines of Broadcast Journalism.* New York: Houghton Mifflin, 1996.

Cray, Ed, Jonathan Kotler and Miles Beller. *American Datelines.* New York: Facts on File, 1990.

Cronon, E. David. *Black Moses: The Story of Marcus Garvey and The Universal Negro Improvement Association.* 2nd ed. Madison, Wis.: University of Wisconsin Press, 1974.

Dates, Jannette L. and William Barlow, eds. *Split Image: African Americans in the Mass Media.* 2nd ed. Washington, D.C.: Howard University Press, 1993.

Donaldson, Sam. *Hold On, Mr. President.* New York: Random House, 1987.

Edwards, Bob. *Fridays with Red: A Radio Friendship.* New York: Simon & Schuster, 1993.

Edwards, Susan. *Erma Bombeck: A Life in Humor.* New York: Avon Books, 1997.

Elledge, Scott. *E.B. White: A Biography.* New York: Norton, 1984.

Emery, Michael and Edwin Emery. *The Press and America: An Interpretive History of the Mass Media.* 7th ed. Englewood Cliffs, N.J.: Prentice Hall, 1992.

Epstein, Edward Jay. *News From Nowhere: Television and the News.* New York: Random House, 1973.

Fedler, Fred. *Media Hoaxes.* Ames, Iowa: Iowa State University Press, 1989.

Fielding, Raymond. *The American Newsreel, 1911–1967.* Norman, Okla.: University of Oklahoma Press, 1972.

Folkerts, Jean, and Dwight L. Teeter Jr. *Voices of a Nation.* 2nd ed. New York: Macmillan College, 1994.

Frank, Reuven. *Out of Thin Air: The Brief Wonderful Life of Network News.* New York: Simon & Schuster, 1991.

Frantzich, Stephen E., and John Sullivan. *The C-SPAN Revolution.* Norman, Okla.: University of Oklahoma Press, 1996.

Gabler, Neal. *Winchell: Gossip, Power and the Culture of Celebrity.* New York: Alfred A. Knopf, 1994.

Gabriel, Ralph Henry. *Elias Boudinot: Cherokee and His America.* Norman, Okla.: University of Oklahoma Press, 1941.

Gans, Herbert. *Deciding What's News: A Study of CBS Evening News, NBC Nightly News, Newsweek, and Time.* New York: Vintage Books, 1980.

Ghiglione, Loren. *The American Journalist: Paradox of the Press.* Washington, D.C.: Library of Congress, 1990.

Goldberg, Robert, and Gerald Jay Goldberg. *Anchors: Brokaw, Jennings, Rather and the Evening News.* Secaucus, N.J.: Carol Pub. Group, 1990.

Goldberg, Robert, and Gerald Jay Goldberg. *Citizen Turner.* New York: Harcourt Brace & Co., 1995.

Goldberg, Vicki. *Margaret Bourke-White: A Biography.* Reading, Mass.: Addison-Wesley Pub. Co., 1987.

Goulart, Ron, ed. *The Encyclopedia of American Comics.* New York: Facts on File, 1990.

Grauer, Neil A. *Remember Laughter: A Life of James Thurber.* Lincoln, Nebr.: University of Nebraska Press, 1994.

Gunther, Marc. *The House That Roone Built: The Inside Story of ABC News.* Boston: Little, Brown, 1994.

Haines, Joe. *Maxwell.* Boston: Houghton Mifflin, 1988.

Hentoff, Nat. *Speaking Freely: A Memoir.* New York: Alfred A. Knopf, 1997.

Herzstein, Robert E. *Henry R. Luce: A Political Portrait of the Man Who Created the American Century.* New York: C. Scribner's Sons, 1994.

Hockenberry, John. *Moving Violations: War Zones, Wheelchairs, and Declarations of Independence.* New York: Hyperion, 1995.

Hogan, Lawrence D. *A Black National News Service: The Associated Negro Press and Claude Barnett, 1919–1945.* London: Associated University Presses, 1983.

Hogan, William, and William German, eds. *The San Francisco Chronicle Reader.* New York: McGraw-Hill, 1962.

Hudson, Frederic. *Journalism in the United States From 1690 to 1872.* New York: Harper & Brothers, 1873.

Ichioka, Yuji. *The Issei: The World of the First Generation Japanese Immigrants, 1885–1924.* New York: Free Press, 1988.

Inabinett, Mark. *Grantland Rice and His Heroes: The Sportswriter as Mythmaker in the 1920s.* Knoxville, Tenn.: University of Tennessee Press, 1994.

Inge, M. Thomas, ed. *Truman Capote: Conversations.* Jackson, Miss.: University Press of Mississippi, 1987.

Kane, Hartnett T. *Dear Dorothy Dix.* Garden City, N.Y.: Doubleday, 1952.

Kerrane, Kevin, and Ben Yagoda, eds. *The Art Of Fact: A Historical Anthology Of Literary Journalism.* New York: Scribner, 1997.

Karolevitz, Robert F. *From Quill to Computer: The Story of America's Community Newspapers: Commemorating the Centennial of the National Newspaper Foundation.* Freeman, S. Dak.: Pine Hill Press, 1985.

Kluger, Richard. *The Paper.* New York: Vintage Books, 1989.

Kobre, Sidney. *Development of American Journalism.* Dubuque, Iowa: W. C. Brown, Co., 1969.

Koppel, Ted, and Kyle Gibson. *Nightline: History in the Making and the Making of Television.* New York: Times Books, 1996.

Kroeger, Brooke. *Nellie Bly: Daredevil, Reporter, Feminist.* New York: Times Books, 1994.

Kuralt, Charles. *Charles Kuralt's America.* New York: G.P. Putnam's Sons, 1995.

Kurth, Peter. *American Cassandra: the Life of Dorothy Thompson.* Boston: Little, Brown, 1990.

Lande, Nathaniel. *Dispatches From The Front: News Accounts of American Wars, 1776-1991.* New York: H. Holt and Co., 1995.

Leonard, Thomas C. *News at the Hearth: A Drama of Reading in Nineteenth-Century America.* Worcester, Mass.: American Antiquarian Society, 1993.

Lewis, Anthony. *Make No Law: The Sullivan Case and the First Amendment.* New York: Random House, 1991.

Lewis, Tom. *Empire of the Air: The Men Who Made Radio.* New York: Edward Burlingame Books, 1991.

Lubow, Arthur. *The Reporter Who Would Be King: A Biography of Richard Harding Davis.* New York: Scribner, 1992.

MacDonald, J. Fred. *Don't Touch That Dial! Radio Programming in American Life, 1920–1960.* Chicago: Nelson-Hall, 1979.

Maier, Thomas. *Newhouse.* New York: St. Martin's Press, 1994.

Manoff, Robert Karl, and Michael Schudson, eds. *Reading the News: A Pantheon Guide To Popular Culture.* New York: Pantheon Books, 1986.

Marton, Kati. *The Polk Conspiracy: Murder and Cover-up in the Case of CBS News Correspondent George Polk.* New York: Times Books, 1992.

Matusow, Barbara. *The Evening Stars: The Making of the Network News Anchor.* Boston: Houghton Mifflin, 1983.

Mauldin, Bill. *Up Front.* New York: Norton, 1991.

McLuhan, Marshall. *Understanding Media, the Extensions of Man.* New York: McGraw-Hill, 1964.

McLuhan, Marshall, and Quentin Fiore. *The Medium is the Massage.* New York: Random House, 1967.

Mencken, H. L., ed. *A Mencken Chrestomathy.* New York: Alfred A. Knopf, 1949.

Mencken, H. L. *Thirty-five Years of Newspaper Work: A Memoir.* Baltimore, Md.: Johns Hopkins University Press, 1994.

Meyer, Karl E. *Pundits, Poets, and Wits: An Omnibus of American Newspaper Columns.* New York: Oxford University Press, 1990.

Mickelson, Sig. *The Electric Mirror: Politics in an Age of Television.* New York: Dodd, Mead, 1972.

Mitchell, Dave, Cathy Mitchell, and Richard Ofshe. *The Light on Synanon.* New York: Seaview Books, 1980.

Monk, Linda R. *The Bill of Rights: A User's Guide.* Alexandria, Va.: Close Up Publishing, 1991.

Mott, Frank Luther. *American Journalism: A History: 1690–1960.* 3rd ed. New York: Macmillan, 1962.

Negroponte, Nicholas. *Being Digital.* New York: Alfred A. Knopf, 1995.

Newseum. *News History Content Book: 100,000 B.C. to 1995.* Eric Newton, ed. Arlington, Va.: Freedom Forum, 1995.

Newseum. *News History Gazette.* Eric Newton, ed. Arlington, Va.: Freedom Forum, 1997.

O'Rourke, P. J. *Age and Guile Beat Youth, Innocence, and a Bad Haircut: Twenty-Five Years of P. J. O'Rourke.* New York: Atlantic Monthly Press, 1995.

O'Sullivan, Judith. *The Great American Comic Strip.* Boston: Little, Brown, 1990.

Paine, Albert Bigelow. *Th. Nast: His Period and His Pictures.* Princeton, N. J.: The Pyne Press, 1904.

Paisner, Daniel. *The Imperfect Mirror: Inside Stories of Television Newswomen.* New York: Wm. Morrow, 1989.

Paneth, Donald. *The Encyclopedia of American Journalism.* New York: Facts on File Publications, 1983.

Parker, Tony. *A Life in Words: Studs Terkel.* New York: H. Holt, 1996.

Pratte, Paul Alfred. *Gods Within the Machine: A History of the American Society of Newspaper Editors, 1923–1993.* Weston, Conn.: Praeger, 1995.

Pyron, Darden Asbury. *Southern Daughter: The Life of Margaret Mitchell.* New York: Oxford University Press, 1991.

Rather, Dan. *The Camera Never Blinks.* New York: Wm. Morrow, 1977.

Reston, James. *Deadline: A Memoir.* New York: Random House, 1991.

Ritchie, Donald A. *American Journalists: Getting the Story.* New York: Oxford University Press, 1997.

Ross, Ishbel. *Ladies of the Press.* 6th ed. New York: Harper, 1936.

Rowan, Carl T. *Breaking Barriers: A Memoir.* Boston: Little, Brown, 1991.

Seib, Philip M. *Rush Hour: Talk Radio, Politics, and the Rise of Rush Limbaugh.* Fort Worth, Texas: Summit Group, 1993.

Shawcross, William. *Murdoch.* New York: Simon & Schuster, 1992.

Sloan, W. David. *The Great Reporters: An Anthology of News Writing at Its Best.* Northport, Ala., 1992.

Smith, Anthony. *The Newspaper: An International History.* London: Thames and Hudson, 1979.

Smith, Sally Bedell. *In All His Glory: The Life of William S. Paley: The Legendary Tycoon and His Brilliant Circle.* New York: Simon & Schuster, 1990.

Smith, W. Eugene. *W. Eugene Smith: His Photographs and Notes.* New York: [Aperture, Inc.], 1969.

Snyder, Louis, and Richard B. Morris, eds. *A Treasury of Great Reporting.* New York: Simon & Schuster, 1949.

Stamberg, Susan. *TALK: NPR's Susan Stamberg Considers All Things.* New York: Random House, 1993.

Steinbeck, John. *The Harvest Gypsies: On the Road to the Grapes of Wrath.* Berkeley, Calif.: Heyday Books, [1988].

Stephens, Mitchell. *A History of News.* Fort Worth, Texas: Harcourt Brace College Publishers, 1997.

Stephens, Mitchell. 3rd ed. *Broadcast News.* Fort Worth, Texas: Harcourt Brace Jovanovich, 1993.

Sterling, Christopher H. and John M. Kittross. *Stay Tuned: A Concise History of American Broadcasting.* 2nd ed. Belmont, Calif.: Wadsworth Publishing Co., 1978.

Streitmatter, Rodger. *Raising Her Voice: African-American Women Journalists Who Changed History.* Lexington, Ky.: University Press of Kentucky, 1994.

Streitmatter, Rodger. *Unspeakable: The Rise of the Gay and Lesbian Press in America.* Boston: Faber and Faber, 1995.

Strunk, William and E. B. White. *The Elements of Style.* 3d ed. New York: Macmillan, 1979.

Sugar, Bert Randolph. *The Thrill of Victory: The Inside Story of ABC Sports.* New York: Hawthorn, 1978.

Talese, Gay. *The Kingdom and the Power.* New York: World Pub. Co., [1969]

Taylor, S. J. *Stalin's Apologist: Walter Duranty, The New York Times's Man in Moscow.* New York: Oxford University Press, 1990.

Thurber, James. *The Years with Ross.* Boston: Little, Brown, 1959.

Thomas, Helen. *Dateline: White House.* New York: Macmillan, 1975.

Thomas, Isaiah. *The History of Printing in America: With a Biography of Printers and an Account of Newspapers.* New York: Weathervane Books, 1970.

Thompson, Hunter S. *Better Than Sex: Confessions of a Political Junkie.* New York: Random House, 1994.

Tonkovich, Nicole. *Domesticity with a Difference: The Nonfiction of Catharine Beecher, Sarah J. Hale, Fanny Fern, and Margaret Fuller.* Jackson, Miss.: University Press of Mississippi, 1997.

Trahant, Mark N. *Pictures of Our Nobler Selves: Native American Contributions to the News Media.* Nashville, Tenn.: The Freedom Forum First Amendment Center, 1995.

Wallace, Mike and Gary Paul Gates. *Close Encounters—Mike Wallace's Own Story.* New York: Wm. Morrow, 1984.

Watson, Mary Ann. *The Expanding Vista: American Television in the Kennedy Years.* Durham, North Carolina: Duke University Press, 1994.

Wertheimer, Linda, ed. *Listening to America: Twenty-five Years in the Life of a Nation, as Heard on National Public Radio.* Boston: Houghton Mifflin, 1995.

White, William Allen. *The Autobiography of William Allen White.* New York: Macmillan, 1946.

White, William, ed. *By-Line: Ernest Hemingway: Selected Articles and Dispatches of Four Decades.* New York: Scribner, 1967.

Wilson, Clint and Felix Gutierrez. *Minorities and the Media.* Beverly Hills, Calif.: Sage Pub. 1985.

Witcover, Jules. *Marathon: The Pursuit of the Presidency, 1972–1976.* New York: Viking Press, 1977.

Yagoda, Ben. *Will Rogers: A Biography.* [San Francisco, Calif.]: HarperCollins West, 1994.

Yardley, Jonathan. *Ring: A Biography of Ring Lardner.* New York: Random House, 1977.

Index

"Journalists should be honest, fair and

courageous ... treat sources, subjects

and colleagues as human beings deserving of

respect ... be free of obligation to any interest other

than the public's right to know ... accountable to

their readers, listeners, viewers and each other."

Society of Professional Journalists

Congress shall make no law respecting

an establishment of religion, or prohibiting the free

exercise thereof; or abridging the freedom of speech,

or of the press, or the right of the people peaceably to

assemble, and to petition the Government for a

redress of grievances.

First Amendment

"Facing the press is more difficult

than bathing a leper.'

Mother Teresa